DATE DUE

DE 2 0 00			
JE 1 1 01			

DEMCO 38-296

The Assault on Equality

R

THE ASSAULT ON EQUALITY

Peter Knapp,
Jane C. Kronick,
R. William Marks,
and
Miriam G. Vosburgh

Praeger Series in Political Economy
Rodney Green, Series Editor

PRAEGER

Westport, Connecticut
London

Library of Congress Cataloging-in-Publication Data

The assault on equality / Peter Knapp . . . [et al.].
    p. cm.—(Praeger series in political economy, ISSN
1072–2882)
   Includes bibliographical references and index.
   ISBN 0–275–95545–1 (alk. paper).—ISBN 0–275–95619–9 (pbk. :
alk. paper)
   1. Equality—United States. 2. Intelligence levels—United
States. 3. Intelligence levels—Social aspects—United States.
4. Intellect. 5. Nature and nurture. I. Knapp, Peter.
II. Series.
JC575.A77   1996
323.42′0975—dc20   96–10436

British Library Cataloguing in Publication Data is available.

Library of Congress Catalog Card Number: 96–10436
ISBN: 0–275–95545–1
ISBN: 0–275–95619–9 (pbk.)
ISSN: 1072–2882

First published in 1996

Praeger Publishers, 88 Post Road West, Westport, CT 06881
An imprint of Greenwood Publishing Group, Inc.

Printed in the United States of America

The paper used in this book complies with the
Permanent Paper Standard issued by the National
Information Standards Organization (Z39.48–1984).

10 9 8 7 6 5 4 3 2 1

Contents

Preface

Issues about equality stand at the center of American values, but they are highly contested. The United States stresses values of social equality heavily, and the two phrases from our political tradition best known to most citizens are Jefferson's "We hold these truths to be self evident: that all men are created equal," and Lincoln's "a new nation, conceived in liberty and dedicated to the proposition that all men are created equal." Both affirm equality. However, there is considerable conflict over the meaning of these phrases, and the United States has one of the highest levels of inequality in the world. The phrases were interpreted as consistent with chattel slavery. Into the twentieth century, they were interpreted as consistent with denying women the right to vote and with legally segregated schools. In the 1940s Gunnar Myrdal labeled the position of blacks in the United States *An American Dilemma* because of conflicts between deep-seated values of equality and the pervasive reality of inequality. In a broader sense, the values of equality as a whole constitute an American dilemma. The conflict continues today.

Debate about fundamental values often centers around the question, equality of what? Equalizing one thing will almost certainly make others unequal. Equal resources, equal political rights, equal opportunities, equal moral concern, equal social value, and equal capacities are in sharp contradiction with one another, with other kinds of equality and with other values. These powerful contradictory forces and contradictory interpretations have led to a very discontinuous historical development.

Over long periods of time, nothing seems to change. Our political debates operate within assumptions and party structures that seem virtually
immovable. Then, in rare moments of change, there are decisive, rarely
foreseen shifts in the central assumptions of the political system. For example, the shifts associated with Andrew Jackson, the Civil War, the Progressive movement, the New Deal, the movements of the 1960s, or the
1980s Reagan/Bush administrations, all took analysts by surprise. There is
speculation, today, about whether we are beginning a new shift. Certainly there is a sharpening of the central contradictions about equality
within American life.

Ordinary political debate on the floor of the Congress and in the
popular media is often a grab bag of arguments. Policies are supported
by appeals to many different kinds of arguments; some are appeals to different values, some of which are contradictory to each other. More rarely,
tight arguments, similar to those of the Supreme Court are developed
where policies are justified as the only right decision by appeal to a distinctive and salient list of values. The Republican *Contract with America* is
distinctive in attempting to develop such a value-driven, ideologically coherent form of debate, appealing to values such as individual responsibility, liberty, opportunity, security and limited government. These values
are used to justify policies such as the Balanced Budget Amendment,
elimination of federal programs, tax cuts, work requirements for AFDC,
or prison construction. This agenda will drive political battles through
the 1990s.

To the extent that the *Contract with America* captures widely held values, it cannot be effectively contested by a mere denial. But if the opposition contests policies and programs one by one, yielding the value frame,
then the battle is over before it begins. The crucial issue is neither the
value frame in itself, nor the individual policies, in themselves, but the
linkage between them. This linkage is built by an argument that says that
certain kinds of policies promote or inhibit individual responsibility, liberty, opportunity, or limited government. On the face of it, inequality
does not appear to promote responsibility, liberty, opportunity, or limited
government. In this society, as in others, the poor appear to be caught in
a vicious cycle in which lack of resources and skills leads to lack of responsibility, autonomy or opportunity, feeding an immense apparatus of
police control. Therefore, those who would defend inequality must construct an argument that such problems stem not from inequality but from
the innate characteristics of the poor.

While there are many works that try to fill this need of the political
right, there is one basic work, and we shall focus on it. Of all the arguments attempting to consolidate this new movement of the right, *The Bell
Curve* is by far the most important. *The Bell Curve* is enormously more

systematic and comprehensive than other works, and as a media event has had a vastly larger audience. It takes a host of particular social theories that have led a marginal existence in the American Enterprise Institute, Mankind Quarterly, or networks of right wing management theorists, education theorists, psychologists, or geneticists, and consolidates them. It formulates basic and radical assumptions about innate inequality in a way that leads to a systematic philosophy and policy implications.

The central agenda of *The Bell Curve* is a new form of an old argument justifying inequality. The argument says that social progress depends upon competition and the survival of the fittest demanding unrestricted competition, producing immense inequalities. *The Bell Curve* popularizes its positions with highly technical arguments, surrounded by an impenetrable hedge of statistics. Citizens who have no interest in the technical issues now find themselves compelled to penetrate and master them because the techniques that it uses to give the impression that inequalities are natural and benign will reappear in other works. *The Bell Curve* popularizes analyses that challenge the basic insights of the social sciences, and it formulates the agenda of the political Right, which will be crucial to political debate in the next decade.

The Bell Curve is a huge, amorphous work, and so it is unclear what criteria are appropriate to analyze it. Some parts of it clearly claim to be ordinary social science, but some others are evidently political ideology—a clarion call for a political platform and an outline of a political philosophy. We think that it is only fair to evaluate it according to the claims that it makes for itself, but these are of several different kinds. *The Bell Curve* speaks with many different voices. It makes scientific claims, scholarly claims, political claims, and moral claims. Often it is unclear what kind of claim is being made or how it should be evaluated. Therefore, we will analyze and evaluate the arguments on several different levels.

In the first place, we evaluate the claim that the book is to be considered a piece of social science. The question is whether it is social science or whether it is pseudo-science. There have been repeated efforts, particularly in the analysis of race inequality, to use the trappings of science to legitimize a position that is fundamentally nonscientific or antiscientific. Much of creationist "science" or the Nazi studies of race are examples.

In the second place, while every single analysis of the book might be flawed as social science, the book might still have something to say. There are questions, issues, and arguments that are not a matter of science but that need to be discussed. For such issues, we use looser and more lenient criterion: is the argument fair and honest? A fair analysis is one that takes into account all the facts, that correctly locates the source of the problems, that is sensitive to the real choices of people, and that avoids global judgments of groups of people and demeaning characterizations. An honest analysis is one that does not manipulate data to make a point, that consistently follows rules, that does not withhold important information, and that neither obscures nor misleads. We shall suggest that much of the analysis of *The Bell Curve* is unfair in that it involves a selective and polemical presentation of facts. It is dishonest in that it often withholds important information from the reader and arbitrarily changes assumptions in order to mislead.

In the third place, for many of the issues in political ideology, even these looser criteria may be too restrictive. Since the main effect of earlier forms of racial and eugenicist theory was clearly antidemocratic and elitist, and since Murray claims to have overcome these characteristics, we ask to what degree the analysis is democratic. The final criterion of our analysis of *The Bell Curve* will be its consistency with democratic politics. Like the other criteria, this is not a criterion external to the analysis. We will suggest that one of the central strategies of *The Bell Curve* is to develop an analysis of inherited inequality whose clear policy implications are hierarchical, coercive, and even genocidal. Herrnstein and Murray try to give the impression of being tolerant and open-minded by expressing grave concern about such implications. Nevertheless, the essential thrust of the analysis is toward producing arrangements and policies whose direct and indirect consequence is to undermine democratic politics.

In the early twentieth century, the old Social Darwinism led to the abyss of the Great Depression and the Holocaust. The new Social Darwinism of *The Bell Curve* leads in the same direction.

Acknowledgements

We are deeply grateful to Rachel Schaller who patiently and carefully typed and retyped this manuscript over the past year. Without the assistance of Rick Eckstein, chapter four and the whole manuscript would be less than they are. A host of colleagues, including Robert Sternberg, Tom Powers, Claude Fischer, Bill Tucker, Steve Rosenthal, and Susan Ptak read the manuscript and offered useful advice. We thank our colleagues for convincing us that our ideas were not as bad as we feared and we thank Rachel for showing us that our handwriting was not as good as we hoped. The members of the Villanova Honors Science Seminar usefully and systematically explored the characteristics of the frequency polygons and logistic regressions of each of *The Bell Curve*'s 19 dependent variables.

The Assault on Equality

Chapter 1

Introduction

Are all men and women created equal?

The current aim of the radical right in the United States is the elimination of policies that equalize opportunities or provide a safety net for the disadvantaged. During 1995, in line with the *Contract with America*, the Congress moved to cut Aid to Families with Dependent Children and low-interest loans for education.[1] This is part of a more general policy initiative in which programs of public health, education, and welfare are all to be cut, federal programs are to be returned to the states by block grants, and federal regulation in areas like food and drug administration is to be sharply curtailed.

A fundamental consideration governing the political support of such policies is equal opportunity. Most Americans believe that all men and women are created equal, at least in the sense that they deserve equal opportunity. Accordingly there is wide support for policies to redress inequalities of opportunity. At the same time, there is now a campaign to redefine equal opportunity to make it compatible with inherited, ascriptive[2] inequalities. According to this campaign, different groups are born with different average abilities and thus programs that try to assure them equal life chances are unjust. *The Bell Curve* (Herrnstein and Murray, 1994) gives a central theoretical justification for this campaign.

The concept of innate differences in ability informs a systematic assault on federal programs for the disadvantaged. It is directed, first,

against affirmative action for minorities and women. The large differences in rewards that persist are legitimate if and only if they reflect major differences in ability. More generally, the abolition of welfare,
unemployment compensation, or programs providing opportunities for
poor children are legitimate only if equal opportunities already exist. The
view that inequalities reflect individual merit serves as a more general
justification of inequality and of government inaction with respect to it.

The *Contract with America* puts forth individualistic moral arguments
that move from individual actions to individual consequences. The arguments in *The Bell Curve* are different in form, but in practice the two kinds
of arguments depend on each other. The common element of all the
main justifications of inequality is an individualistic bias—a view that social success, social failure, or social problems all result from individual
traits rather than from social structures, social policies, or the rules of the
game. *The Bell Curve* develops the ideas that current inequalities have resulted from individual differences in ability, that such inequalities are inherited because the abilities are, and therefore that the inequalities are
legitimate and unavoidable. However, analyses, apparently diametrically
opposed to these genetic ones, that ascribe social problems to moral and
cultural sources can lead to the same result. For example, in D'Sousa's
The End of Racism (1995), the main argument is that there is a culture gap
between blacks and whites.[3] D'Sousa denies that there are genetic differences between blacks and whites, but his belief that a black subculture
makes its members inferior colleagues, employees, or neighbors leads to
many of the same policy conclusions.[4] Gingrich, in his *Contract with America*, rests his policy proposals on premises different from either of these:
the moral values of autonomy and independence. He suggests that the
problem is dependency. Those with values of independence do not need
to be protected from job discrimination or provided with job training;
they can "make jobs for themselves."[5] Thus, analyses of social problems
and inequalities in terms of individual inadequacies come in several different forms. But in all such arguments, social inequalities are pictured as
the natural operation of an invisible hand by which virtue is encouraged
and vice is discouraged. In this world the rich get richer and the poor get
poorer. It is no one's fault, but rather the working of Inscrutable
Providence.

But this is not the nineteenth century. Individualistic arguments coming into a public arena confront existing knowledge. While social science
analyses of social problems vary, virtually none sees problems such as
crime, illegitimacy, or school failure as inevitable consequences of biological differences. The understanding of the social causes of such problems
as poverty, unemployment, school failure, or crime has led to their wide
perception as socially generated and requiring a social response. The

only way that individualistic moral argument can dominate is if the arguments to social genesis are countered and driven from the public domain. This is the function of an argument that can claim to be social science and, as such, argue that collective or social responses to these social problems do not and cannot work because the problem is unfit individuals.

The Bell Curve argues that social inequalities are the natural result of inherited differences in cognitive abilities.

The Bell Curve is an elaborate, systematic, and widely read argument for inherited cognitive differences between groups. It legitimates and introduces all the other arguments. With the formidable backing of several right wing foundations and the active collaboration of such journals as the National Review and New Republic, it was able to accomplish two tasks that seem, at first glance, incompatible. As a popular media event, it was able to shift the public agenda toward the consideration of biogenetic theories of race relations. Within the social sciences, it was able to legitimate biogenetic models and to set an agenda of individualistic models of social problems such as crime and unemployment, according to which inherited cognitive ability plays a preponderant role. It argues that the inheritance of different mental abilities is increasingly the basis of social position in the United States. Part I argues that this has come about in the last generation as intelligence tests and related general ability tests have been increasingly used to select people for education and for jobs. Part II argues that innate intelligence is the major determinant of socially problematic behaviors such as school failure, unemployment, divorce, having an illegitimate child, or committing crimes. Stupid people do stupid things. Part III argues that genetic differences may well account for the substantial difference in test scores of different ethnic (racial) groups, and that those differences account for the different social outcomes for different groups. Richard J. Herrnstein and Charles Murray, the authors of *The Bell Curve*, argue that Asians and Jews are smarter than Europeans, blacks and Hispanics are more stupid, and that this difference accounts for the bulk of the racial/ethnic differences in school success, unemployment, crime, etc. Finally, Part IV consolidates the general policy implications of the analysis. The authors argue that the increased meritocratic sorting by test scores, combined with inheritance of mental abilities, leads to a highly unequal caste system. As people are increasingly allocated to social position on the basis of ability, there is increased inequality, segregation, and lack of social mobility.

Herrnstein and Murray argue for a society in which there is "a place for everyone." This requires, at least, a radical reduction of federal responsibility, reduction of the complexity of moral-legal systems, elimination of most affirmative action programs, and reduction of welfare. They believe that reducing federal responsibility will revitalize local communities and neighborhoods. Simplification of the criminal justice system and the simplification of the dominant moral framework as it appears on TV and in schools will teach right from wrong in a way that can be understood by even the most stupid persons. The elimination of welfare will discourage the propagation of the "unfit," and the position of single mothers will be so uncomfortable that most illegitimate children will be given up for adoption. Arguments such as those of Herrnstein and Murray form the crucial link between the moral value assumptions of the New Right[6] and their policy proposals. Those arguments attempt to counter the understanding that most social problems stem from vicious cycles of poverty that must be broken. The New Deal articulated a counter-vision in which the society must protect groups such as the poor, the elderly, children, and the infirm, breaking vicious cycles of poverty. Today, many of the foundations of the New Deal are being questioned once again, and *The Bell Curve* is the theoretical basis of this reaction, establishing a counter-vision of inequality and individual responsibility.

If illegitimacy, poverty, inequality, and crime are viewed as the result of vicious cycles originating in social causes, public policy will gravitate to eliminating those social causes. To convince the public that such policies are wrong, structures of poverty, inequality, discrimination, racism, and lack of opportunity must be disguised as differences in ability. The role of investments in education, science, health, and transportation in creating public wealth must be obscured and attention focused on individual abilities, themselves pictured as unchangeable. Thus, debate about the causes and consequences of social problems, particularly about their social structural or individual origin, is crucial to the debates about social policy. The Bell Curve's arguments about the individual origins of success and social problems is crucial to reorienting public debate toward social policies that reward individual success.

The Matthew principle governs a system in which the rich are rewarded and the poor are penalized.

A great deal is known about the functioning of cycles of privilege and lack of privilege. The ability of those with some resources to attract other resources is often called the "Matthew principle,"[7] from the biblical parable of the servants. Servants are given different amounts of money. The richest servant uses the money, it grows, and so he is given more. The poorest servant buries his and so it is taken away from him. "For unto every one that hath shall be given, and he shall have abundance; but from him that hath not shall be taken away even that which he hath" (Matthew 25:29).

It is a puzzling moral vision that takes from the poor and gives to the rich. Biblical parables are subject to different interpretations. Certainly, it is often true that those with one kind of resource are, in fact, often in a better situation to acquire others. For example, the wealthy are in a better position to acquire more wealth as well as social status or political influence, and political influence can be used to promote policies that entrench privileges. Unless these tendencies are counteracted, a cycle of self-reinforcing privilege is established at the top and cycles of self-reinforcing deprivation and powerlessness at the bottom. The result is the situation described by the saying "the rich get richer, but the poor get pregnant." Moreover, if one does not use the gifts one has been given, they atrophy.[8] But the fact that there are such tendencies does not mean that they are morally desirable or that we must allow them to operate unchecked. Indeed, such cycles are one basis of the vision that dominates Christian ethics of a duty to help the weak. Against any such duty, the central political agenda of the New Right is to allow cycles of privilege and lack of privilege to operate without interference.

The argument that reward for individual success drives progress was the center of the Social Darwinist program of the 1870s.

There have been times when similar agendas have become dominant. The Social Darwinists of the last century viewed people and groups as unequal, and they advocated the principle of unrestricted competition—the "survival of the fittest." Herbert Spencer elaborated the vision of progress, driven by free competition that raised the question of the treatment of the poor or the weak, who lose in the competition. Spencer argued,

> Pervading all nature, we may see at work a stern discipline, which is a little cruel that it may be very kind. It seems hard that a laborer incapacitated by sickness from competing with his stronger fellows should have to bear the resulting privations. It seems hard that widows and orphans should be left to struggle for life or death. Nevertheless, when regarded not separately, but in connection with the interests of universal humanity, these harsh fatalities are seen to be full of the highest beneficence—the same beneficence which brings to early graves the children of diseased parents and singles out the low-spirited, the intemperate, and the debilitated as victims of an epidemic. (1851, p. 289)

Spencer was the most popular social theorist in the United States at the end of the nineteenth century, and his harsh vision of individualistic competition was elaborated by those who came to be called Social Darwinists.[9] While most of the population did not view the starvation of widows and orphans as a "stern beneficence," that view on the part of some academics and politicians was able to immobilize any social response for decades. Social Darwinists viewed competition as both inevitable and the source of progress, self-reliance, and freedom for the society. Today, we again face a choice between having an inegalitarian society or one that stresses equality and equal human dignity.

The United States today is characterized by large inequalities of resources, particularly among children. Millions of children live in poverty, often lacking food, shelter, and basic security. They lack the resources to use any of their gifts, and their education often leaves them functionally illiterate. This is the group for which the New Right argues there should be "taken away even that which (s)he hath," and *The Bell Curve* legitimizes those policies. The central device sugar-coating this grim picture is the soothing reassurance, often repeated, that the very fact that (s)he is reading the book shows that the reader is part of the cognitive elite, to whom all doors are open, rather than one of the poor incompetents, doomed to educational, family, and economic failure.

This analysis is in the service of a political agenda on the political Right, directed toward the preservation of wealth and the removal of all programs that might drain finances from the wealthy. Within modern society, inherited inequality is problematic. The children of the dozens of billionaires in the United States inherit economic and social resources comparable to the great emperors, aristocrats, sultans, or slave owners of the past. At the other end of the system, tens of millions of people live in poverty, often sleeping in the streets and train stations. Their children are lucky to escape infancy alive, biologically and psychologically intact. Such inequalities were relatively non-problematic in traditional aristocratic, slave, or caste societies, but they are the center of value conflicts, political conflicts, and ambivalence in contemporary societies.

The concluding chapter of *The Bell Curve* calls for "a place for everyone," arguing that for thousands of years the great political thinkers in both East and West have tried to harmonize human differences by finding meaningful positions for all. Herrnstein and Murray stress the idea that Confucius, the great Hindu thinkers, the Greek and Roman philosophers, and Western thinkers such as John Locke, Thomas Jefferson, and John Adams all believed in the intrinsic inequality of human talents. And certainly the societies of ancient China, India, Greece, or Rome were highly unequal and hierarchical, as was the United States in the time of Jefferson and Lincoln. Such societies may have supplied a place for everyone but they were certainly organized to keep everyone in his or her place. In modern society, however, such social arrangements are highly problematic. In the United States, the principle that all men and women are created equal underpins other moral, legal, and constitutional structures. The old Social Darwinism fought determinedly against institutions that aimed at the ideal of equality of opportunity, such as universal, free public education, child labor laws, and workers' compensation.[10] The new Social Darwinism of *The Bell Curve* signals a new assault on such policies and institutions.

Concepts of innate genetic human inequality often justify systems of inequality and domination. Privileged groups often believe that they possess their privileges because they are superior, mistaking socially created differences for biologically innate ones. An example of this mistake was the justification of slavery—attributing the effects of socially generated deprivation and brutalization to biologically innate inequality. The classic case of this mistake was the justification of slavery by Aristotle, and so we can call it "Aristotle's fallacy." Aristotle justified slavery as both necessary and desirable because of the innate inequality among humans.[11] He argued that people vary in their ability to rule and that it was better (for both slaves and citizens) if those who were not able to rule (slaves) were under the control of those who were (citizens). Slavery brutalized slaves and stripped them of autonomy, resources, citizenship, and even language. Aristotle's fallacy mistook these social differences for natural differences of ability and justified them.

The idea of unequal inherited ability exerts a fascination for privileged groups because it reconciles equality of opportunity with large inherited inequalities. Inherited inequality of social position is particularly problematic when whole groups of people (racial, sexual, religious, or linguistic) are born with unequal life chances. The idea of individual competition and survival of the fittest has often been closely associated with collective (often racist) conceptions of group inequality. Herrnstein and Murray stress the fact that the founding fathers of the United States believed in intrinsic inequalities of talent. Certainly, the eighteenth century understanding of the value of human equality was extremely limited. Its application was restricted to men. It was reconciled with slavery and with the disenfranchisement and subordination of women, children, Indians, Mexicans, and other groups. However, throughout the nineteenth and twentieth centuries there has been a constant struggle to expand the concept of equal human dignity.

For the old Social Darwinism, inequality was the engine of progress.

While history does not repeat itself, one of the best ways to understand the implications of social analyses today is to see their relation to those in the past. The central elements of *The Bell Curve* all appeared in the Social Darwinism of the late nineteenth and early twentieth century. Herrnstein and Murray draw together four strands of analysis that unraveled sixty years ago.

Social Darwinism resulted from the confluence of these four powerful strands of social theory. The primary strand, often called nineteenth century liberalism, was the demand for individual competition and limited government. Exemplified by writers such as Herbert Spencer and William Sumner, it opposed measures such as public education, child-labor laws, or a progressive income tax.[12] But while individual competition, leading to the "survival of the fittest," has always been attractive to some privileged groups, it has never had mass appeal for obvious reasons. By the early twentieth century it was defunct as a mass political force except through its link to the three other strands of social theory: eugenics, psychometrics, and mass racism.

Eugenics, the second strand of Social Darwinism, was a popular movement associated with the emerging discipline of genetics. Eugenicists believed in inherited inequality and promoted policies to encourage superior genetic stock. Francis Galton and Charles Davenport popularized the theory of inheritance, ideas about choice of mates, and a concern with the inheritance of intelligence.[13] Geneticists such as Davenport gave crucial scientific legitimation to social policies that treated the poor as the source of social problems. Diseases such as pellagra (now known to be caused by vitamin B deficiency) were ascribed to hereditary causes.[14] The effects of widespread debilitating diseases like endemic hookworm were ascribed to hereditary shiftlessness. The central policy concern of the eugenicists was that the "feeble minded" or retarded population would breed, using up resources and degrading the gene pool. Even tuberculosis, whose bacterial cause was understood, was ascribed to heredity. Davenport argued, correctly, that even when an infectious agent is known, one must also take account of resistance. But he then concluded that

> The fact that of all occupations of females, that of servant shows the highest death rate for consumption does not imply that this occupation is extra-hazardous to the lungs or to body-resistance rather than that servants are largely Irish (who as a nation lack resistance to tuberculosis) or that they are below the average in mental and physical development, including disease resistance. (Davenport, 1911:19)

Servants were susceptible to tuberculosis for the same reasons as the rest of the poor. The resurgence of tuberculosis today has nothing to do with genetic susceptibility and everything to do with public health—and the growth of homelessness, poverty, and HIV. The eugenic focus on alleged genetic causes allowed policy makers to suppose that particular populations were the problem.   Bad science served bigoted, anti-immigrant politics.   Even if Davenport were right, the policy implications of his analysis were to distract attention from treatment, nutrition, poverty, or housing of the tubercular, and to focus on the elimination of undesirable groups, either by limitation of immigration or by sterilization.

Psychometrics, the intelligence testing movement, constituted the third stream of Social Darwinism, linked to classical Spencerian liberalism and to eugenics, on the one hand, and to racist and nativist movements, on the other.[15]   Figures such as Goddard, Lewis Terman, Robert Yerkes, and Carl Brigham adapted IQ tests and administered them to thousands of army recruits.[16]   Laughlin, one of Davenport's followers, was the Expert Eugenics Agent of the U.S. House of Representatives Committee on Immigration and Naturalization.   He wrote *Eugenical Sterilization in the United States* (1922), which proposed a model eugenics law requiring sterilization of "the socially inadequate classes," defined as:

(1) Feeble-minded; (2) Insane (including psychopathic); (3) Criminalistic (including the delinquent and wayward); (4) Epileptic; (5) Inebriate (including drug habitués); (6) Diseased (including the tuberculous, the syphilitic, the leprous, and others with chronic infections and legally segregable diseases); (7) Blind (including those with seriously impaired vision): (8) Deaf (including those with seriously impaired hearing); (9) Deformed (including the crippled); and (10) Dependent (including orphans, ne'er-do-wells, the homeless, tramps and paupers). (Laughlin, 1922, p. 369)

Eugenicists particularly urged the forced sterilization of the feeble minded, and involuntary sterilization laws were enacted in about 30 states (still on the books in many) under which tens of thousands of Americans have been involuntarily sterilized.   American sterilization laws served as models in Nazi Germany that, in turn, led to the extermination of "socially inadequate persons."   After the exposure of Nazi methods and procedures, eugenics fell into disrepute.

A broad stream of nativism, racism, and bigotry in both Europe and the United States had given political muscle to the union of classical liberalism, eugenics, and psychometrics.   Racist analysts had a wide audience, and the Ku Klux Klan mentality dominated many state legislatures, even outside the South.   However, after World War II these ideas were eclipsed.   By mid-century, although the psychometric movement had a powerful impact on the testing and selection of people within schools, the army, and other bureaucratic organizations, its ideas were in retreat.   The acceptability of racist ideas declined, and the interpretation of performance on IQ tests as a measure of genetically determined cognitive ability had been subjected to withering scientific criticisms.

The New Social Darwinism of *The Bell Curve* reunites these four political tendencies.

Unfortunately, Social Darwinism is not of purely historical interest. Each of its four strands is resurgent today, and *The Bell Curve* knits them back into a more or less coherent ideology. In the political system, criticism of government has become more strident and more active. The bombing of the Oklahoma City federal building in 1995, killing more than one hundred people, shows the violence of some elements of this strand of social thought. Within the social sciences, massive funding of the genome project and the expansion of ability testing in the military, in education, and in business has led to organized movements analogous to the eugenic and psychometric movements early in the century. An upsurge of racial conflict and racism provides the last element to the Social Darwinist configuration. Herrnstein and Murray draw the four movements together and consolidate them in a highly technical form, characterized by series of ellipses, disclaimers, and distortions. Murray, in particular, is a brilliant polemicist, a master magician who can make apparently solid findings appear and disappear with a wave of his wand. As in all magic, the key to the tricks is timing and in getting the audience to look where the magician wishes them to look—at the hat when the hand goes behind the back for a rabbit. We shall analyze some of the more important tricks and show how they are done.

Specifically, the magic concerns the claims, the concepts and assumptions, and the use of sources and data in *The Bell Curve*. For example, there is even doubt about what the central claims of the book are. Many analysts have taken the central claim of *The Bell Curve* to be that blacks are genetically inferior to whites. Herrnstein and Murray claim that to be a terrible misrepresentation. *The Bell Curve* is careful never to say that blacks are less intelligent than whites, and Murray has claimed that his critics must have read a different book from the one he wrote, or that they are misrepresenting his argument. Murray claims to be agnostic over whether the lower performance of blacks on IQ tests is innate; to be a scientist uncovering the facts of large differences in performance on such tests and reviewing conflicting theories about it.

Yet this is not the whole story. An illusionist is able to make people see things that have not happened, and Herrnstein and Murray are able to make readers hear what they have not explicitly said. They are careful not to *say* what they spend a great deal of effort constructing an argument to *imply*. *The Bell Curve* mounts a sharp and determined argument that the tests on which blacks do poorly are unbiased measures of intelligence, and that intelligence is innate. The evident implication of these arguments is that there is a genetic racial difference in intelligence, and this implication is reinforced by the book's handling of prior sources. Despite its enormous bibliography *The Bell Curve* systematically fails to cite or acknowledge the major works dealing with the processes it analyzes: race, poverty, the family, crime, and affirmative action (see our Appendix 2). Instead of dealing with or even acknowledging the bulk of the relevant scholarship, Herrnstein and Murray give the reader more than one hundred references to a small group of theorists, often referred to as "the professors of hate," associated with Mankind Quarterly and with explicitly racist groups such as the Pioneer Fund.[17] On the question of the genetic origin of racial differences, Herrnstein and Murray represent themselves as determinedly agnostic, but compelled by the facts and the body of expert opinion to inform us of "evidence" for the genetic basis of racial differences in academic performance. This is a kind of Michael Jackson moonwalk, in which the performer appears to push determinedly against a trunk that, with a force of its own, drives him back across the stage, when the simple fact is that he is pulling it.

Concepts in *The Bell Curve* often do not mean what they seem to mean. "Heritability," "genetic trait," "capacity," "intelligence," or "test bias" all have technical and narrow meanings considerably different from their common usage. Often Herrnstein and Murray are able to accomplish remarkable illusions by substituting the common usage for the scientific term. For example, "heritability" as a technical term is a statistical concept that has nothing to do with genetic causation. Anything associated with a heritable trait will be heritable, and so a socially caused trait can be entirely heritable. Slave status and everything that went with it in the antebellum South was fully heritable, but to regard it as genetic is Aristotle's fallacy.[18] In a racist society, any consequences of racism will be as heritable as skin color. But then, like a goldfish transformed into a bunch of flowers—presto chango!—Herrnstein and Murray take "heritability" to mean unalterable genetic capacities. The last half of *The Bell Curve* mounts a determined campaign to abolish compensatory education, and other programs to equalize opportunities, on the grounds that the disadvantages are innate and for many people there is nothing they can learn that will repay the cost of the teaching.[19]

Words in *The Bell Curve* must be examined closely. For example, it uses the concept of a socially constructed ethnic group rather than of a biological race. An ethnic group is a component of the social and cultural system and is defined by how others respond to a given person. Genetic arguments are utterly irrelevant to ethnic groups, which are culturally and socially constructed.[20] With respect to race many theorists believe that this concept is a kind of myth—indeed the most powerful and dangerous of all such myths. Although *The Bell Curve* uses the language of "ethnic groups," its treatment ignores or dismisses all of the work that

established the concept of an ethnic group. Instead, it fills the verbal construct of an ethnic group with the old, nineteenth century concept of a
biological race. It then shifts to arguing that it does not matter whether
problems such as family breakdown are or are not a matter of genetic
ability; they may as well be, because we cannot change them.[21] The argument is remarkable and the issues are slippery. In one sense, it obviously
matters. It is possible that a policy intervention might change a person's
social situation without changing their genes. If the disadvantage of their
children is a consequence of the social situation, then it would have been
ameliorated or removed; whereas if it were a consequence of their genes,
it would not.[22] D'Sousa (1995), Murray's colleague at the American Enterprise Institute, shows one way in which it sometimes does not matter.
D'Sousa argues that blacks have cultural pathologies so that they are culturally, rather than biologically, inferior,[23] but comes to the same policy
implications as *The Bell Curve*. Nevertheless, in terms of justice, it makes a
great deal of difference whether such effects are socially or biologically
created.[24]

Not only the sources and concepts but also the arguments of *The Bell
Curve* must be read with great care. They are always written with an eye
to their mass political effect, and often do not say what they mean or
mean what they say—or, at any rate, they often do not mean what they
seem to say at first glance.[25] For example, many commentators have criticized *The Bell Curve* as racist.[26] Those commentators have suggested that
the view that there are innate biological race differences in intelligence is
the archetype of racist beliefs. Herrnstein and Murray say that they "cannot think of a legitimate argument why any encounter between individual whites and blacks need be affected by the knowledge that an
aggregate ethnic difference in measured intelligence is genetic," and they
even italicize the idea (*The Bell Curve*, p. 313).

Reviewers have asked how *The Bell Curve* can develop hundreds of
pages of argument that there are racial differences in intelligence, depending upon racist sources, belaboring every existing racist stereotype,
implying that social problems such as welfare, illegitimacy, unemployment, and crime stem from inferior intelligence, and then suggest that
people treat each other as individuals. It is evident from closely reading
the argument that, actually, Herrnstein and Murray do not assert that
these ideas will not promote racism or lead to racist practices and conflicts. They only say that they can think of no *legitimate* argument why *individual* encounters *need* be influenced by that "knowledge."[27] The
question whether a work like *The Bell Curve* will promote or inhibit racism
is an important one.[28]

The political agenda of a new Social Darwinism is what really holds
the book together and drives its arguments. Theoretically, Herrnstein

and Murray link political individualism (neo-Spencerianism), genetic determinism, and psychological analyses of IQ to produce a reductionist argument. Reductionism involves the explanation of the properties of wholes in terms of the properties of their parts. Herrnstein and Murray analyze social structures and social problems in terms of four reductions, corresponding to the Spencerian, the psychometric, the eugenic, and popular racist strands of nineteenth century Social Darwinist theory. *The Bell Curve* explains all personality, skills, and self-concept effects in terms of cognitive ability. It explains all social, cultural, and ethnic behaviors in terms of genetic constitution. It treats race as a genetic, essential characteristic. And it explains all larger social structures as individual choices. These reductions constitute the logical skeleton of Herrnstein and Murray's argument, the analytical machinery that allows them to produce the illusions and to reach the conclusions central to the book.

The new assault on social services argues that these services produce a custodial state for the cognitively inferior, rather like a giant Indian reservation. The analogy is apt, but not in the way that Herrnstein and Murray suppose. The population of Indians in North America, some twenty million in the eighteenth century, had declined to about 300,000 by the end of the nineteenth century.[29] Tens of millions had been wiped out by disease, starvation, lack of legal protection, and, whenever there was armed resistance, active military intervention. The fate of American Indians was clearly not due to an overly generous federal government. Hitler, in discussions with his inner circle, greatly admired the treatment of American Indians. That treatment was a Social Darwinist dream (or nightmare) come true. The abolition of affirmative action, welfare, and social services, leaving poor black and Hispanic neighborhoods to their own devices in dealing with health, education, jobs, and welfare—often in the face of endemic AIDS, drug traffic, and gang warfare—could produce a similar result. But this result would not be safely distant—out on the frontier. Rather, occurring in the heart of every American city, it would produce escalating violence and coercion.

The central theoretical arguments of *The Bell Curve* rest on four related reductionisms that treat complex systems as fully explained by the characteristics of their components.

In support of this policy, much of the argument in *The Bell Curve* is merely ingenious and opportunistic manipulation. By choosing what sources to look at, what data to consider, and how to interpret sources and data, the authors construct a kind of lawyer's brief for the idea of genetic racial differences. However, their claim to do more than construct a lawyer's brief requires the impression of an austere logic. Problems of illegitimacy, poverty, crime, racism, or education are complex. All complexity has to be swept aside if the moralistic interpretations and policies of the New Right are to dominate. *The Bell Curve* reduces complex social structures to individual actions which are further reduced to genes, race, or IQ.[30] The reductions underpin analyses that are misleading, and at the same time they give the argument a false sense of an underlying logic. The persistent reductionism of the analysis constitutes the conceptual scaffolding of the work and its central linkage to the movements of the New Right.[31] Specifically, it adapts and synthesizes the four reductionisms characteristic of nineteenth century Social Darwinism.

Reductionism can be successful under certain conditions. Successful science sometimes makes heroic simplifications, cutting through a host of nonessential details to get to the bottom line. The bottom line of combustion is the presence of oxygen and a combustible substance. No oxygen, no combustion. The bottom line of many diseases is the presence of a disease agent: no HIV virus, no AIDS. Many successful scientific advances have been reductionist in this sense. Of course, false science, fake pseudo-science, and failed science also have often stemmed from reductionist forms of analysis. For the medieval alchemists, the bottom line was that substances can often be transformed into each other, and they sought a philosopher's stone that could transform common substances into gold. The question about the analysis in *The Bell Curve* is whether its reductionist arguments are essentially correct or whether they form a false pseudo-science like the search for a philosopher's stone.

While some of the advances of science have hinged on the discovery of simple, basic processes, others stemmed from the discovery that it is necessary to take account of structures in addition to elements. Many of the arguments of *The Bell Curve* have a bottom-line character. The bottom line of Head Start, according to *The Bell Curve*, is that it is trying to do the impossible: to improve the performance of children who are defective. The bottom line of affirmative action programs is that they force schools and employers to accept applicants who are not smart. The bottom line of the War on Poverty is that it increased the size of the defective population, thus making social problems worse. Linked reductionist conceptualizations promote these analyses. We shall see that many of *The Bell Curve*'s explanations have the failed, simplistic character of the search for a philosopher's stone. Race relations and social problems such as crime and illegitimacy are not likely to be explained by any flaws in individuals, certainly not by IQ.

Within the framework of the argument, four linked reductionisms justify the neglect of all social, cultural, and motivational factors in favor of alleged individual differences in cognitive ability: (1) individualistic reductionism treats all social structures and outcomes as the result of individual choices; (2) cognitive reductionism treats all human actions as ultimately a function of rational calculation; (3) genetic reductionism treats all relevant differences between people as a function of their genetic endowment; and (4) racial reductionism treats all major differences in social and cultural organization as resulting from racial differences in the population.

Individualistic reductionism will be the focus of Chapter Four, below. Genetic and cognitive reductionism will be discussed in Chapter Two, and racial reductionism will be discussed in Chapter Six. The individualistic reductionism of Herrnstein and Murray assumes that the relevant aspects explaining social structures such as crime are individual capacities. Complex social structures are explained in terms of individual actions, that are in turn explained in terms of rational calculations. This, then, grounds an analysis that reduces personality to smartness and the human situation to biogenetic capabilities.

1. Individualistic reductionism explains social structures in terms of individual actions, producing identifications such as: social structure = individual actions = rational calculation of rewards and costs.

It is misleading to explain larger social structures in terms of the choices of its individual members without adequately describing the constraints under which those choices are made. This is particularly true in the ghetto where those constraints are very tight. But what do we mean by a social structure? One example comes from the well known analysis of ghetto social structure by William Julius Wilson, which takes the flight of jobs to be central to the formation of a tangle of pathology.[32] Wilson argues that more than ten million jobs were lost from the "rust belt" during the Reagan-Bush years, which meant that a large number of unemployed men could not support a family. As a result, there were fewer positive role models, limited aspirations, and changes in family structure to adjust to the absence of a working father.[33] He further suggests that this not only led to a subculture in the next generation characterized by anger, violence, and street hustling, but also to "weak labor force attachment." This is not defined by the set of attitudes toward work, although they accompany it, but by the existence of a set of people who are socially isolated, do not have job histories that an employer would find convincing, do not have a network of friends who know how and where to get and keep jobs, and do not have appropriate work habits.

We are not trying to evaluate this model but rather to understand what a social structure is and what will happen if it is viewed reductionistically. The tangled connections between unemployment, broken families, role models, networks of friends and their jobs or lack thereof, street hustling, anger, job habits, and violence is a social structure. If one ignores this structure, and instead treats individual attitudes and dispositions (e.g., work aspirations or crime) as though they dropped from the sky, they will seem to hang in mid-air, to result from mysterious incapacities of the people themselves. In any case where a Matthew principle is operating, explanations in terms of individual choices will substitute a blaming of the victim and a legitimation of the present arrangements for a real analysis of the structure. This is the case even when the individual explanation is, in its own terms, quite correct.[34] An example from medical science and public health, where these issues are relatively non controversial, may illuminate social processes involving poverty and mobility, where the issues are more contested. Tuberculosis, at the individual level, is unquestionably caused by the tubercular bacillus. At the individual level, overcoming the body's defenses by the bacillus is the necessary and sufficient condition for tuberculosis, and the treatment of the bacillus will remove the infection. Yet older theories that ascribed tuberculosis to poor housing, malnutrition, and despair were not entirely wrong. Among the factors producing the vulnerability of a population to tuberculosis, poor housing and malnutrition played a significant role. In fact, the main reductions in the infected population in Europe occurred as a result of public health measures prior to the development of the antibiotics for treating cases at the individual level.[35] The inhibition of such public health solutions in the United States, due to individualistic ways of thinking about the problems, was the main legacy of the old Social Darwinism. The reemergence of tuberculosis as a major killer in the United States is partly the result of new strains that are antibiotic resistant, but it is even more closely related to increases in homelessness and the size of vulnerable populations such as people with AIDS.

The individualistic reductionism of *The Bell Curve* consists of the explanation of social structures such as crime, unemployment or illegitimacy in terms of the attributes of individuals. *The Bell Curve* emphasizes intelligence, and neglects cultural, attitudinal, and motivational characteristics of behavior. However, once the social structure of jobs, friends, schools, and contacts have been ignored, it hardly matters whether genes, IQ, culture, morals, or Divine Retribution are then stressed. Individualistic accounts of rates of unemployment, poverty, crime, or illegitimacy may blame the victims for the social structure in which they are trapped.[36] In fact, the important processes and issues in *The Bell Curve* are sociological, not psychological. *The Bell Curve* uses "expert opinion" (i.e., the conventional wisdom among psychometricians) to reduce all aspects of personality to the single dimension of cognitive functioning.

2.   Cognitive reductionism treats all mental abilities as one-dimensional, ranking people in a single scale that identifies: IQ = G = SAT = WAIS[37] = AFQT = cognitive capacity = smartness.

Justified by the psychological arguments of psychometricians about the intercorrelation of test scores is the substantive assumption that there is one and only one kind of "smartness," measured in an unbiased way by the Armed Forces Qualification Test and essentially unmodifiable by schooling. [It is worth noting that any such trait is one that Madonna (IQ=140) or Reggie Jackson (IQ=160) have considerably more of than J. D. Salinger (IQ=104) or J. F. Kennedy (IQ=119)].[38]

The simplest statement of this strand of Murray's analysis is that there is one and only one kind of smartness. While other things like morals, motivation, creativity, social connections, or manners may be relevant to social success in other societies, Herrnstein and Murray argue that only cognitive capacity is relevant in modern society. For reasons we describe in chapter two, Herrnstein and Murray's assumptions of a one-dimensional intelligence are implausible.[39] Social characteristics such as creativity, motivation, capacity to relate to others, and moral outlook, which cannot be ranked in linear order, are far more important to different kinds of academic and occupational performance.[40] Inherited advantages such as access to adequate food, nice neighborhoods, fine education, good manners, social contacts, or a million dollars worth of stock still play an enormous role in educational and occupational success.

Cognitive reductionism requires that there be a measure that ranks people in a single order with regard to all or most tasks of importance. If the characteristics required to be a successful lawyer, businessman, or scientist are different, or if the characteristic is not well measured by performance on an IQ test, then the argument falls apart. Compelling critiques of their cognitive reductionism have appeared and will continue to do so.[41] Herrnstein and Murray's analysis requires that tests such as the SAT or the Armed Forces Qualifications Test measure a single immutable cognitive ability.[42] Fischer and his colleagues have shown that such test scores mainly measure the amount and quality of ones exposure to formal schooling.[43] We shall focus on the genetic causal assumptions that underpin Herrnstein and Murray's analysis.

A third strand of Murray's analysis treats all relevant aspects of functioning as genetic. The reduction of cultural and personality functioning to IQ is in turn connected to their bio-genetic orientation. Social inheritance and the reproduction of group differences are conceived as heritability, which is identified with genetic mechanisms and assumed to be socially unmodifiable. Traits like near-sightedness, poor hearing, or dyslexia are probably genetic, and they have certainly caused millions of people to do poorly in school, but they cannot sustain the policy recommendations of *The Bell Curve* because they are modifiable. The effects of many of them are probably contextual. Poor hearing might help one do better in a noisy school which requires shutting out the noise.

3. Genetic reductionism treats individual variation as determined by genetic endowment, identifying: heritability = inherited = genetic = biological = natural = unmodifiable.

Herrnstein and Murray admit that it is not possible to identify heritability with genetics or with unmodifiable traits, but then use language that blurs the distinction. They give a false picture of immutability of individual variation by the assumptions they make and the way they interpret their data. For example, they identify performances on the Armed Forces Qualification Test in 1980, when the subjects ranged up to 24 years old, as measures of childhood IQ.[44] Without the strong assumption that such tests measure a socially unmodifiable ability, the analysis is totally implausible. If there is an effect of poverty, schooling, etc. on performance on the Armed Forces Qualification test, the measurement of the effect of IQ is biased upward by the reverse effect of schooling or poverty on the test. Even with the assumption that test performance is mainly genetic, that procedure gives an inflated estimate of the effect of IQ.

The genetic reductionism of Murray's argument leads to the justification and legitimation of inegalitarian, oppressive arrangements (Aristotle's fallacy). Arguments that biology is destiny have always been peculiarly comforting to privileged groups aiming to legitimate their privileges. However, they represent an attempt to turn the clock back to the racist, sexist, sharply class-divided society of the robber barons, justifying the privileges of the well-bred in terms of efficiency and intelligence instead of industry and virtue. Chapter two will show that the conceptions of genetics, environment, and adaptation to which Herrnstein and Murray appeal are hopelessly simplistic and outdated. Chapter six will show that "heritability" gives absolutely no information about the genetic or environmental source of the differences between groups (races).

There are considerable tensions between the individualist, cognitive, and genetic assumptions of Herrnstein and Murray's arguments and their focus on racial differences. Their analysis of racial differences brings them into sharp conflict with most contemporary social science. Herrnstein and Murray are forced to treat race as a biological and essential trait that corresponds to deep, essential aspects of persons, particularly their cognitive capacity. In the late nineteenth century, popular racism generated a body of literature that developed an elaborated world view, interpreting human development and history as governed by race.

Despite a small clique of theorists in South Africa, the southern United States, and Northern Ireland, no significant set of social theorists today is willing to accept the assumptions of that analysis. In order to get us to accept it as mainstream, *The Bell Curve* must engage in very clever staging.

4. Racial reductionism treats visibly different or ethnically constructed groups as distinct genetic populations, identifying: Race = skin color = ethnic group = breeding populations = gene pools.

Nineteenth century views of discrete racial groups (e.g., Nordic, Jewish, or African "races") are no longer viable. Skin color, hair texture, and other visible markers do not correspond to the differences such as blood type that seem to indicate relatively stable populations. The Australian aborigines may appear similar to some African groups, but they are actually at opposite extremes from each other with regard to most genetic markers.[45] In order to construct their argument, Herrnstein and Murray have to vacillate between biological and social concepts of ethnic group. They construct their central concept, the bell curve itself, around the concept of the mean and variation of groups, asserting that there are important differences between the means of different groups. There is, however, substantial variation around the means, so that differences in group means make little difference at the level of individuals.

Herrnstein and Murray vacillate over the significance of race. Their treatment of race represents the sharpest set of contradictions in *The Bell Curve*, continually saying one thing and implying another. The racial arguments are in tension with individualism.[46] However, race is the center of huge ascriptive inequalities. Race and racism[47] have been driving forces of United States politics from the Civil War to the present.[48] What makes no sense theoretically or logically makes perfect sense historically, politically, and ideologically. Historically the Spencerian, psychometric, and eugenic strands of Social Darwinism have always gained their political muscle from popular racism. Politically, a defense of concentrations of wealth requires a representation of the recipients of social services as being the urban ghetto poor, rather than groups such as the aged, the disabled, the orphaned, or the abused. Further, the ghetto poor must be seen as responsible for their own plight. Ideologically, if redistributive policies and social supports are to be stopped, the disadvantages and disabilities must be represented as biologically, not socially, created, and most readers must feel that such social supports go to restricted (and unworthy) groups. Groups such as the working poor, the aged, and the blind have to be conjured out of sight, and attention focused on a group of which the reader is not a member.

All four types of reductionist argument converge and reinforce one another in their tendency to direct social policy away from strategies to reduce inequalities and socially produced disadvantages. This was also the principal legacy of Social Darwinism. Social Darwinists focused on the elimination of "unfit" populations rather than the amelioration of social problems. They were obsessed with the reproduction of the "feeble minded." By focusing on the alleged genetic component of retardation, they directed attention away from all the public health and family support policies that have reduced many kinds of retardation.

As with German measles, childhood immunization, prenatal and postnatal nutrition and health care, and a host of other issues, the essential question is whether to treat the problem as a structural one, requiring a social (public health) solution, or to treat the issue as an individual set of problems requiring individual, market (fee-for-service) solutions, sometimes supplemented by spotty welfare-type supplements. Indeed, the whole issue of *The Bell Curve* is whether issues such as racism, education, employment, or housing should be treated as structural, with solutions such as full employment policies and affirmative action programs, or whether they should be left to individual survival of the fittest.

In a structure of cumulative causation, reductionist explanations are exceptionally misleading.

In all the social sciences, oversimplified representations of complex dynamics are a danger. When structure of self-reinforcing advantage or disadvantage are operating, this danger is particularly acute. In no area of sociology is this more evident than in the field of race and ethnic relations. For more than a generation, the issues have been well understood.

Deceptive oversimplifications using reductionist explanation are notorious for providing justifications for racist policies. Fifty years ago, in *An American Dilemma*, Myrdal developed a model of cumulative causation to describe race relations. Some theorists had argued that white racism and discrimination was the only problem faced by blacks in the United States.[49] Other theorists had argued that blacks were held back only by themselves by high rates of crime, unemployment, illegitimacy, and the like, and had advocated self-help rather than anti-discrimination.[50] Myrdal's analysis included both points.[51] It documented the fact that structures of white supremacy, Jim Crow, powerful and pervasive structures of economic, educational, health, and housing discrimination, extending to the social etiquette of race relations, formed a powerful racist system that constrained blacks. Poverty, unemployment, low education, family breakdown, and other components of a low standard of living and morals form a powerfully self-reinforcing system. These conditions themselves reinforce white racism and discrimination, which reinforce the low standard of living.[52] Myrdal argued that lack of economic resources, lack of social status, lack of political power, scapegoating, lack of role models, and a host of other processes are mutually reinforcing. In such a system, governed by a kind of self-reinforcing Matthew principle, one improvement can lead to others—but conversely, deterioration in one area will lead to deterioration in the others.[53] In such a system, to take any single original variable as the source of the others is misleading.

Figure 1-1 is a representation of Myrdal's analysis, showing ways that a low black standard of living and white racism each consist of a complex of mutually reinforcing elements and that each complex mutually reinforces the other.[54] Moreover, Myrdal's analysis is not only relevant to race relations. It has been generalized to describe other processes between nations, ethnic groups, religious groups, socioeconomic classes, genders or any other social group. Social processes often operate on the "Matthew Principle," taking from the disadvantaged and giving to the already advantaged, so that advantages and disadvantages will accumulate. In that case, an individualist explanation of the result in terms of the attributes of individuals will be misleading.

Figure 1-1.
Myrdal's analysis of cumulative causation.

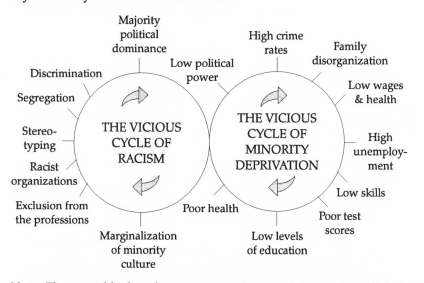

Note: These variables have been represented as two vicious cycles. All the interconnections of each cycle and the further interconnections between them have not been represented. But a structure of cumulative causation is defined as one in which each characteristic is reinforced by and reinforces each of the others.

Specifically, whenever the larger structure produces cumulative effects, treating the resulting differences as caused by initial endowment will be deceptive. For example, an infant who is a hair's breadth more verbal and as a consequence is showered with encouragement may well become more and more verbal. More verbal children may be rewarded in school and at work. If so, tiny initial differences would lead to huge differences in verbal ability perfectly correlated with huge differences in income. It is easy to see that it is a complete fallacy to believe that the differences in income were caused by the differences in verbal ability. Rather, they were caused by the rewards showered upon this ability. This is most obvious when there are no initial differences in verbal ability at all. If babies with beautiful blue eyes are showered with rewards and encouragement while brown-eyed babies are not, the result is a verbal, rich, educated blue-eyed population and a nonverbal, poor, uneducated brown-eyed population. Again, the inequality will appear to have been generated by the genes for eye-color, when it was created by the structure of social rewards.

Chapter 2

The History, Biology, and Psychology of IQ

Policies that increase inequality require scientific legitimation.

Policies that reinforce or accommodate privilege and inequality are fundamentally problematic in the twentieth century, so they require special justification. The central proposals of the New Right are policies that reinforce the advantages of the privileged and the disadvantages of the poor (cutbacks in welfare and schooling, a general reduction of federal budgets) while increasing military and prison expenditures and increasing the use of unregulated markets (such as voucher systems in schooling, and the reduction of affirmative action). The social sciences cannot prove that a policy such as welfare or affirmative action is right or wrong. Yet, both now and in the past, social scientific analysis has been central to justifying such policies. Scientific analysis of the causes of social problems plays a role in justifying social policies. Without the support of analysis that purports to be science, no new policy of this sort is likely to gain general acceptance; without the opposition of such analyses, such policies are unlikely to be abolished.

When the question of segregated schools was being heard by the Supreme Court in 1954, social theorists argued that separate schools could not be equal; that unequal, segregated schools damaged minority children. For most Supreme Court Justices, these arguments were not decisive. What was decisive were constitutional guarantees of equal treatment. Yet questions about the consequences of unequal treatment were important, both for law and for mass politics. Policy debates need to be informed about the causes and consequences of social problems.

Causes and consequences of problems such as racial inequality, crime, illegitimacy, or unemployment set constraints on social policy. Views of the appropriate policy response depend in part on whether such problems are regarded as a natural and inevitable result of people's genes, a free moral choice of perverse individuals, a result of intolerable social conditions, or the result of privileged people taking advantage of the helpless. While the social sciences cannot establish social policies, they can powerfully influence them.

The Bell Curve attempts to establish an overall view of society and social problems. It assumes that the obstacles to success represented by race, gender, or being born into poverty have all been eliminated and that racism, sexism, and other forms of institutionalized privilege were eliminated some time ago. As a consequence, society is seen as basically open, allowing all to advance to the limits of their abilities. The main social problems of society are seen to stem from the limited abilities of some of its members. The argument is an elaboration of one Herrnstein presented more than twenty years ago in the *Atlantic Monthly*[55] and his book, *IQ and the Meritocracy*.[56]

Herrnstein wrote as a defender of IQ tests. He argued that such tests had opened up higher positions in the society to talent, breaking down the traditional barriers to social mobility (i.e., class, status, religion, race, ethnicity, gender, etc.). He believed that this tendency had already created a meritocracy, in which intelligent people rise to the top. He presented his argument as a rejection of the possibility of an egalitarian society, and he believed that substantial inequality of rewards was just and inevitable:

- If differences in mental abilities are inherited, and
- If success requires those abilities, and
- If earnings and prestige depend on success,
- Then social standing will be based to some extent on inherited differences among people (*The Bell Curve*, p. 105).

The syllogism organizes major portions of the analysis. It says that inequalities and "success" are based on inherited abilities "to some extent." *The Bell Curve* will elaborate on the nature of that "success" and that "extent." Herrnstein argued that IQ tests measure inherited abilities and that the increased use of them makes the society more "meritocratic," opening up education and hiring to talent. Moreover, he argued that the more that social positions come to depend on ability, the more they come to be inherited. The increased use of objective testing enhances mobility during a transition, and finally creates a state where there is little mobility because the intelligent people are born at the top and the stupid people are born at the bottom. At that point the meritocratic encouragement of mobility produces a caste system, in which genetic inferiority of those born at the bottom is an insuperable obstacle.[57]

The central ideological implications of the syllogism stem from the meritocratic caste paradox.

The meritocratic caste paradox is the source of the most striking policy consequences of the syllogism. We may formulate the paradox as a corollary: since social position depends on the combination of environmental and genetic differences, as environmental differences in opportunity decrease, social position comes increasingly to depend on genetic differences, producing an increasingly inegalitarian caste system of people with unequal abilities.[58]

This paradox says that the more open the society becomes, the more it becomes a closed caste system. Against the view that most inequalities in the society stem from privilege and will be reduced by equal opportunity, it suggests that increased equality of opportunity produces increased inequalities. Policies promoting equality of opportunity (e.g., universal free public education, access to health care) increase segregation, inequality, and caste. If greater equality of opportunity causes greater inequality and caste-like segregation, then relative equality is an unachievable ideal. This view motivates many policies of the New Right that reinforce the advantages of the advantaged and the disadvantages of the disadvantaged.

This analysis is politically useful to privileged groups. Exclusive neighborhoods, schools, clubs, tax breaks, contacts, culture, and information: all are desired not only for the privileged themselves but also for securing the future life chances of their descendants. At the same time social arrangements that create unequal opportunities are highly problematic in American society. The value system of social equality—of blue jeans and "just plain folks"—is violated by caste, privilege, and segregation.[59] Less privileged groups have aspirations for an equal shot at schooling, jobs, and life chances for *their* children. In the absence of scientific-looking justifications that treat caste-like arrangements as "really" meritocratic, caste arrangements are extremely vulnerable. For example, the number of people believing that whites have a right to live in racially segregated neighborhoods has steadily declined.

In this situation, the meritocratic caste paradox seems to reconcile the ideology of achievement, openness, and equality of opportunity with a reality of segregation, increased inequality, and other caste-like structures. It seems to say that not only are these apparent opposites compatible but also, as a matter of logic and as a matter of science, one causes the other. It allows privileged groups to have the best of all worlds and to ally either with the upwardly mobile middle class or with working class people. Over the course of the twentieth century, the view that inequalities resulted from unequal opportunities has led to support for programs such as compensatory education and affirmative action.[60] Few privileged groups have supported these programs. *The Bell Curve* provides a systematic argument that inequalities do not result from unequal opportunities but from fixed differences in ability.

The parts of this argument that depend on factual and causal analyses will be dealt with in later chapters. Here, we will deal only with the logic of the analysis, and with some of the assumptions necessary to the argument. The most important assumptions made are those that link heritability, inheritance, genetics, and immutability. Those assumptions are the magic wand that allows social policies reinforcing privilege to be defended as openness and that allows privilege to be portrayed as the inevitable result of openness and inherited differences in ability.

The meritocratic caste paradox is internally inconsistent and rests on counter-factual hidden premises.

A syllogism is only as good as its premises. A hidden premise is an unstated assumption that is used to get to a conclusion. The basic hidden premise here is that there has been a decline in environmental inequalities in the United States. Part I of *The Bell Curve* aims to convince the reader that inequalities of opportunity (environmental differences) have been eliminated, are being eliminated, or tend to be eliminated without government intervention; that, for instance, there has been an end of racism and an end of sexism. In Chapter three, we will argue that no such decline has taken place.

However, the argument is not only factually mistaken, but also logically incoherent. An equivocation is an argument in which a term is used with one sense in one place and in another sense in another. Herrnstein and Murray are fond of equivocation. What appears to be an informal, down to earth, homey use of terms such as "race," "heritability," "leveling," "partitioning, "churning," or "advantage" conceals slippery shifts from one meaning to another. In cases such as "heritability," Herrnstein and Murray use a technical term, but apply it non-technically. In cases such as "leveling" and "churning," they coin their own term, carefully avoiding specific social science terms that were constructed precisely to avoid elusive colloquial connotations. In the case of the meritocratic caste paradox, they vacillate between the relative importance of genetics to inequality and its absolute effects.

It is logically true that if all sources of inequality are either environmental or genetic, and if the environmental components decrease, then the relative importance of genetic components increases. But this relative increase would not lead to absolute increases in inequality or caste. Herrnstein and Murray sketch a number of inexplicit and implausible mechanisms, such as assortative mating (people's tendency to marry others like themselves), to generate the genetic basis of meritocratic caste.[61] There is, of course, a rich sociological literature about who marries whom. The authors never discuss it, possibly because the literature does not support any plausible model by which assortative mating would produce increasing caste inequalities. In the United States, where parents do not arrange marriages, the opportunity for interaction is a principal requirement for choice of marriage partners. Residence, organizational memberships, work, school, and leisure time activities all play a role. Throughout history, people have usually tried to marry others like themselves in cultural identity—race, religion, ethnic background, and age—but the structural limits of who is available determine whether this preference is accomplished.[62] Social class is a primary determinant of marital choice, and has been as long as we have studied marital patterns.[63] It is neither increasing nor decreasing in importance.[64] In any case, the time scale of the analyses in *The Bell Curve* is too short, by an order of magnitude, for genetic divergence of intelligence due to assortative mating or other genetic processes.

Another hidden premise of the meritocratic caste corollary is the assumption that the effects of genetic inheritance on success have remained constant. This is also implausible. Most of the effects of genetics on success do not rest on anything so mysterious as IQ. Not being able to see a blackboard or an oncoming car, or to hear a teacher or a coworker, or to withstand a disease does not promote success. But genetic effects are not independent of the environment. With the growth of modern medicine and optometry, the adverse effects of genes for myopia, poor hearing, and many other conditions have vanished.

The meritocratic caste paradox and *The Bell Curve* as a whole are based on reductionist analyses that ask the wrong questions for social policy.

The incoherent arguments and misleading analyses result from a simplistic idea of the relationship between an individual and his or her environment. In an analysis of socially developed capacities, it is highly deceptive to represent the outcome as the result of genetic mechanisms alone. But it is also deceptive to pose the question of whether the result is due to genes or to discrimination. The search for a particular racist, sexist, or bigoted discriminator is just as misleading as the search for a bad gene. Both environment and genes are seen to act in a simplistic way.[65] However, even a careful, sophisticated, multifactorial model might have been diversionary because the essential point is even more basic.

Herrnstein and Murray appeal to genetic mechanisms, incorrectly identified with heritability, to argue against taking social action to reduce inequalities. The disadvantages and inequalities that they justify could be entirely inherited without being genetic, but even if entirely genetic would not necessarily be unalterable. The question of the extent to which social position results from genetic abilities is misleading. The inference they draw, that if such inequalities are mostly genetic then they are legitimate, does not follow.

Herrnstein and Murray use statistical methods that presuppose this simplistic way of conceptualizing the issue. As evidence that low intelligence is the major or a major source of social problems they compare standardized statistics. Test scores (conceived as a measure of genetic cognitive ability) are sometimes more highly correlated with socially problematic behaviors than with socioeconomic status. The standardized[66] statistic does not tell us how "important" an apparent cause is from a policy point of view. Rather, that analysis requires that we estimate how effective interventions with regard to several possible causes are for reducing effects.[67] It is easy to see why Herrnstein and Murray cannot acknowledge this well-known result. Now, as earlier, the view that social problems are genetic serves to legitimate government inaction with respect to the social sources of social problems. From the standpoint of social policy, we are usually interested in how we can reduce the problem. Analysis in terms of genetic predisposition treats people as the problem and fosters the delusion that by sterilizing people or preventing the immigration of unfit populations we could get rid of such problems. This delusion allows the society to fail to address the problems. Much could have been done to lower rates of retardation. One legacy of Social Darwinism is that the United States still lags behind virtually all advanced industrial nations in terms of infant immunization, prenatal and postnatal child care and nutrition.[68]

The analysis rests on individualistic reductionism that blames the victims.

The dominant theoretical strand of Social Darwinism is its individualism. The individualism of the analysis is connected to the moralism of the traditional conservative analysis of social problems that sees social problems as the result of individual moral failings. In some circles, they are further viewed as divine retribution—the sins of the fathers visited on the sons. *The Bell Curve* presents a type of analysis that appears very different from the traditional moralistic one. Its aseptic statistical tests focus on biological predisposition. Yet not only are the two types of analysis compatible but they often say the same thing in different terms.

In order to produce their analysis of meritocracy and meritocratic caste, Herrnstein and Murray must assume that the bases of success, failure, or social problems lie within individuals. This chapter will focus on the genetic reductionism of Herrnstein and Murray's argument, the assumption that there are fixed additive contributions of genes and of environment to intelligence, and that genes contribute the lion's share. We will see that their question of whether some persons or groups have superior genes for intelligence, independent of environments, is a bad question or, at the least, it rests on implausible hidden assumptions. The simplistic assumption that you can add the effects of genes and of environment will be important because it is the basis of Herrnstein and Murray's methods of analyzing the contribution of IQ (assumed to be genetic) and of socioeconomic status (assumed to be environmental) to various social problems, as well as their analyses of race, ethnicity, and social policy. In these analyses, the genetic, cognitive, racial, and individualistic assumptions are all problematic, but these problems are often obscured by the ways they combine. This is not the first time that this combination of reductionist assumptions has been used to promote a pseudo-scientific legitimation of inegalitarian policies.

Their one-dimensional and genetic conception of intelligence was the theoretical basis for the political linkage of the psychometric, eugenic, and racist movements.

As we noted in the first chapter, the rise of a concern with IQ in the United States early in the century followed mass immigration and the establishment of mass education. Under these circumstances, the notion of a short, inexpensive test to rank students according to innate intellectual ability proved very attractive. The children of privileged groups did well on such tests, and so movements to expand their use often appealed to and reinforced the beliefs of privileged groups that they were superior and that inferior groups should be restricted or eliminated. This is one reason that the pioneers of the intelligence testing movement were often entangled with both eugenics and racist movements. Expressing concern about the propagation of the feeble-minded was also a way of appealing to the political opponents of the expansion of public services. Instead of expensive educational, social, or health programs, eugenicists suggested that the social problems could be eliminated by eliminating the populations that needed such programs. They aimed to show that a host of social pathologies, such as crime, unemployment, illegitimacy, all stemmed from a single cause: low intelligence. If that deficiency could be discovered by a simple test, then the size of defective populations could be reduced—by sterilization, by incarceration, or by restriction of immigration.

In the United States, Henry Goddard championed the institutionalization of the retarded. His history of the Kallikaks is now recognized to be scientifically worthless.[69] The pioneers of the intelligence testing movement were also entangled with racist theorizing. This was the period when the nativist movement to restrict immigration was extremely powerful. Goddard administered intelligence tests to immigrants at Ellis Island, arguing that the bulk of Jewish, Hungarian, Italian, and Russian immigrants were at a moronic level. Carl Brigham, the founder of the Educational Testing Service, reported that "Negro," "Alpine," and "Mediterranean" immigrants were inferior to "Nordics."[70]

The Bell Curve rests on outdated cognitive reductionism.

The idea that is indispensable for the arguments in *The Bell Curve* is that intelligence is immutable—that IQ and related tests measure an innate capacity that cannot be changed. The book cannot present direct evidence for this assumption of immutability since all available evidence shows that the measured intelligence of societies, groups, and individuals changes. In every country for which we have data, there has been a substantial rise in tested IQ. Ethnic groups such as Eastern European Jews, who tested low on intelligence early in the century, test high today. When there have been intensive interventions, IQ and related scores have increased significantly. While Herrnstein and Murray dismiss or downplay such direct evidence, they cannot leave it at that or they would end up with an entirely unconvincing argument that merely explains away all the available facts. Therefore, they must construct a positive argument for immutability. Given the nature of the direct evidence, that argument must be indirect.

Herrnstein and Murray's cognitive reductionism—their view that intelligence is a simple, one-dimensional ability, well measured by tests such as the SAT or the Armed Forces Qualifications Test—is designed to sustain that indirect argument. It dismisses the whole body of research showing intelligence to be a multidimensional ability whose process of development is influenced by motivational and social supports in many different ways (See for instance, Sternberg, 1993; Fischer et al., 1996). It ignores the fact that test scores are much more powerfully related to the amount, recency, and quality of education than they are to age (Fischer, 1996). Herrnstein and Murray resuscitate "g," the notion of a single general intelligence factor. Charles Spearman, early in the century, had noticed that performance on one test of academic or mental ability is always positively correlated with performance on others. Using the technique of factor analysis, he postulated a single general intelligence factor, which he called "g," to account for this positive correlation.[71] The assumption of some single intelligence factor allows Herrnstein and Murray to treat many different tests, some of which are more powerfully influenced by schooling than others, as interchangeable.[72]

The notion of a single general intelligence factor has been subject to compelling critiques over the last twenty years.[73] There are many reasons why all tests should be positively correlated, not the least that they are all constructed similarly and that they are all paper-and-pencil tests. With more varied kinds of tests intelligence appears to be more multidimensional. What this means has been explored by theorists such as Howard Gardner and Robert Sternberg. By studying the mixtures of abilities impaired by various kinds of damage to the brain, Gardner suggested that there are some seven distinct kinds of intelligence.[74] Sternberg has argued that there are at least two other kinds of general intelligence, that he found to be poorly correlated with "g." Sternberg calls the ability to size up an ambiguous and novel concrete situation, to estimate the other people in that situation, and to decide what needs to be done, "practical intelligence." Many people who are notably high on academic intelligence are notably low on practical intelligence, but practical intelligence is important to both academic and business achievement. Sternberg calls the ability to challenge assumptions and think in a radically novel and unconventional way "creative intelligence," a type of intelligence that is uncorrelated to the other two kinds. Sternberg and his associates have shown that practical intelligence and creative intelligence play at least as great a role in academic and occupational success as test scores. Not surprisingly, groups that stress practical and creative intelligence are less likely to do well on the "g-loaded" IQ tests stressed by Herrnstein and Murray.

Most of the central claims to a genetic, fixed, one-dimensional capacity were abandoned during the second half of the twentieth century. Many of the founders of the movement had abandoned their earlier claims. By 1975, most American psychologists would agree with the American Psychological Association Board of Scientific Affairs that

> A distinction is drawn traditionally between intelligence and achievement tests. A naive statement of the difference is that the intelligence test measures capacity to learn and the achievement test measures what has been learned. But items in all psychological and educational tests measure acquired behavior.... An attempt to recognize the incongruity of a

behavioral measure as a measure of capacity is illustrated by the statement
that the intelligence tests contain items that everyone has an equal opportunity to learn. This statement can be dismissed as false.... There is no
merit in maintaining a fiction. (Kamin and Eysenck, 1981, p. 94)

To the extent that real psychological abilities and capacities develop
like a snowflake, building upon prior structures, a measure of innate ability at birth would be utterly useless for schools or employers. Capacities
have to be fitted to motivational frameworks, identities and skills, which
in turn usually require social and contextual supports. This mixture then
serves as a foundation for further development.

Herrnstein and Murray's analysis rests on the assumption that they
are dealing with a trait that is well measured by IQ tests and is substantially inherited. They slide from measures of heritability to the inference
that heritability means genetic mechanisms and unmodifiable traits. This
incorrect inference was common to the older literature that they employ.
Their analysis further supposes that the effects of genes and of environment are simply added together and that heritability allows them to be
disentangled. This is a simplistic, outdated view of the way genes and
environments interact.

There are also problems with their estimates. The best direct evidence
for an estimate of heritability would be monozygotic twins reared sepa-
rately.[75] There are relatively few such cases, and the independence of the
environments of the twins is almost always suspect. For more than a generation, the principal data used to argue the heritability of intelligence
were the work of Cyril Burt, who obtained findings that were too perfect
to have been validly obtained. While Herrnstein and Murray suggest that
his work may be valid, Burt's work is generally recognized as scientifically worthless.[76] Therefore, they must largely depend on a single small
study of a Minnesota group. The work is based on a very small number
of cases, the independence of whose twins has the same problems of correlated environments as the other studies. In 1979, the Minnesota twins
study, which Herrnstein and Murray describe as "a model of its kind," began with a pair of separated identical twins. No population was sampled
in an unbiased way, and the process by which twins were selected into
the study insured that their environments were not uncorrelated.[77]

**In _The Bell Curve_, arguments rely on biological determinism or genetic
reductionism.**

A key part of the argument of Herrnstein and Murray is the first premise of their "syllogism," the assumption that intelligence is inherited. In
support of this they muster arguments from geneticists, but in so doing

they substantially misrepresent what can be concluded from the genetic findings and theory. Here we will examine these authors' genetic argument. Unlike the nineteenth century eugenic arguments where traits like feeble-mindedness were treated as entirely inherited, Herrnstein and Murray attempt to give the appearance of a more sophisticated analysis by making the question a matter of degree: how much of the variation in intelligence is inherited? Similarly, they give the appearance of being open-minded by appearing to make the answer hinge on their reading of empirical studies. Both the sophistication and the empirical basis of their formulation, however, are fraudulent. We shall see that their analysis rests on the same reductionist, oversimplified view of nature (heredity) and nurture (environment).

In order to evaluate their argument, we must first examine what it is that genetic findings can tell us. Much of the confusion about genetics arises from a misunderstanding (or possibly a willful misrepresentation) of different uses of the notion of attributes being heritable. Herrnstein and Murray sometimes grant that the effects of genetics and environment are not additive and that heritability does not indicate the degree to which traits are genetically caused or inherited. But in appearing to grant these points, they often trivialize them so as to permit themselves to continue making fallacious arguments. Since the issues are absolutely central to arguments about heredity, we shall describe the central points in some detail.

In everyday language, the claim that a trait is inherited (or heritable), means that offspring resemble their parents. But everyday experience also tells us that offspring are not identical to their parents, not even to the degree that they are a simple mix of the characteristics of mother and father. Our genetic models tell us why this is so. First, it is not the traits themselves that are transmitted to offspring, it is the individual genetic elements that are part of the determination of the trait. Second, the trait itself arises from the interplay between multiple genetic elements and the environment in which those genetic elements express themselves.

The simplest genetic model involves single genetic elements.

The question of a trait being heritable is further complicated by the nature of the trait being discussed. Most people are familiar with the simplest sort of genetic determination of a trait: individual genes causing distinct categorical differences between individuals. We know of genes that cause baldness (in men and women), the presence or absence of a widow's peak, myopia, bent or straight little fingers (clinodactyly), brown sticky or gray crumbly ear wax, dwarfism, and gigantism. We also know of genes that cause more important sorts of differences, such as those causing sickle cell anemia or phenylketonuria. *Mendelian Inheritance in Man*[78] catalogs these differences in many thousands of pages. For these sorts of genetically determined traits, assigning individuals to a small number of different groups is a simple task. For example, it is easy to divide people into those with widow's peak and those without, or those with sickle cell anemia and those without. This assignment will reflect differences in genetic makeup. Given these differences, we can make some predictions (with varying degrees of certainty) about the nature of the offspring of individuals with these traits. That is, with a little work it will be easy to say that an individual has a widow's peak, to determine that the cause of the widow's peak in that individual is genetic, and on the basis of this genetic model, to talk about the probability that this individual's offspring will have a widow's peak.

Notice that even in these simple cases there are problems of interaction with other genetic elements and with the environment. Suppose we are interested in characterizing a group of people, known only to us through pictures, for presence or absence of widow's peak. We can make this characterization only if these individuals have hair. Anyone whose hair is missing or invisible for environmental reasons (including, but not limited to, skinheads and nuns) or for genetic reasons (various forms of baldness) would defy categorization. Furthermore, the pictures will certainly include individuals whose hair line is difficult to see because of differences in hair styling. These difficulties may be overcome with additional study or analysis: in most of the cases just mentioned, the remedy is obvious. In other more complex cases, these kinds of interactions present more difficult problems. Certainly in the case of intelligence, any measures of innate ability will be affected by other factors, partly for the reasons stressed earlier that all psychological tests measure acquired characteristics.

Many traits of fundamental importance cannot be explained with simple genetic models. What we see is the result of genetic elements interacting with each other and with the environment.

No one thinks that intelligence can be accounted for with a model as simple as baldness or myopia, but the simple cases help us make sense of the more complex one. Even for these very simple characteristics, environment and genetics do not have the simple and additive relation that they would have to have in the analysis of Herrnstein and Murray.

In most cases, what we observe is the end product of the interaction between particular genetic elements and the environment. Geneticists use the terms *genotype* and *phenotype* to refer to the genetic elements and to the end product of all these interactions: the genotype is the genetic makeup of the individual, the phenotype what the individual looks like. If the only thing affecting how one looked were genetic inheritance the relationship between genotype and phenotype would be quite simple, and the logic of the analysis in *The Bell Curve* would hold.

Genetic determination is more complex when the characteristic with which we are concerned involves a number of different genes and environmental influences. Offspring may resemble parents (i.e. the trait is heritable) in characteristics that cannot easily be assigned to one of a small number of groups. Thus, we recognize that there may be a tendency for tall parents to have tall offspring and short parents to have short offspring. Quantitative traits, such as height, defy the sorts of genetic analysis discussed above. For these, environmental factors and genetic differences will interact with each other to determine the value of the trait (phenotype) in an individual. We would quite reasonably expect that individuals raised in a nutritionally rich environment would grow to be taller than individuals who are substantially malnourished. Furthermore, it is clear that the timing and exact nature of nutritional deprivation will change the effects on height.

Notice that for traits such as these, individuals generally defy simple categorization. For the purposes of this argument we will exclude from analysis those individuals who are abnormally short (genetic dwarfs) or abnormally tall (genetic gigantism) in such a way that makes them easy to categorize into the height categories "dwarf" and "giant." However, it should be obvious that the analysis of height will involve very different kinds of mechanisms, some genetic and some environmental. If one fails to distinguish them, throwing all variation into a common pot, which one then partitions into "genetic" and "environmental," and if, further, one then uses forms of analysis that artificially emphasize extreme cases (dwarfs and giants), the result will be highly deceptive. We are concerned with the relationship between parent and offspring for individuals of heights that correspond to the normal range of variation in height. Among individuals with the normal range of variation in height, it is not possible to divide individuals into a small number of groups and make the same sorts of genetic analysis that we might make with hairlines. Thus, an analysis equivalent to the one we carried out with respect to widow's peak isn't possible here because of the variety of influences.

In the genetic model of many genes acting together, the heritability of a trait characterizes the relative importance of genes and the environment in a specific population.

Our understanding of how such quantitative traits are determined involves the action of many genes interacting with each other and with the environment. All the sorts of interactions that we discussed for traits determined by single genes come into play here, too. The combined effects of many different genes and the varied effects and influence of the environment give us the smooth distribution of phenotypes that is often referred to as a bell curve.

The form that a geneticist's analysis takes in these cases focuses not on the characteristics of individuals, but rather on the characteristics of the population to which these individuals belong. We know that in any population there will be variability in the character under study. In the specific example we are looking at, different individuals will have different heights.[79] It's easy to see that there are at least two simple sources for this variation: variation caused by differences in genetic makeup and by variation in environments. (We'll suppose that we've conquered the sorts of variation imposed by age and by time of day.) Geneticists define a quantity, called the *heritability* of a trait, that simply measures what fraction of the total *variation* in a trait is caused by *variation* in genes. In its simplest form, then, heritability = (variation caused by genes) ÷ (variation caused by genes + variation caused by environment).[80] This will take values between zero and one: zero if none of the observed variation in a population is caused by variation in genes; one if all of the observed variation in a population is caused by variation in genes. The name of this measure is misleading, because it does not measure the degree to which any individual owes his or her phenotype to genes. As we will see, this simple misunderstanding leads to substantial misinterpretations. The center of Herrnstein and Murray's argument is the view that some part of intelligence is due to genes; some part is due to the environment; and that "heritability" tells one how much is due to each. This key assumption undergirding their analyses involves a misleading oversimplification of the concepts "environment" and "heritability."

In the first place, it is clear that the heritability of a trait applies only for a specific population and only in the specific environment in which the measurements have been carried out. If we assess the heritability of the same trait in another population or in another environment, both genetic and environmental variances will be different, and the specific value of the heritability will change. Thus, heritability is not a characteristic of the trait, but rather a characteristic of the trait in a specific group of individuals in a specific environment.

The norm of reaction is a useful characterization of the relationship of genotype, phenotype, and environment.

We have seen that the environment can have dramatic effects on the phenotype produced. Indeed, identical genotypes can be expected to produce different phenotypes in different environments. Thus, what we really want to understand is the relationship among the three: how genotype and environment interact to produce a phenotype. This is neatly summarized as a norm of reaction. The norm of reaction for a particular genotype can, in theory at least, be summarized in the form of a simple graph. Several possible norms of reaction are shown in Figure 2-1. Each line represents the way in which the phenotype of a person (or population of genetically identical persons) would react to changes in some environmental variable. In the graph on the top left, the phenotype changes dramatically with environmental changes: small changes in the environment produce dramatic changes in phenotype. The top right graph represents a phenotype that is insensitive to changes in environment. Here even large environmental changes will produce only very small changes in phenotype. In the graph on the bottom, the effect of changes in the environment depend critically on the value of the current environment. On the left side of the graph, phenotype is quite sensitive to environmental changes; on the right, it is quite insensitive. Why might phenotype be exquisitely sensitive to environmental differences in poor

Figure 2-1.
Three hypothetical norms of reaction showing how environments might affect IQ scores.

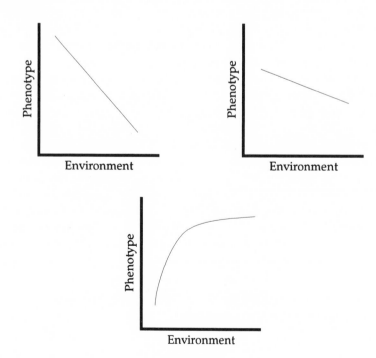

environments and insensitive in better ones? In thinking about the inter-action between genetic and environmental effects it is worth keeping in mind that IQ scores on a test such as Herrnstein and Murray use will be affected by functional illiteracy, functional deafness, or chronic illness. Therefore, anything about the environment that affects such conditions will affect whether and how they affect test scores. Thus genetic deafness might be completely handicapping without a hearing aid, but environ-mental changes might have little effect beyond that.

What does this sort of analysis tell us about how something such as IQ might behave? As an example, the graph at the top left would describe what is usually called a sensitive child. In a supportive environment, the child reaches high levels, but in a poor environment the child fails misera-bly. The graph at the top right represents a less sensitive genotype that achieves about the same in all environments, while the graph at the bot-tom represents a genotype sensitive to environmental disabilities but not to environmental enrichment. In dealing with these different genotypes, it makes absolutely no sense to ask which has a higher overall intelli-gence. The question is poorly formed because the answer depends on the environment and the norms of reaction. Unless they have the same slopes and never cross, the questions which is higher in general or how much higher are meaningless. A hidden premise in much of *The Bell Cur-ve*'s analysis is the assumption of implausible norms of reaction.

Herrnstein and Murray are aware that genetic and environmental fac-tors may interact with each other. When it suits their purpose, they even assume such interactions. For example, they assume that such interac-tions will increase the effects of intelligence when there is greater educa-tion, which involves higher sensitivity to enriched environments. When it suits their purpose they assume a curve like that at the bottom, in which the effects of environment hit a ceiling. They do not justify any of these assumptions or notify the reader of the implausible character of the assumptions. Most of the time, it suits their purpose to assume that the phenotype is almost entirely insensitive to environmental variation.

These three figures illustrate the sorts of relationships between geno-type, environment, and phenotype that we might see. Unfortunately, the norms of reaction are known for very few traits, and for these only for a limited range of environments. For the cases that have been studied, the situation is not so simple as any of these figures might suggest. As we shall see, the exact nature of the norms of reaction are critically important in assessing the arguments that Herrnstein and Murray are advancing.

Norms of reaction can help us interpret heritability.

With a little extension, the graphs of norms of reaction can be used to help examine what heritability does and does not mean. First, we recognize that populations of individuals are exposed to a range of environments, but a range that is limited somewhat. We can represent this by assuming that most individuals will be exposed to environments in the middle of the range, smaller numbers of individuals exposed to environments in the extremes of the range. On our norm of reaction diagram, this might look something like Figure 2-2. The small bell-shaped curve on the bottom represents the normal range of environments for this population.[81]

However, the assumption that the effect of genes and environment can be added is simplistic. The bottom graph in Figure 2-2 shows two different genotypes, one for which environmental differences have little effect on phenotype, and a second for which environmental differences have a dramatic effect on phenotype. In the case of a real population distributed in a real set of environments, the variation will be more complex. Consider two populations, one composed solely of individuals of the first

Figure 2-2
Three hypothetical norms of reaction for two genotypes.

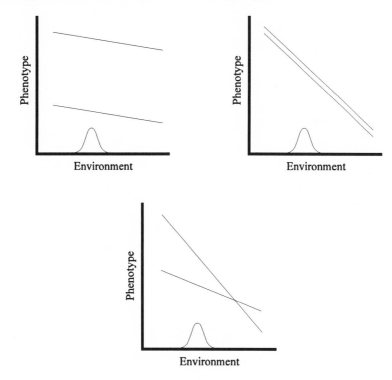

genotype, and the other composed solely of individuals of the second genotype. Clearly, for the genotype 1 population, there will be very little variation in phenotype; for the genotype 2 population, there will be considerable variation in phenotype. Since real populations are composed of a large number of genotypes, a more realistic view would include the norm of reaction for every genotype found in the population. Fortunately, the behavior of the heritability can be understood just by considering a population with a couple of genotypes. This is illustrated by the other graphs in Figure 2-2.

In the figure on the top left, each individual genotype is quite insensitive to environmental changes, but the genotypes themselves give rise to remarkably different phenotypes. Therefore most of the population variation is caused by genotype, and the heritability will be high. In the figure in the top right, there is not much difference from genotype to genotype, and both genotypes are very sensitive to environmental changes. Most of the variation in the population will be the result of environmental variability, and the heritability will be small. In the case on the bottom there is a substantial amount of variability between genotypes over the normal range of environments, and heritability would be substantial. Thus, the first two panels illustrate what we might mean if we claimed that phenotypic variation was "mainly genetic" or "mainly environmental."

The third panel illustrates a case in which asking which genotype is superior is nonsense. Notice that if we were to make changes to the environment such that there was a uniform increase in the environmental variable, the differences between the genotypes would decrease and the heritability would go down. Furthermore, if the environmental variable increases enough, the ranking of the phenotypes changes: the genotype that had a higher phenotype at low values of the environmental variable becomes the lower of the two for large values of the environmental variable. In a case such as this, the question of how much one of the genotypes is superior to the other is, of course, absurd.

As these examples make clear, the exact nature of norms of reaction is critical to an understanding of just what we can and cannot infer from estimates of heritability. For the few cases for which norms of reaction are known, the relationships among genotype, phenotype, and environment are complex, and the usual assumptions of *The Bell Curve* are not met. Figure 2-3 shows norms of reaction for the number of abdominal bristles in fruit flies raised at different temperatures for ten genotypes. Genotypes have significant interactions with the environment, so that their norms of reaction cross over each other. Assertions about the superiority of one is meaningless. Though these norms of reaction are known only for simple traits such as this, it is unlikely that the norms of reaction for intelligence are simpler. When the environment is not one-dimensional, and the effects of environment and heredity are not additive, as in Figure 2-3, the analysis of *The Bell Curve* makes no sense at all.

Herrnstein and Murray make very weak claims about the inheritance of intelligence; to say that something is somewhere between 40 percent and 80 percent says very little. It is important to recognize that the crucial part of the argument is not the number, which they stress, but the assumptions, which they conceal. In fact, they have little support for claims that heritability must lie between 0.40 and 0.80 and it would not matter for their argument. We will not contest their assumption that heritability is between 0.4 and 0.8, giving their analysis every benefit of the doubt, although that assumption does not seem well grounded to us.

Studies of heritability cannot answer the question of how much IQ is a function of genes.

The arguments that are advanced in *The Bell Curve* can be examined in the light of this understanding of what the genetic measures can and cannot tell us. For the sake of this discussion, we will also set aside the controversy over whether standardized tests measure a one-dimensional capacity accurately. Let us suppose that there is some standardized test that does a good job of measuring a quantity that we will call IQ.

Figure 2-3.
Norms of reaction for abdominal bristle number as a function of temperature for ten genotypes of fruit flies. (after Griffiths *et al.*, 1996, p. 837)

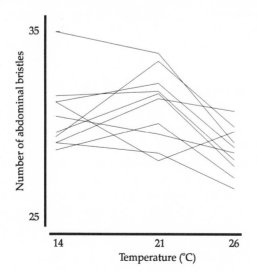

The Bell Curve contains two main foci for the genetic arguments. The first of these, on pp. 105-110, poses the question, "How Much Is IQ a Matter of Genes?" The next sentence contains the putative answer: "IQ is substantially heritable." Herrnstein and Murray base this answer on studies that suggest that the heritability of IQ is somewhere between 0.40 and 0.80.

However, the question they pose cannot be addressed by studies of heritability. Heritability is the answer to a very different sort of question. An accurate section heading, "How Much Is (Total Variation in IQ) a Matter of (Variation in Phenotype Caused by Different Genes for Specific Populations in Specific Environments)?" is not catchy, but is substantially more honest. This difference in phrasing changes the argument fundamentally and makes it impossible to support the later arguments they make.

A muddy view of the relationship between genes and environment serves several functions in *The Bell Curve*. In the first twelve chapters, it is used to justify the assumption that intelligence test scores of young adults are not influenced by their family, schooling, friends, or neighborhood. Those test scores are taken to reflect innate ability, and their correlations with social problems are taken to indicate that the problems are not susceptible to social policy. Moreover, in Chapter Six, which contains the second focus for genetic arguments, we will see that there are particularly serious problems when heritability is used to analyze group differences. A high heritability does not tell us that the phenotype of an individual is caused by genes. Heritabilities tell us nothing about the causes of differences in the average value of some trait in a group. Heritability is a partitioning of variance, and as such is completely independent of the average. Statements about the sources of variation cannot tell us anything about average values. The heritability of a trait contains no information about the average value of that trait.

"Substantially heritable" does not mean immutable.

A corollary of this argument is that "substantially heritable" does not mean that a population is forever fixed with this average value of the trait. For well-known[82] reasons a trait might be highly heritable and environmental modifications might affect it dramatically. Even in a trait that is 100% "heritable," environmental intervention could cause a substantial improvement. Even if the heritability of IQ is "substantial," the IQ of neither individuals nor groups is fixed. Environmental changes can bring about dramatic changes in phenotype for traits with a heritability of 1.0.

On page 109, Herrnstein and Murray ask us to consider "the limits that heritability puts on the ability to manipulate intelligence." In fact, of course, a high heritability puts absolutely no limits on the ability to manipulate anything. Changes in environments can still improve the mean value of the trait, and changes in environments can still alter the heritability of a trait. Their misrepresentation of heritability continues later on p. 109 with the claim that "what most interventions accomplish is to move children from awful environments to ones that are merely below average, and such changes are limited in their potential consequences when heritability so constrains the limits of environmental effects." Our point bears repeating: a high heritability places *absolutely no* limits on the effect of environmental changes.

"Substantially heritable" does not mean that the phenotype of any individual is the result of genes.

"Heritability" is used in *The Bell Curve* to suggest a genetic mechanism operating in each individual to produce an immutable result. Only with this assumption are Herrnstein and Murray's interpretations of data or policy implications plausible. But heritability says nothing about the relation between an individual and its progeny. By changing the environments that populations encounter, heritability can be made larger or smaller without changing the underlying genetic structure of individuals.

"Substantially heritable," even 100 percent heritable, also does not mean that any *individual* is forever fixed with a particular phenotype. As we shall see, the jump from "heritable" to "inherited" is fallacious. Since heritability is a statement about the relative contributions of environment as sources of variation within a population, it cannot be used to determine whether the trait possessed by any individual is caused by genes. Indeed, the question itself makes no sense. The phenotype of every individual is the result of the expression of genes in a particular sequence of environments—one cannot think about a phenotype in the absence of the genes or in the absence of the environment.

The syllogism reexamined.

In the light of this discussion, what do we conclude about the basic syllogism? From the premise that intelligence is inherited, the syllogism derives the inevitability of social inequality. The syllogism is an elaborate form of the view that social inequality is increasingly a matter of the survival of the fittest. Herrnstein and Murray claim that if social standing has a high correlation with measured IQ, and if IQ has high heritability, then differences in social standing are caused by genes and are therefore fixed. But the exact value of the heritability of IQ or of social standing contains no information about the causes of differences between individuals or between groups.

Herrnstein and Murray cannot be ignorant of these facts about the nature of heritability. In the more than twenty years since the publication of Arthur Jensen's work, the point has been made repeatedly.[83] Their willful misrepresentation of the genetic argument suggests that the conclusions they wish the reader to draw precede the argument. The misrepresentation continues, in an even more malignant form, in their discussion of the relationship between races, ethnic groups, and IQ. We will deal with that argument directly in Chapter Six.

Central to all their legitimating claims is the claim that a scientific analysis will lead us to the bottom line about the causes of various social problems, and for Herrnstein and Murray that bottom line is no more scientific or sophisticated than the popular saying that "you can't make a silk purse out of a sow's ear." They suggest that some people just do not have the stuff to be doctors, lawyers, or businessmen. Herrnstein and Murray are aware of the weakness of their genetic and psychometric arguments. After hundreds of pages of pseudo-scientific arguments and calculations based on a genetic account of individual and group differences, they will say, it does not matter; even if the cause is not genetic,[84] IQ cannot be changed.[85] This argument is dishonest. In the first place, the "even" makes it seem (as they know is untrue) that if it were genetic then that would set limits on the degree to which it could be changed. Moreover, many of their central arguments are not really about whether it can be changed, but about whether the society is genuinely meritocratic.

Chapter 3

A Meritocratic Social Structure?

The Herrnstein syllogism explicates a historical vision of the increase of segregation and inequality in the United States during the Reagan years.

During the 1980s, inequality rose sharply in the United States. From 1973 to 1995, real per capita production in the United States increased by more than a third, but for the vast majority of the work force (non-supervisory workers), hourly wages declined. During the 1980's, all the earning gains went to the top twenty percent of the work force and sixty-four percent of those gains went to the top one percent.[86] At the bottom of the social structure there was a sharp increase in poverty and homelessness, especially among children. The political agenda of the New Right in the United States today will increase that inequality. The theoretical analysis of *The Bell Curve* defends it.

Many of the reasons for the increase in inequality are well-known. Throughout the period, the Reagan-Bush administrations made a conscious effort to give incentives to the upper class. Policies such as large tax cuts, especially for the wealthy, deregulation of the savings and loans, changes in regulation of occupational health and safety and bankruptcy, as well as policies facilitating the movement of millions of jobs away from the "rust belt", all helped the upper class to make a killing. The flip side of those changes was the slashing of welfare rolls and the lowering of the real size of welfare payments, the reduction of many social services, and the creation of massive areas of high unemployment, poverty, and segregation at the center of most American cities, as well as an increasing income gap between the rich and the poor.[87]

As noted in the last chapter, Herrnstein's thesis of the rise of a meritocracy achieved instant notoriety in the early 1970s. However, it remained without political influence. *The Bell Curve* reintroduces these ideas in a different political climate. The thesis of a meritocracy purports to be descriptive and explanatory, but its main purpose is a justification of social inequalities. The thesis says that inherited traditional privilege has disappeared, so that now top positions of the society are staffed by the most able. At the same time, it argues that inherited inequalities are bound to increase. As environmental differences decline in importance, inherited differences increase, creating a new caste system with the bright, able people on the top and the dregs on the bottom. The argument requires considerable sleight of hand. It is predicated on the decline of environmental inequalities at the same time that it predicts increasing environmental inequalities.

Despite, or perhaps because of, its conceptual slipperiness, the argument is politically useful. It suggests that government action to assure equality of opportunity does not reduce those inequalities, but increases them. By reducing environmental differences, social policy increases the effects of genetic differences. By encouraging breeding by the unfit, it creates the ultimate welfare dependency: the creation of a fundamentally unfit, dependent population. Nineteenth- and early twentieth-century eugenics policy was led inexorably from these assumptions to the policy conclusions that the only effective responses were sterilization, euthanasia, restriction of immigration, and, in Germany, genocide.[88] Characteristically, Herrnstein and Murray lead the reader to that point and then disavow those traditional eugenicist conclusions.[89] However, in the 1990s these assumptions motivate at least a systematic assault on the main structures of government intervention on behalf of the poor.

To serve as a legitimation of the assault on equality, Herrnstein's schematic account, which depended mainly on the use of IQ tests had to be given a more plausible mechanism, to be articulated with social science literature in neoconservative economics and management, and to be connected to policy issues on affirmative action, taxes, and welfare. Murray is a master of constructing historical interpretations by splicing together a number of time series and producing a startling interpretation with considerable political importance. *Losing Ground* in 1984 was a major document legitimizing Reagan cutbacks. As a result of mild cutbacks in the Carter years and sharper ones in the early Reagan years, a number of social problems were intensified, such as homelessness, urban collapse, an illegal second economy of drug dealing and crime, and endemic AIDS in poor black and Hispanic communities. *Losing Ground* argued that such problems were not the consequences of cutbacks of welfare. Murray argued that welfare breaks down the family structure (i.e. it creates a disincentive to marry) and the cultural system (i.e. it provides a disincentive to work). Thus he concludes that it was the excess of welfare in the 1970s, not the cutbacks of social services in the 1980s, that produced these social problems. A truly startling account: giving money to the poor makes them poorer; taking money from them makes them richer. The analysis contradicted the fact that the great majority of welfare recipients stayed on welfare for only a short time.[90] But it was politically useful in justifying welfare cutbacks for the poor.

Part I of *The Bell Curve* extends and radicalizes that argument. Like *Losing Ground*, it argues that social services, or income maintenance such as Aid to Families with Dependent Children produce more of the very social problems they seek to remedy. While *Losing Ground* suggested that they produce defective subcultures and motivations, *The Bell Curve* argues that they produce defective people.[91] Policies promoting equality merely produce intractable inequalities.

The first four chapters of *The Bell Curve* describe an implausible transformation.

The first chapter of *The Bell Curve* attempts to make this thesis plausible by concentrating on education. Specifically, it takes the transformation of Harvard University as emblematic of the transformation of education and of the whole society. Murray, a graduate of Harvard, and Herrnstein, a professor there, seem to mistake Harvard for the whole society, at the same time that they overlook (or obscure) some of the best-known and best-documented facts about that institution. The single fact around which Chapter One revolves is that during the 1950s the average SAT scores of Harvard students rose sharply. They transform this into the central paradox of meritocracy. On one hand, old barriers of social background, wealth, religion, ethnicity, race, or social status are torn down in a great social leveling. On the other hand, the more cognitively able are increasingly partitioned; they are segregated and associate with one another; they marry one another and bear cognitively able children, creating a new, meritocratic system based on cognitive ability. This increasing caste is supposedly demonstrated by the sharpened distinctions between the elite colleges and the bulk of American institutions of higher education. Herrnstein and Murray play the processes of leveling and partitioning off against each other.

Chapter Two of *The Bell Curve* argues that occupations have also become more selective. College graduation and graduate study are now required for the top positions in the occupational hierarchy. Since education is presumed to be dependent on IQ, personal cognitive ability is increasingly separating the smart from the dumb in the world of work. Chapter Three then develops the cornerstone of the argument, the specification of "success" as work productivity. This produces the argument that without any government programs supporting equal opportunity, an invisible hand will eliminate privilege. Any employer, regardless of his or her personal prejudices, must try to become a little Harvard University giving preference to more intelligent applicants because they are more productive workers. Smart people do better than dumb people in every job in society. To fail to distinguish between the smart and the dumb in hiring necessarily reduces productivity and, thus, the GNP. The last chapters of the book argue that affirmative action policies interfere with naturally meritocratic, color-blind labor market processes.

Chapter Four anticipates the down side of meritocracy, the unfortunate but inevitable development of a new caste system, namely the partitioning of society into the smart and the dumb. The smart will do better and better as the dumb remain locked in low-achievement, low-reward positions. "Success and failure in the American economy, and all that goes with it, are increasingly a matter of the genes that people inherit." Since this partitioning is separating the smart from the dumb in their everyday interactions, smart people will marry smart people, and this process, creating a fundamental division in society, is accentuated through advances by women.[92]

A defense of meritocracy, the rule by a narrow, self-perpetuating, high-IQ caste, is politically important. It is not a view that immediately recommends itself as attractive, politically popular, or consistent with democratic politics.[93] However, high income professionals and businessmen, who did very well under the Reagan policies of the 1980's, are predisposed to see themselves and their children as superior to the rest of the population and to see their success as tied to efficiency and productivity. The Reagan era enormously increased inequality and an accompanying host of social problems such as homelessness. The political Right needs an alibi for these social problems. *The Bell Curve*'s fantasy about the increased cognitive partitioning, segregation, and assortative mating of the cognitive elite portrays the problems as fixed. The present assault on women, children, minorities, and social services will produce inequalities and social problems that could dwarf those of 1995. For those who support inequality, it is politically indispensable to develop an alibi for these problems, even before they fully manifest themselves.

At the same time, the argument does damage control on holes in Murray's earlier argument in *Losing Ground*. Murray had argued that welfare produced a general disincentive to work. But analyses had shown that most welfare recipients are on welfare for only a short time.[94] Murray responded by arguing that long-term welfare dependents are the problem. Since most of these long-term SSI or AFDC recipients are ill, disabled, elderly, or otherwise relatively unemployable, he needed the argument that welfare somehow produces that disabled population. Only thus can cutting benefits to poor women, the disabled, and their children be represented as being "a little cruel to be very kind."

The argument requires a magical transformation: There is both a leveling (increasing mobility) and partitioning (decreasing mobility).

The concept of meritocracy is a general political justification of differential power, rewards, and status for those at the top of society. Because inequality reflects differences in ability, there is no reason for societal intervention. Because inequality is inevitable, government action to reduce inequality is utopian.

The historical sketch in the first chapters of *The Bell Curve* must convince the reader that there has been a fundamental, irresistible, and desirable change in the basis of class position in the recent period—that privilege associated with wealth, ethnicity, religion, race, or connections has disappeared in a "great social leveling." In place of such privilege, the authors intend to convince us that there is a meritocratic system in which intelligent people are being rewarded for their intelligence. Essentially, the chapters must perform a great magic trick. The lion of class privilege stalks across the stage. It enters the intelligence testing box in schools, professions, the military, or business. Presto chango! Out comes the beneficent, productive golden retriever of meritocracy.

Using Harvard as a model for the entire university system, Herrnstein and Murray reach the conclusion that, because a higher proportion of people are going to college, universities have become more democratic, and so a more diverse population is employed in the executive offices of corporations. Insofar as lion-like obstacles to equal opportunity remain, few people are willing to jettison instruments of equal opportunity. *The Bell Curve* must convince us that the changes are a result of greater selection on the basis of ability, rather than of the broad social changes, for that focus will motivate their later policy recommendations. It must convince us of the transformation without giving any data that show a great social leveling. No such data exist. In the real world, lions do not change into retrievers through the results of IQ tests. Indeed, even though there is an immense literature on social mobility in the United States, Herrnstein and Murray must ignore it because studies of occupational achievement have consistently supported the conclusion that not much has changed. Sons repeat the position of their fathers.[95] There were earlier, and there are now, structural supports that maintain most people in their relative positions. Wealth and status make it possible for children from higher income families to continue the achievement of their parents. Without the friendships formed in private schools, membership in private clubs, and other contacts, many channels of information and recommendation remain closed to those with lower social status.

How is the magic trick accomplished? It is a masterpiece of rhetoric. To give the illusion of a startling increase in equality of opportunity, the reader's attention must be focused on education, and within education on individualist processes of selection into elite institutions, and within those, on selection criteria, all the while ignoring social structural changes. SAT scores must be accepted as a measure of fixed genetic ability, independent of education or privilege. Only then can the increase in SAT scores at elite institutions be represented as a great social leveling. Inherited structures of privilege must be spirited away. Among the most visible of such structures of differential access to opportunity are racial and gender differences. Herrnstein and Murray's arguments cooperate with those of Murray's colleague at the American Enterprise Institute, D'Sousa (1995), to convince us that such racially restrictive structures of access, support or information, usually viewed as components of "institutional racism", have disappeared.[96]

The trick begins in the first chapter. In that chapter, we must look at rising SAT scores at Harvard and be convinced that we are looking at increased meritocracy (and great social leveling) in the society as a whole. Then, in Chapter Two, we are suddenly shifted to business and find that the education of managers and executives has increased. We must conclude that if education is more meritocratic and businessmen are more educated, that the society is more meritocratic. Then, finally, an invisible hand—an irresistible mechanism—has to be presented. Chapter Three has to convince us that a flood of new evidence has shown that more intelligent workers are more productive, so that all businessmen or administrators, no matter what their personal prejudices, are compelled by institutional interests to hire the more intelligent.

This will lead to the fanciest trick of all, the surprise ending implicit in the Herrnstein syllogism: *The Bell Curve* will change the retriever back into a lion again! Meritocracy becomes increasingly partitioned, increasingly inegalitarian, and increasingly caste-like. But now, strengthened by its productivity and technological efficiency, it is invincible and irresistible. America has become more unequal because it has become more equal! Millions of children are trapped in awful conditions of ghetto poverty not because of any lack of opportunity, but precisely because there is equal opportunity that has drained those communities of anyone with ability. A final puff of smoke, and the final form of *The Bell Curve*'s "meritocracy " appears: a (racist) caste system, with the children of those at the bottom doomed to stay there by their alleged innate inferiority.

The illusion of a great leveling and partitioning is produced by selective focus on individual selection criteria at elite institutions, and those criteria are then misrepresented.

As in all magic tricks, the first requirement is that the audience must want to believe. The whole story represents a deep American myth. Central to the politics of the Right is the view of the world as one where everyone is able to reach his or her full potential and to claim a position based solely on his or her individual ability. This is powerful rhetoric because Americans are socialized to a belief in individual opportunity. It is, however, an argument that is possible only by denial of continued differential opportunity in society and by ignoring the changing social meaning of different levels of education over time. If we consider the high school diploma of the past as equivalent in its social power to the college degree of today, Herrnstein and Murray present no evidence that education is more important today or that cognitive ability was less recognized in the past.

Most magic tricks require harsh lighting against a stark black and white stage. All kinds of wires and other devices can be made invisible against the black background, particularly when the eye is distracted by the magician's white gloves. Here, and in subsequent chapters, the reductionist conceptualization of ability serves as the harsh light to deceive the eye. Specifically, the broad social changes of urbanization and industrialization must be rendered invisible so that their consequences can be ascribed to meritocratic selection. Herrnstein and Murray must misrepresent the institutional struggles and their institutional consequences (such as the funding and growth of high schools or land grant colleges) as being instead the automatic consequence of the invisible hand of meritocratic selection. They must ignore and misrepresent the processes and institutions as they affected the experience of women and ethnic or religious minorities. Herrnstein and Murray first restrict our attention to education; and among educational processes, they concentrate on SAT scores. These must be treated as measures of cognitive ability, even though later chapters of *The Bell Curve* will treat SAT scores as a measure of effectiveness of education. In complete contradiction to this later analysis, SAT scores are treated here as a measure of biologically fixed cognitive ability. This allows the increase in the SAT scores at elite universities to be represented as the replacement of privilege by merit.

The argument rests on comparisons over time of the proportion of young people attending college and the percentage of those with high

SAT scores who do so.[97] Herrnstein and Murray represent the rise of SAT scores in elite schools as the disappearance of traditional privilege. To narrow our focus to selection criteria, they ignore the main processes of urbanization, industrialization, change in gender relations, and growth of education. By doing so, they give the impression that selectivity in the past was on the basis of privilege, while it is now on the basis of merit. All one needs to do to eliminate privilege is to use the magic box of ability testing. The analysis intentionally fails to take into account the expansion of education over time. Jobs that required a high school diploma, at most, early in the century, required a college degree after World War II, but it is not clear what is intrinsically meritocratic about that. The principal changes involved credential inflation, the growth of high schools, increasing higher education of women, and the G.I. Bill. Only by ignoring these institutional changes can Herrnstein and Murray represent the mid-century increase in SATs as a great social leveling.

In the nineteenth century the United States was a primarily rural nation. Most people lived on farms. It was also a time when rural people were heavily served by one-room country schools. It is not until the 1930s that high schools were built in many areas serving a wider geographical area. The consolidated rural school, which brought together the children of many one-room school districts in a modern educational system, followed World War II. (Even rural communities close to New York City had no high school in the first decade of the twentieth century. Children had to board in a city like Albany or Poughkeepsie to attend high school. Few girls were sent away from home to board. Without access to high school, few children could go on to college.) In the cities where high school was more easily available, women were a significant proportion of the top-achieving high school graduates. Yet college education was precluded for most women in the early part of the century. Only the women's colleges admitted women in large numbers. Sending women to college did not become a norm until after World War II, and women's educational achievement remained behind that of men until the last quarter of the twentieth century.

When the lion of class privilege emerges from the black box of ability testing, its mane, its claws, and any traces of class privilege have been carefully removed. *The Bell Curve* must assume that SAT scores fairly represent individual ability and that all individuals have an equal chance to do well on these tests (contrary to the explicit claims of the Educational Testing Service), ignoring the influence of different quality of educational opportunity on the scores. Privileged children have been in an environment where the credentials of teachers are high, classes are small, and the curriculum is fully developed to ensure mastery of advanced academic material. A full network of supports is provided for the weaker students.

These schools offer special classes to prepare their students for the PSAT and SAT exams. Further, the parents support an entire business designed to enhance performance on these exams.

Contrast this with the environment of the poor kids in center city coming from homes without space for study, where even basic nutrition is dependent on the federally subsidized school breakfast and lunch. Their schools are overcrowded, deprived of basic educational material, without extracurricular or even basic advising resources, housed in decrepit buildings, and with teachers who have low expectations for their students, often poor credentials, and high turnover. Yet Herrnstein and Murray expect these children to perform as well as those in private schools or the schools of the wealthy suburbs. The shocking conditions detailed in such accounts of center city schools as Kozol's *Savage Inequalities* are not conditions in which children of equal ability can shine equally. Children from these schools do not do as well as others on any measure of performance. Without adequate preparation, without effective guidance, and without parental resources, these students do not have the same incentives to adopt academic roles or the same opportunity to go on in education. To claim, therefore, that they are of lower cognitive ability is to blame the victims for what has happened to them.

In its treatment of both education and of occupation, the analysis is highly selective. A reductionist conceptualization directs attention away from real institutional changes to the selection standards that follow from or justify them. The selection of the beginning and end points of that time series carefully conceals the main social structural changes such as the growth of high schools or social policies such as the G.I. Bill behind a black curtain. By ignoring the growth of public schools or the land grant colleges, and by beginning the analysis during the height of the Great Depression, the postwar shift at elite institutions can be represented as a great transformation, with the counter-transformation of cognitive partitioning waiting behind the curtain, to account for the fact that no magic has really occurred. There is no analysis of the contribution of an increasing proportion of young people as the baby-boomers entered college, and no attempt to separate the experiences of men and women. By ignoring the institutional supports that made possible the advance of many groups since World War II, Herrnstein and Murray minimize the social costs of eliminating those supports.

Moreover, by exaggerating the benefits of meritocratic testing practices, they imply that untrammeled labor markets will eliminate remaining privilege. However, while there has been a sharp increase in SAT scores at elite schools, that indicates little about meritocracy in the society as a whole. Broad social changes have led to an explosion of applications to places such as Harvard. This could increase their average SAT scores without shorting any of their other traditional criteria of selection. Institutional self-interest does encourage such institutions to accept students who will undoubtedly make their mark in the world. But, contrary to the claims of Herrnstein and Murray, institutions such as Harvard explicitly decline to make SAT scores their primary basis of admission. In the first place, they believe that many other indicators (such as having sailed around the world, having scored fifty touchdowns, or having composed a symphony) might be better indicators of ability. Even more important, such institutions have policies about "legacies." The preferential admission of sons and daughters of alumni, of graduates of top preparatory schools like Exeter and Andover, and policies of recruitment through Harvard Clubs encourage the future elite to apply. Contrary to the analyses in *The Bell Curve*, the future elite are not always the brightest, and it is the future elite that institutional self-interest serves. There are categories of possible students, such as the young Rockefellers, Fords, or Kennedys, who may make their mark on the world regardless of SAT scores or any measure of ability. The rich and powerful still use the elite institutions to preserve and maintain their position in society. The invisible hand of institutional self-interest dictates following the Matthew principle of attracting those with wealth and power, rather than concentrating on academic ability.

The occupational transformation: ability is treated as now sufficient as well as necessary for success.

Chapter Two of *The Bell Curve*, "Cognitive Partitioning by Occupation," is the shortest chapter of the book. Yet it is the crucial argument for the magical transformation. No matter how meritocratic or non-meritocratic the educational system, it is occupations that are central to the policy argument of the New Right. Chapter Two must convince the reader that the processes by which Harvard and other elite universities increased their SAT scores are writ large in the recruitment processes to the top occupational positions of the society. It claims that positions at the top of the occupational hierarchy select the brightest, leaving those with lower cognitive ability to lower-status occupations. This argument is dependent on the accuracy of the prior argument about education, but it does not follow from it.

If programs of compensatory education and other attempts to equalize opportunities are to be rolled back, we must be convinced that intelligence is not only necessary to occupational success, but also sufficient. No one, or virtually no one, is left behind. Neither gender, race, poverty, being a member of a religious minority, nor any other childhood disadvantage any longer holds back a significant number of people. The claims in the chapter are impressionistic. It gives the impression that there has been a qualitative transformation and that virtually all obstacles have disappeared without actually claiming any more than that, "an extremely high proportion of people of the labor force with IQs above 120 are already working in a high-IQ profession or in an executive or managerial position. One could easily make a case that the figure is in the neighborhood of 70 to 80 percent" (*The Bell Curve*, p. 60). Given these high percentages, Herrnstein and Murray imply that all those who can make it in society are making it, and therefore they will eventually conclude that "[f]or many people, there is nothing that they can learn which will repay the cost of the teaching" (*The Bell Curve*, p. 520).

To sustain the policy agenda of the New Right, *The Bell Curve* must try to show that selection is so meritocratic that relatively few children get left behind. Among the potent arguments against Social Darwinism early in the century was the argument that, regardless of whether ability is necessary for success in the United States, it is not sufficient.[98] To counter the argument that much talent is wasted, *The Bell Curve* must argue that virtually everyone with ability rises to the top. Almost no one worth worrying about is wasted.[99] Further, we must be convinced that this is not because of the efforts to provide public education or to equalize opportunity, but rather because of the automatic and invisible hand of meritocratic selection.

The argument is presented in three stages. First, Herrnstein and Murray argue that about one third of the high-IQ pool is drawn off into the pool of high-IQ occupations such as doctors, lawyers, and engineers. Then they argue that upper-level managers and chief executives draw off many more. And finally, they present a pseudo-scientific calculation to show that most intelligent people get ahead. While they admit that nobody knows what the IQ of executives was at the turn of the century, and therefore whether it has changed at all, they suggest that it is almost certainly the case that in 1990 a large proportion of the top IQ decile who are not in the high-IQ professions are business executives. They present a calculation that, they say, shows that "the constraints leave no other possibilities." But their calculations merely say that there are about thirteen million people in the high-IQ decile, of whom 11 million are in the labor force. Only about 4.6 million of them could be in high-IQ professions. Therefore, they conclude, the rest must be in executive positions. And they suggest that this is consistent with the fact that executives are often educated and/or mobile (*The Bell Curve*, pp. 59-60).

But this "broad envelope of possibilities" and this fountain of numbers represent nothing but the assumptions that have been put into the analysis. Herrnstein and Murray first define a grab bag of high-IQ occupations constructed to maximize the average IQ of the people in it, including accountants, architects, engineers, scientists, lawyers, college professors, and physicians. These professions account for only a small minority of the people testing high on academic ability.[100] So what happens to the rest? The "constraints which leave no other possibility" is the unrealistic assumption that most intelligent people succeed. And so Herrnstein and Murray must assume that they become businessmen. The difficulty with the argument lies in its assumptions that those occupations are homogeneous in their requirement of the kind of ability tested by SATs or IQ tests; that the same is true of business and management more generally; and that such abilities are not only necessary but nearly sufficient for success in those occupations, so that 70 to 80 percent of the high IQ respondents are in them.

Since the analysis depends on meritocracy in education, and since we know that education and SAT scores are influenced by factors other than innate ability, the argument about the partitioning of high-IQ occupations is weak. The argument for a fundamental transformation of the recruitment patterns of the thirteen million people classed as working in executive, administrative, and managerial positions is so weak and insubstantial that it is hard to deal with it. Certainly it is impossible to take it seriously. Ultimately the argument depends on a short Fortune article[101] and a tissue of arbitrary assumptions.

We know an enormous amount about social mobility. Herrnstein and Murray ignore this literature. They depend, instead, on a *Fortune* report of a survey of the chief executive officers of the *Fortune* 500 to demonstrate that there has been a qualitative increase in the education of management as well as a decline in its recruitment from wealthy families or traditional groups. They assert that from 1900 to 1950 the proportion of chief executive officers coming from wealthy families and traditionally privileged groups went from nearly 50 percent to about 33 percent, and then "[i]n the next twenty five years, the picture changed. The proportion of CEOs who came from wealthy families had dropped from almost half in 1900 and a third in 1950 to 5.5 percent by 1976" (*The Bell Curve*, p. 58). If true, the change from 50 percent to 5 percent would be startling, but in fact the argument depends on comparing apples and oranges. The argument quite characteristically shuttles back and forth between different, nonequivalent groups (chief executive officers of the *Fortune* 500; presidents of the *Fortune* 500, "typical" chief executive officers; executive, administrative and managerial positions) without flagging the fact for the reader. The reader is forced to assume that they are equivalent because if they are not, the argument is gibberish. The *Fortune* article's argument, if true, is not relevant to the thirteen million executive, administrative, and managerial positions in *The Bell Curve*'s argument; we know that the groups referred to in the *Fortune* article are not typical. They are not even typical of CEOs, and when Herrnstein and Murray label the results of the *Fortune* survey "the typical CEO" (p. 59), this is frivolous and misleading.

The article does not describe enough of its methods to allow one to explore why its results contradict the many scholarly studies of elite mobility. It is, after all, a four-page article in a popular magazine. The article is based on self-report, from one small survey in 1976, that it compares to another from 1950. Further, contrary to what is asserted in *The Bell Curve*, the 1976 survey is not comparable to that in 1950. The sampling is different. For example, the finding of an increase in the numbers of Jewish chief executive officers in 1976 results largely from the fact that the later survey, but not the earlier one, included retail trade. Moreover, on the plausible assumption that presidents need to be more comparable to major stockholders, the whole shift in background is an artifact of the noncomparability of the groups. The proportion of fathers of CEOs from 1900 to 1976 who could have come from blue-collar or from clerical positions depends on the population proportions of such positions, which are not controlled for. In general, to construct an argument on such evidence is the scholarship of a pack rat. A pack rat scavenges through garbage to find shiny bottle caps. Herrnstein and Murray scavenge through the library finding studies that correspond to their presumptions, failing to consult any of the main works in the field. Of course, there may be jewels to be found in garbage, but these are bottle caps.[102]

What drives the whole argument is a tissue of arbitrary assumptions. Herrnstein and Murray splice together a set of noncomparable studies. By arbitrarily choosing beginning and end points, they give the impression of a set of uniform trends. By ignoring the scholarly literature, they give the impression that the one survey they cite is typical. When they find that on no plausible assumption could the high-IQ occupations account for even half of the high-IQ respondents, they merely assume that the bulk of managers must have the specifically academic skills tested by IQ tests, and they "demonstrate" this by looking at the rising education of a totally different group, chief executive officers.

The whole argument about the alleged role of tested intelligence in success in business ignores the position of women, whose intelligence no more assures them success in business than it does success in the military. (This is a good example of an occupation in which opportunity has been historically closed to one whole group in society regardless of relative cognitive ability or achievement in school.) No one would deny that certain jobs have skill requirements. Not everyone can be a good musician. Not everyone can be an artist. Not everyone has a facility in mathematics. The requirements for different jobs are not the same and do not tap the same strengths of individuals. Further, without opportunity many who could be successful in particular jobs will not be. This is a society that has experienced long struggles to open the channels for occupational achievement. Women as a group face the "glass ceiling," a limit to their potential occupational achievement independent of their ability. The struggle for comparable worth or equal pay for equal work continues, with women consistently under-rewarded for the same work and relegated to more marginal employment. Top achievement in the occupational world belongs predominantly to men. There are still few women among the scientists, the partners of major law firms, the medical establishment, and the boardrooms of major corporations. Women share discrimination in the workplace with the pervasive discrimination against minorities.

Herrnstein and Murray's view of the world is intentionally blind to institutional racism or institutional sexism. While they grant that some individuals may have behaved in a discriminatory way in the past, they suggest that there is now a level playing field. The cumulative effect of multiple disadvantages of groups as a whole, built into institutional structures, standard operating procedures, segregation and group identities, and producing such well known phenomena as tokenism, glass ceilings, or revolving doors, is eliminated from consideration. There is no consideration of the impact of massive segregation by race prior to the civil rights movement, where schools, professions, unions, restaurants, and housing were closed to blacks. The civil rights movement opened educational opportunities including access to the professional schools. This change helped to create a substantial black middle class. There have been other major changes in the labor force, however, that have dampened the effects of the civil rights movement. As desegregation spread across the country in the 1970s, blue-collar jobs were decreasing in number. Companies reduced their work force and whole industries closed down or moved out of the country. Families in the inner city remained trapped in poverty. None of these barriers is considered.

Is ability one-dimensional?

Chapters Three and Four of *The Bell Curve* develop a critical justification for an increase in inequality in education and in occupations, viewing such inequality as an economically efficient meritocracy. Chapter Three argues that intelligent people do any job better than dumb people and attacks the received wisdom, articulated most sharply by Harvard's president Bok, that test scores are important in helping one to get education, but do not determine what one can do with it. Herrnstein and Murray aim to overturn this "received wisdom" by showing that "a flood of studies" has demonstrated that test scores correlate highly with productivity. They believe that the correlation is not because education teaches one anything useful, and certainly not because it allows one access to jobs of responsibility and power, but because education and tests indicate "g," the assumed general intelligence factor. Moreover, they argue that not only are occupations that require intellectual work affected by intelligence, but that any job, from ditch digger and secretary to corporate boss or mathematician is done better by those who score higher on SATs, AFQTs, GATBs (General Aptitude Test Battery), or other general ability tests.

The Bell Curve argues that bright people can do any job better than dumb people and further that no employer should hire anyone of low intelligence because these employees will depress productivity, which Herrnstein and Murray see as reflected in pay. But a whole range of factors including favoritism, gender, personality, and position influence how much people are paid. Witness the struggle of women for equal pay for equal work. Nor is the assumption that bright people can do any job better than dumb people correct. Different jobs require not only different talents but different tolerances. People who test high on tests do routine jobs poorly. Further, high test scores are no guarantee that people have the skills or interests that a particular job may require. The construction trades prefer to hire certain Native American tribes for jobs high on the girders because they seem to be more comfortable and skillful at heights. Ignoring different requirements for different jobs allows Herrnstein and Murray to make a simple-minded efficiency argument.

In fact, the "flood" of evidence that bright people do every job better turns out to be the work of a few theorists committed to that idea, principally John E. Hunter and his colleagues.[103] In a section "The weakness of individual studies," Herrnstein and Murray admit that none of the individual studies of this group is very convincing. It is only by inflating the importance of the work of these few theorists and distorting the disagreements in the field that The Bell Curve can make it seem that the limitations of "general ability tests" are no longer generally recognized in the social sciences. Herrnstein and Murray represent the continuum of positions as running from Hunter to Hartigan. Hunter is an advocate of the General Aptitude Test Battery and estimates its predictive ability as around 0.45. Hartigan, and the National Research Council Committee he chaired, oppose its unqualified use and estimate its predictive validity as around 0.25. When one gives a general ability test to applicants for a job, the actual correlation between their performance on the test and their performance on the job (usually measured by supervisor ratings) is about 0.25. Here, Herrnstein and Murray proceed to ignore what they have told us elsewhere about correlation coefficients. If the correlation is 0.25, that variable explains only about 6% of the variation in performance (0.25 squared). Herrnstein and Murray have to give the impression that much of the variation in performance is being explained, for otherwise their view that such tests should become the central mode of hiring would be totally implausible.

Hunter or anyone else generating estimates higher than 0.25 usually do so by making corrections for restriction of range. They argue that any number of people in the general population who would have scored low on the test and performed badly on the job did not take the test; nor did others who would have scored high on the test and performed well on the job. Therefore they inflate the observed correlation to an estimate of what it would predict from the general population.[104] Herrnstein and Murray used the football analogy: you have to be heavy to be a pro football player, but heavy pro football players aren't much better, because all pro football players are heavy. All this begs the main questions. Do we use a test to discriminate among applicants, or among the general population? Suppose a little guy in fact plays football as effectively as the heavy guys. Isn't that what counts? Is it fair to apply a test that does not give him a chance, especially when even Hunter's inflated correlation explains only about 20% (0.45 squared) of the variation in performance?

The argument that general ability tests would give all persons an equal opportunity to reach their full potential in society ignores the discriminatory practices in education and employment that are still evident for many groups. The views that the United States has suddenly become a meritocracy and that there is a single all-important ability well measured by SATs are not plausible. The principle that drives the argument is protection of economic productivity. What gives the arguments an appearance of plausibility is the pervasive force of social class in our society. Those at the top have more resources and more ability to control the destiny of their children. Those at the bottom are constrained in many ways from achieving their full potential. Because the limitations of their environment affect every aspect of their lives—including the very survival of their offspring at birth—we see the inadequacies at every point in their careers.

The Bell Curve's argument plays on the reader's desire to believe in the American myth of equal opportunity, and also plays on our desire to be among the saved and the superior. This is a deterministic model, an argument that one's destiny is determined by one's genes. The twentieth century has seen the consequences of doctrines that find the differential superiority of different groups a fundamental characteristic of their inheritance. The cognitive superiority of one group over another justified that phase of the Holocaust that exterminated mental defectives and it continues to justify attacks on equality. The argument that genes determine ability and that those who achieve less are less valuable is a dangerous ideology for a democracy.

A truer picture: The same people are achieving the same positions; only the legitimating myths have changed.

Inheritance is important. There was a lot of inherited privilege in the nineteenth century, and there is a lot of inherited privilege today. Then, as now, privileged groups could claim to be more literate, more cultured, and more able, but the fact is that such differences were socially created. By the twentieth century, some limited inroads had been made into this block of privilege. Free universal public education, the vote for blacks and for women, affirmative action, and the policies of the New Deal, the New Frontier, and the Great Society have pried open some of the gates. *The Bell Curve* spearheads a campaign to slam them shut again.

It is important neither to underestimate nor to overestimate the changes that have occurred. The situation is not monolithic, and there is some variation from school to school and from job to job. But, in general, one can say that because of the coincidence of broad social changes with important changes in social policy, some real opportunities were opened for women, for blacks, for the poor, and for ethnic, religious, and other minorities. There was no sudden, massive, automatic transformation, and such openings have been limited and contested. Class privilege, race privilege, male privilege, and WASP privilege remain alive and well. No invisible hand eliminated privilege in the 1950s. Indeed, the many people who are losing ground today, often "angry white males," are doing so because their gains were recent and insecure; and under these circumstances it is very tempting to blame other groups, whose gains are even more recent and even more insecure.

The limited gains were spearheaded by groups at the bottom. Movements for public education, open admissions, civil rights, women's rights and unions all produced gains, and many of these gains are now being taken away. Ranking, sorting, and classifying people by their test scores was not a way of opening the privileged positions of the society to those at the bottom but a way of closing them off. In this context, the argument that the society is a meritocracy has served the interests of those wishing to protect privileged positions and roll back minority gains in two ways. The supposed transformation into a meritocracy—a transformation magically teleported back in time to the Eisenhower era—says that the laws, rules, and private commitments to affirmative action are unnecessary. The invisible hand of the market will do all the opening that is needed. In fact, however, institutional self-interest and the natural results of markets are as likely to produce institutional racism, sexism, and privilege as they are to produce openings. All such institutions tend to operate on the Matthew principle "To him who has, shall be given"; but when we have made progress it is because we have operated with a more general view

that "to everyone, based on their simple human dignity, shall be given."
Second, the argument to meritocracy generates the view that it impossible as well as unnecessary to open up the society. Failure at meritocratic tests is presented as the indication of genetic inability. In contrast, we shall see how and why the societies such as Japan improve their test scores. Treatment of tests as measures of ability, as in the Mandarin examinations of the Imperial Chinese Empire, leads only to the consolidation of privileges. To relabel the remaining structures of segregation, inequality, and privilege as merit insures that they will grow.

Chapter 4

Schools, Poverty, and Opportunity

Cutbacks in social services and compensatory programs require legitimation because the American public supports governmental approaches to reduce inequalities.

In our society, the conventional route to a successful life is through good education, paid work, and marriage. Herrnstein and Murray claim that social barriers to achieving these have been progressively removed; by this time virtually all citizens have equal opportunity to attain them to the extent that they are individually able. The facts do not support this; enormous inequalities in opportunity still exist.

The American public in general finds these inequalities unacceptable and worrying. The abysmal quality of large proportions of inner city and rural schools; the sharp differentials in unemployment rates among racial, gender, and age groups; the absence for some groups of the conditions basic to a good marriage or even to marriage, are important examples of inequalities seen as problematic in a modern society. Furthermore, it is widely recognized that poverty compounds the effects of the other social impediments to getting ahead.

How these inequalities should be eliminated is, however, a different question. Is it the responsibility of government to implement policies to reduce or eliminate these inequalities? Should it be a community responsibility? What sorts of programs would be effective? What programs might have undesirable side effects? Although opinions on these issues vary greatly, there are some clear majority preferences.

There is strong support for government to establish policies to reduce the inequalities in universal social services—for example, the vast differences in the quality of schools in different localities. The great majority also think that government through its policies and programs should play a part toward equalizing the opportunities for a good life among different population groups. American public opinion may be sampled from a December 1994 study of American policy attitudes that reported on its survey results and those of other recent polls.[105] The survey, *Fighting Poverty in America*, conducted by the Center for the Study of Policy Attitudes in Washington, D.C. (CSPA), found widespread public support for policies and programs that attempt to satisfy basic needs and equalize opportunity. Based on feelings of moral responsibility and beliefs that reducing inequalities would result in a more prosperous and less crime-ridden society, an overwhelming number of respondents (85 percent) asserted that society in general had a responsibility to try to eliminate poverty, and almost as large a percentage (80 percent) believed that government should be involved in this task. The survey results clearly reflected the well-known recent decline in public confidence in government to run programs efficiently, but there was almost no support for the elimination of existing government poverty programs. The majority of respondents wanted the programs to be more generously funded. Despite the substantial majority support for poverty programs, a large percentage of respondents (68 percent) believed that the programs could make people dependent and destroy initiative. There was majority support for limiting the length of time people could receive welfare, but this was accompanied by strong support for job training programs and job guarantees. Preference was shown for programs designed to eliminate barriers and increase opportunity rather than just satisfy immediate need. For example, while support was shown for increased spending on all programs discussed in this survey, the increase was supported more strongly for educational and incentive programs such as Head Start, Job Corps, and Vista, than for welfare programs such as AFDC and food stamps (CSPA, 1994).

In summary, most Americans support the retention and improvement of government efforts to eliminate poverty and to increase opportunity for the disadvantaged. There is some concern that a side effect of the programs may be the creation of dependency and lack of ambition in their recipients, but this concern is not sufficient to overcome the strong majority support for programs to assist all citizens to participate fully in our society and its opportunities.[106]

The New Right legitimizes cutbacks in services and programs by appeals to values of independence, opportunity, and limited government.

The New Right justifies its intentions to cut back programs for the disadvantaged by appealing to social values of limited government and individual responsibility. Most Americans, however, see a major role for government. Thus the New Right appeals to public concerns about potential dependency. It asserts that provision of assistance programs weakens the ability and willingness of people to take responsibility for their own lives, damaging both society and the individual. The *Contract with America* reflects this belief in the title of its welfare reforms, namely the *Personal Responsibility Act*. In the book *Contract with America*, Newt Gingrich expresses the same opinion in the rhetorical question, "Isn't it time for Government to encourage work rather than dependency?" The question reveals the single-minded way in which the New Right has translated the value of individual responsibility into a guideline for social policy decisions. Dependency is designated as a destroyer, and any policies that the decision makers can even remotely accuse of creating dependency must be shot down, even those that reduce dependency by opening the doors of opportunity.[107]

Concerns about the development of dependency, however, have not succeeded in preventing strong public support for these social programs. If a majority of the public is to support the cutbacks advanced by the New Right, a more effective rationale is needed to convince people that social programs are useless, that they cannot open the doors to new opportunities for the disadvantaged, or even satisfactorily meet basic needs. Using so-called scientific findings, *The Bell Curve* lays out a new analysis of social programs in an attempt to convince the public that the programs can be legitimately abolished.

Part II of *The Bell Curve* develops a rationale for abolishing social programs by purporting to show that low cognitive ability is the major cause of America's most serious social problems.

Herrnstein and Murray set out to convince their readers that social programs cannot alleviate social difficulties. Problems, from broken families to crime, reflect the inadequacies of those afflicted. The authors, then, blame individuals for social problems. However, they now define the problem-producing characteristic as genetically inherited low cognitive ability, a claim that is clearly different from the view—advanced by Murray in *Losing Ground* (1984)—that dependency is the source of many of the same social problems. *The Bell Curve* does not specifically reject the dependency argument. It tries to bridge the gap between the two theories by affirming that chronic welfare dependency may develop and be transmitted from one generation to the next through a culture of poverty, but that this occurs primarily among people of low intelligence.

Murray's primary commitment is not to any empirical or theoretical or conceptual position, but to the political program involving cutbacks of social programs. His most characteristic arguments appeal to economic efficiency, and they either inflate the costs or deny the benefits of such social programs. The argument to dependency implies that there are hidden costs. Those to genetic incapacity minimize the benefits. Herrnstein and Murray's assumption that IQ is minimally affected by social factors after childhood implies that almost nothing can be done through social programs. We have already argued against their claims about the immutability of cognitive ability, and now we shall analyze the way they have built up other parts of their case.

The first step was to present a series of statistical analyses showing a linkage between low cognitive ability and a range of personal inadequacies (see Appendix 1). Data were derived from the National Longitudinal Survey of Youth (NLSY) findings from 1979 to 1990. The NLSY collected information on the Armed Forces Qualification Test (AFQT), which Herrnstein and Murray take to measure intelligence. Another crucial variable, socioeconomic background, was measured by a socioeconomic status (SES) index of parental education, income, and occupation at the time the respondent was fourteen years of age. Logistic regression was used to measure the strength of the effect of cognitive ability (AFQT) and social class background (SES) on selected dependent variables such as educational level, marital status, poverty, crime, unemployment, and welfare dependence.[108]

The statistical methods of Part II are a textbook case of how to lie with statistics.

Part II of *The Bell Curve* presents results in the form of 22 graphs, and Appendix 4 presents regression equations that show the numerical value of the coefficients. These results are the basis of the argument that IQ powerfully affects and explains a very large number of social variables such as schooling, crime rates, unemployment, or family breakdown.

Many technical questions are raised by the ways the variables are measured, the choices of variables included, the graphic presentation, and the interpretation of the results. *The Bell Curve* is a very useful demonstration of how to lie with statistics.[109] Appendix 1 of this book covers the issues crucial to understanding their analysis for those not trained in the statistical methods of the social sciences. We will mainly be concerned with the question of whether the graphs of the partial effects of

AFQT and SES provide fair and honest evidence on the relative effects of intelligence and the socioeconomic environment.

Herrnstein and Murray's graphs purport to show the effects of IQ and social environment on such other variables as unemployment, illegitimacy and crime. These graphs are remarkably opaque. They represent a very particular set of spectacles through which to view the data. With a few exceptions, the authors do not present the raw data, nor is it possible for a reader or analyst to recover the data, either from the text and graphs or from the appendices. The graphs show theoretically predicted relations between the behavior that they wish to explain, such as poverty status in 1970, and SES or AFQT, controlling the other and age. They give the impression that in most cases the effect of AFQT is greater than that of SES, and that innate genetic factors are more important than environmental ones. These impressions, however, are largely a result of the inappropriate way of measuring and presenting the results.

The analysis exaggerates the effects of extreme cases. Herrnstein and Murray, however, repeatedly state that focusing on the extremes was exactly what they wanted to do. They suggest that they would have included only the top 1 percent or 2 percent of people in their top cognitive class, had their sample size been large enough (*The Bell Curve*, p. 121).

The effect of this presentation is to give the illusion of a scientifically accurate, theoretically meaningful measure of the relative importance of socioeconomic status and cognitive ability. At the same time, it distracts attention from the theoretically appropriate question of *how much* change in SES or AFQT it takes to produce *how much* change in conditions such as poverty or the effects of illegitimacy. We can see the effect of this procedure in the few cases where Herrnstein and Murray allow us to see the data. For example, their model case for the power of intelligence (test scores) is as a cause of poverty. Their logistic regressions show diverging curves in which the ostensible effect of test scores on poverty appears qualitatively stronger than that of socioeconomic background. But when we look at their data, we get a different story (*The Bell Curve*, p. 131-2):

Table 4-1.
Chance of being in poverty by SES and AFQT

PERCENT IN POVERTY		PERCENT IN POVERTY	
Top 5% of SES	3%	Top 5% of AFQT	2%
Next 20% of SES	3%	Next 20% of AFQT	3%
Mid 50% of SES	7%	Mid 50% of AFQT	6%
Next 20% of SES	12%	Next 20% of AFQT	16%
Lowest 5% of SES	24%	Lowest 5% of AFQT	30%

The principal difference between the subjects with very low AFQT and very low socioeconomic backgrounds, measured on Herrnstein and Murray's index, was that 24 percent of those from very low socioeconomic backgrounds were in poverty, as compared to 30 percent of those with very low test scores. This is a 6 percent difference. It is 6 percent of the 5 percent in the very low categories, or about one third of 1 percent. The 4 percent difference of the next 20 percent represents another fraction of 1 percent. The method by which Herrnstein and Murray present the data inflates this to a huge divergence between the two curves. There are sound reasons why the social sciences avoid this procedure, which focuses on the effects of a very small number of cases, particularly when these cases are subject to various biases.

Is it ever appropriate to exaggerate the effects of extreme cases? It might be. If there is the same causality operating for the extreme cases that operates for the bulk of the cases, it will not be deceptive. However, if extreme cases have different causes and consequences from those of the normal range of variation—just as the causes and consequences of being a dwarf are different from the causes and consequences of being somewhat short—then such a graph is deceptive. Herrnstein and Murray give no argument or evidence that the causes and consequences of the extreme cases are the same as those of the cases with modest variation. There are plausible arguments that gross variations in intelligence or social class (e.g., Downs syndrome or homelessness) have a different dynamic from minor variations in either.

Herrnstein and Murray use the comparison between the standardized slopes[110] of AFQT and SES with regard to such variables as poverty, unemployment, or crime to determine which cause is "more important." But standardized slopes are not the appropriate policy-relevant measure of the importance of different factors. Moreover, they are dependent on the amount of variation. Ordinarily, for policy one is interested in how much change in the effect one gets from resources devoted to changing the cause, and comparison of standardized slopes does not tell us that.[111] But it is easy to understand why Herrnstein and Murray obscure the question. Some parts of their argument represent AFQT or SAT scores as essentially unchangeable (and hence entirely unimportant causes from a policy standpoint), while other parts of their argument document that they are changed by education.[112] Furthermore, there are serious problems with their SES index.

The comparison of tests scores (AFQT) with the socioeconomic status index (SES) does not show the relative importance of innate ability and social environment. Armed Forces Qualification Test scores do not measure innate ability. Their SES index does not measure the effects of environment. The variables have not been measured in a comparable way.

The AFQT was constructed to be sensitive to extreme variation, while their measure of socioeconomic status is insensitive to it.[113]

To measure socioeconomic status, they average father's education, mother's education, highest parental occupational status, and family income in 1979. Depending on things like mother's education, the child of a millionaire may not show up as very high on this measure, and a child who grew up homeless may not show up low. A series of later analyses[114] have shown that the measure of SES which Herrnstein and Murray use enormously understates the effect of a deprived environment. For example, Fischer and his colleagues have shown in *Inequality By Design* (1996) that Herrnstein and Murray's SES measure is dominated by parent's education, which has virtually no relation to many of the dependent variables such as poverty. Adding variables to take account of the obvious differences in environment such as siblings, intact family, or living on a farm, the difference between the apparent effect of AFQT and that of SES virtually disappears. Adding other measures such as schooling and the level of unemployment and deprivation in the community, even if these are fairly crudely measured, AFQT score has a qualitatively weaker relation than environment. Effects such as those of gender are even stronger, and the analyses of these components not only does a far better job of explaining conditions such as poverty, but also allows one to see the policy structures that affect such conditions.

Similarly, the very powerful interrelation between AFQT score and schooling is one indication that the test mainly measures exposure to formal schooling. Since the main issue posed throughout Part II is the relative power of SES and AFQT in predicting various behaviors one must ask how any error or insensitivity will affect the apparent influence of these two variables. Whenever a variable is measured less well, its apparent relationship to the dependent variable will be lowered. When the relationship is weak, it will often be decisive.

Indeed, the central question is not whether AFQT is "more important" than SES or SES is "more important" than AFQT. The question is whether Herrnstein and Murray have any evidence that AFQT plays any causal role whatsoever. They treat AFQT as a measure of a genetically fixed cognitive ability. However if this score is influenced by the environment, then it is a symptom of deprivation, which is the real cause of the social problems and conditions that Herrnstein and Murray purport to explain. Appendix 1, below, shows that measures of childhood IQ do not have the same relation to Herrnstein and Murray's dependent variables as do AFQT scores, even though childhood IQ scores are highly correlated with AFQT. That is, Herrnstein and Murray discuss whether intelligence at age fifteen and socioeconomic background are causes of poverty and other conditions. They do not measure test performance at age 15, but in 1980, when the respondents were between 14 and 22. Socioeconomic status, on the other hand, was measured by combining a number of measures, some of which refer to 1980 and some of which refer to much earlier events. Father's education and mother's education had occurred a generation earlier. Family income and parental occupation refers to something contemporaneous.

Herrnstein and Murray assume that both intelligence (test performance) and socioeconomic status are relatively stable. In the case of test score performance, they make this assumption explicit, saying "After the age of about ten the IQ scores are essentially stable within the constraints of measurement error" (*The Bell Curve*, p. 130). We shall present some reasons for doubting that assumption. They also need the assumption in the case of socioeconomic status. Income is not stable.[115] For some people, low income lasts for relatively short periods. This means that within the framework of their assumptions, the SES index is a much less accurate measure of background;[116] its construction makes it a valid measure neither of the respondents' childhood background nor of their present situation. Furthermore, there are other problems concerning the choice of variables and how these authors have interpreted the causal relations between them.

The analysis represents the cumulative effects of disadvantage as being genetic.

Herrnstein and Murray suggest that their regressions show that innate intelligence has a greater effect on such variables as school success, disability or unemployment than do environmental effects. Whether their data show this hinges on the issues of spurious relationships. As our Appendix 1 shows, any regression can only indicate causal influences within a framework of assumptions, derived from theory and previous research, about what influences operate.[117] If one fails to examine conditions that are interrelated with the variables examined, they will often be misled by spurious relationships.[118]

For example, suppose we believe that fire engines reduce fire damage (by putting out fires). From this theory we predict that when there are more fire engines there should be less damage and when there are fewer fire engines there should be more damage. We might collect a lot of data on fire damage and engines, finding, to our surprise, that when more fire engines show up, there is more damage. Suppose that we conclude that fire engines do not really prevent damage; rather they increase it, both directly and indirectly. Directly, we observe firemen committing damage both with axes and with water. Indirectly, they create dependency. The active mobilization of communities used to put out fires, but when fire engines show up—especially many of them—people stand around waiting for the firemen to do the work. Thus we conclude that fire damage can be reduced by eliminating all fire departments.

This is an absurd idea, and the policy implications are likely to increase fire damage. A small town may be able to get by with buckets, but the San Francisco fire of 1906 showed the consequences of trying to deal with urban fires that way. The essential problem is that the presence of many fire engines is a symptom of highly damaging fires rather than a cause. Much of the analysis of *The Bell Curve* suggests that social policies have made social problems worse rather than better. Their analyses fail to examine the degree to which test scores are a symptom rather than a cause of those conditions. Herrnstein and Murray briefly dismiss the issue with respect to poverty, and they make some nonsystematic controls with respect to schooling. Mostly they ignore it.

On the question of whether poor test scores might be a symptom of conditions associated with poverty or poor schooling, Herrnstein and Murray say that these conditions might have a detrimental effect on a person's IQ score. They claim, however, that what produced the score does not matter (*The Bell Curve*, p. 130). This is a central maneuver of *The Bell Curve*, and it is fraudulent. What produces the score does matter. It matters for what they choose to control or not to control in any analysis. It matters for their interpretation of the data and the policy implications they draw from it. Moreover, the problem and bias are even more serious if the causation is not one way or the other but reciprocal, as implied by any structure of cumulative causation. If poverty and schooling and other variables that are treated as effects of adolescent intelligence (test performance) also affect it, then the apparent effect of test performance will be inflated by the reciprocal effects on it. In Chapter 17 and Appendix 3 of *The Bell Curve*, Herrnstein and Murray show that years of schooling does, in fact, have an effect on AFQT score and equivalent tests. There is good reason to suppose that the quality of schooling also has an effect. Herrnstein and Murray sometimes control for the amount of schooling, but they argue that schooling is a special variable in this regard. It is not. Virtually any of the correlates of a poor or disorganized community will behave like schooling in this respect. To the extent that this happens, the regression on AFQT inflates the apparent effect of AFQT. The analyses of Part II look at effects on unemployment, poverty, illegitimacy, or crime one by one, considering each only as an effect, as dependent variables. Their index of socioeconomic status fails to capture such effects of family background. It is a question of hobbling the competition and then having a race.

The conception of a vicious cycle of deprivation highlights the bias and distortion which will be produced by such a method of analysis.

Figure 4-1 portrays the way such a cycle operates at both the aggregate and individual level of analysis. The top two circles of the figure portray the vicious cycles in the dominant and in the subordinate group, from Figure 1-1. At the aggregate level, a series of characteristics of a poor, deprived, or minority community are mutually reinforcing. They reinforce and are reinforced by the social marginalization and stigmatization of that community by the institutions of the majority. In Figure 4-1 each of these elements of the vicious cycle in the minority community are represented as, itself, a cycle of many elements.

At the bottom of Figure 4-1, we have magnified some of the processes that operate with respect to education. At the collective level, the education of a whole group or community contains a large number of different processes such as labeling and stigmatization, lack of funding, low occupational expectations, aspirations and identities oriented to non-academic work, oppositional peer groups, and strains placed on the school system, which produce lower levels of educational achievement and motivation.

Figure 4-1.
Self-reinforcing cycles of deprivation at the aggregate and individual levels.

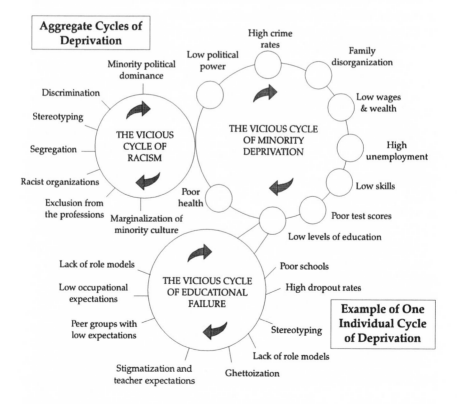

Any individual is not only affected by each of these conditions working directly upon him or her, but also by those that operate on their family, friends, community, or school. However, within the strait jacket of Herrnstein and Murray's analysis, all these processes are only given the distorted reflection of the effect on education of SES and AFQT score when the respondent was between 14 and 23.

The failure to consider the social environment abstracts individual (pathological) behavior from the (brutalizing) social context producing it. Abstracted in this way, it appears to stem from the pathology, stupidity, immorality, degeneracy, or inadequacy of the people in those neighborhoods. Within Part II, the causal language is muted and descriptive. Herrnstein and Murray speak of which variables seem more important. In later chapters they will pretend that they have shown the causal importance of test scores to individual outcomes and that this shows the causal importance of change in test scores to the society.[119] These are not the same. Having a high enough SAT score might guarantee that one could go to an elite college, but if everyone had higher SAT scores, everyone would not be able to go to elite colleges.

One of the problems of these authors' analyses in Part II is the failure to look at the interconnection between such variables or at related conditions such as measured aspirations, alcoholism and other addictions, or stigmatization. A rich sociological literature has analyzed how such conditions can come into being or reinforce each other. Herrnstein and Murray justify their failure to look at any of the conditions of poor communities by saying that statistical analysis can become a bottomless pit. They complain that technical journals often run articles built around the estimated effects of a dozen or more independent variables. In contrast to that procedure, they say that their principle was to explore additional dynamics only when there were clear logical reasons why they might be important "because of dynamics having little or nothing to do with IQ" (*The Bell Curve*, p. 124). They even italicize this proviso, suggesting that it is a misuse of regression analysis to introduce an additional variable that is "mostly" an expression of variables already in the equation.

Our Appendix 1 argues that Herrnstein and Murray are quite correct that multivariate analysis can become a bottomless pit, and that it can be deceptive to control for too many variables, especially variables that are affected by others under consideration. If other factors are solely a consequence of variation in intelligence scores, it would be inappropriate to control those factors in looking at the effect of intelligence.[120] At the same time, it is wrong to suggest that one should not control factors that influence test performance, such as schooling or substance abuse, for those are the very things that it is crucial to control. Herrnstein and Murray later use this proviso as *a priori* grounds to exclude the many known causes of the variation in different groups' test scores. Moreover, they fail to use the same criteria in estimating the effects they wish to demonstrate. For example, if going to poor schools causes one to have poor test scores, which causes one to obtain poor jobs, then in looking at the effect of schools on jobs it would be inappropriate to control test scores, since those show how, not whether, the schools have an effect.[121] By the same token, their failure to consider or control measures of personal motivation or disorganization is incorrect. If variables such as motivation, jobs, or addiction have effects on one's IQ (test performance) and on such things as crime, then their effects will seem to result from IQ.

To a considerable extent, the individualistic and genetic conceptual apparatus of *The Bell Curve* operates to obscure the main social causes of any of the occupational, educational, family, or criminal behaviors. It assumes that nothing affects test performance, even when other parts of the book show that this is not true. It is similar to the most famous magical trick of them all: the floating lady or levitation trick. Black vertical wires are entirely invisible from a distance, under certain lighting, against the background of black vertical drapes. Anything can be suspended or levitated using such wires. Within *The Bell Curve* the individualistic assumptions of the analysis serve as the black vertical drapes against which social processes of disorganization are rendered invisible so that their effects may be ascribed to IQ.

The ideology that informs the book requires Herrnstein and Murray to disguise the social support of those who have risen and to minimize the costs of abolishing programs aimed at providing opportunity to those at the bottom: equal public education, unemployment compensation and other programs of health education and welfare. Thus, it allows them to ignore the fact that the position of the non-wealthy working class and middle class groups will be gravely undercut by removing those programs. At the same time, it also allows them to exaggerate the benefits of "meritocratic" procedures.

The individualistic interpretations of Herrnstein and Murray wipe out nearly a century of advances in the social scientific understanding of social problems.

For most of this century, research into social problems has been grounded in the understanding that people's behavior is shaped by social factors, most notably by the immediate physical, social, and cultural environment. Much of the seminal research was carried out at the University of Chicago in the 1920s and 1930s. This research and its findings rendered the more abstract, individualistic theories of the Social Darwinists obsolete. Dividing the city into many specific social areas from "gold coast" to slum, researchers such as Robert Park, Ernest Burgess, Louis Wirth, Clifford R. Shaw, Henry D. McKay, and Harvey M. Zorbaugh produced a common finding, namely that the social regions of the city differed enormously and consistently in the level of social problems within their geographical borders.[122] The same general problem-ridden neighborhoods had high concentrations of social problems of all kinds, including poverty, broken families, suicide, and crime. Even when the population or ethnic composition of a neighborhood changed completely, that area often continued to have high rates of pathology. The problems stemmed not from the people but from the social structure. In areas where the poor could afford housing, inadequate neighborhood facilities, including schools, encouraged unsuccessful and delinquent behavior, perpetuated through gangs and delinquent subcultures.

As would be expected, there were sharp controversies among members of the Chicago school. They disagreed as to how far social problems were associated with characteristics of the residents and how far with the conditions of the slums; they disagreed about which conditions were most important. Some theorists stressed the development of different value patterns or subcultures; others stressed the extent to which people were reacting rationally to adverse conditions. This controversy has continued into the present with the debate around William Julius Wilson's analysis of the effects of jobs lost during the Bush-Reagan years on the social structure of the slum and its consequences.[123] European theorists showed other ways that people are shaped by their social and cultural environments, and these theories swept away the inadequate individualist theories of Spencer and the Social Darwinists.[124]

Central to all this research, however, is the view that the balance between individual and social causes should not be handled by a priori assumptions, but investigated empirically. It is a methodological axiom of this approach that one should take account of people's situations and of the understandings, customs, and coping mechanisms that arise from those situations. If, in context, the behaviors are rational, reasonable, and understandable, then it is inappropriate to posit some mysterious, genetic, ethnic, or racial cause for the behaviors. Herrnstein and Murray's analysis is striking not because it disagrees with these studies, but because it ignores them without evidence or argument. They falsely imply that by including a single measure of the effects of socioeconomic status, they have taken account of such effects.

The interconnected problems of poverty, inadequate schooling, and unemployment are concentrated in areas with adverse environments.

Newspapers and other accounts have made us all familiar with the environment of poverty, highlighting the day-to-day problems encountered by poor people. The physical environment in which they live is frequently hazardous to health. Deteriorating housing with problems such as broken steps, dangerous appliances or heating systems, and flaking lead paint are common, causing injuries, illnesses, mental deficiencies, and even sudden death. Malnutrition, chronic diseases, and other debilitating illnesses take their toll. Medical treatment, even when available through Medicaid, tends to be used more sparingly by the poor, who are usually sicker than the better off by the time they seek help.[125]

The social environment is also hazardous. Physical violence in poor urban communities is the stuff of everyday life. Strongly linked is the use of illicit drugs, which are pervasive in certain poor inner city districts and are among the greatest concerns of the American public today. These problems have led to poorer functioning by many people in these neighborhoods. Raising themselves out of poverty without help, through the conventional means of education, job training and seeking, and steady employment is sometimes beyond their powers.

Other sociocultural aspects of a slum can also undermine functioning. Someone in Appalachia or in the ghetto who, against all odds, says no to alcohol or drugs, studies hard, refuses to engage in illicit sex or to join a gang, and who gets and holds a job, may still be victimized by a hazardous environment. Problems in the lifestyles of the working poor, street hustlers, welfare mothers, and the homeless are very different, but all involve strains. Consider the welfare mother. Her life is bounded by laws, by social context, and by social conditions imposed for receiving AFDC. The law often prohibits leaving children under certain ages at home alone. The immediate context does not provide day care, job training, or social support; and it is an exceptionally hazardous one. Within that context movement towards a "successful" life is extraordinarily difficult.

Finally, there are many well known "messages" from the environment. Families or members of peer groups may assert that schooling is a waste of time, that it gets you nowhere. Drugs may be touted by someone you trust or someone of whom you are afraid. Agents from inside or outside the community, possibly teachers or police officers, may convince you that you are no good, a piece of trash who will never amount to anything. Many find it difficult to escape such a web of interconnected problems. The nearest that Herrnstein and Murray ever get to considering such problems is to examine background SES. The whole context of the development and persistence of social problems is blatantly ignored.

Identification of who the poor really are greatly undermines these conclusions.

Herrnstein and Murray give no evidence for the assertion that it is primarily the cognitively disadvantaged who have been below the poverty line within the past two decades. Even a cursory examination of who the poor are throws serious doubt on this thesis. An analysis by age group shows that increases in poverty rates were negatively correlated with age.[126] In fact, poverty rates for the 65-plus years age group declined from 16 percent in 1973 to 12 percent in 1990; they have declined almost consistently over the past fifty years due largely to improvements in Social Security. If poverty has increased among the young but not the old, then Herrnstein and Murray's thesis would lead to the conclusion that the old are much smarter than the young. This makes little sense.

Analysis by family composition also questions the Herrnstein and Murray explanation. They assert that the divorce and unmarried parenthood, which result in the creation of single-parent families, occur primarily among those of low cognitive ability. Married people are brighter. If this were true, we would expect that any increase in poverty rates would be steeper for single-headed families than for the smarter two-parent families as, according to the intelligence thesis, adverse conditions are better handled by the smart than by the cognitively limited. However, the increase in poverty rates from 1973 to 1991, which occurred in all family types, was very similar for the two family structures, 1.9 percent for two-parent and male-headed families and 2.2 percent for female-headed.[127] The fact that percentage increases in "smarter" and "dumber" family types differed little further undermines the credibility of the one-factor explanation of the poverty trend.

If, instead of looking at trends, we look at the composition of the poor, we again find a profile that fits very awkwardly with an explanation in terms of genetic low intelligence. In 1990, for example:

- Forty percent of the poor were children.
- Children were twice as likely to be poor as the elderly (rates: 22 percent of children and 12 percent of the elderly were poor).
- Two-thirds of poor adults were women.
- Two-thirds of poor adults were white (rates: 32 percent of blacks; 28 percent of Latinos; 12 percent of Asian Americans; and 11 percent of whites were poor).[128]

Are Herrnstein and Murray really prepared to argue that women and children are significantly lower in intelligence than men or that the elderly are more intelligent than children? What is one to make of the higher-than-average poverty rates *and* IQ of Asian Americans?

The real explanation of the poverty trend is found in social and economic changes.

No argument based on personal defects can explain a poverty trend that so clearly reflects social changes. Research has shown that the decline in poverty between the late 1930s and 1973 was largely due to economic progress that brought increased job opportunities and rising wages. Over the same period, social programs created by the New Deal and the War on Poverty, helped push many above the poverty threshold. Improvements slowed early in the 1970s. During the 1980s the income gap between the wealthiest and poorest families grew appreciably. The heightened inequality stemmed from both economic and social policy changes. Economic changes included falling wage rates, particularly in the lower-paid jobs and in the younger age groups, increased tax benefits for the rich, and periodic increases in unemployment. Social policy changes led to cutbacks in poverty programs, including food stamps, nutrition, housing, health care, and child care. A particularly vulnerable population, female-headed families, increased sharply in number and were devastated by the social and economic changes. If the women worked, they earned impossibly low wages; if on AFDC, their benefits did not raise their families to the poverty line. The absence of subsidized day care or job training reduced their options.[129]

The Bell Curve must demonstrate that poverty is cognitively determined and unalterable if it is to conclude that poverty programs are ineffective and wasteful. Accordingly, Herrnstein and Murray interpret their logistic regressions as showing IQ as the cause and biological foundation of poverty. As the conceptual and measurement inadequacies of their variables and tests have already been thoroughly critiqued, the most important question to ask at this point is whether their independent variables (AFQT, SES, and age) do indeed cover the reasons for being poor or not poor. The answer, from their own statistics, is clearly no. Even at the individual level of analysis, these three variables together explain only around 10 percent of the reasons for being above or below poverty level. As support for policy-relevant explanations of social structures such as poverty, school failure, or unemployment, these data are a fraud. No reader who takes the time and effort to understand the data can accept this claim. The authors appear to be relying on the probability that most readers will simply not examine the calculations closely.

Their analyses are covered by a conceptualization that is like a line of patter, and that has a close fit with the ideas of the New Right in general and with the more negative understanding of poverty in our society. They appeal implicitly to poverty myths pervasive in our society.

Herrnstein and Murray build on and reinforce myths that vilify the poor and so justify their disadvantaged conditions.

The individualistic explanation of Herrnstein and Murray for poverty is based on myths incorporating errors that they ignore either accidentally or on purpose.[130] We find it extremely interesting that these myths continue to sway popular and elite opinion despite their weak factual foundation. Clearly this weak foundation did not deter Herrnstein and Murray from using them. Because we have already challenged the alleged direct link between intelligence and social success, we shall here explore the indirect links between intelligence and social success. Herrnstein and Murray argue that low IQ causes certain undesirable behavioral traits that then lead to poverty. This argument is fueled by the following myths.[131]

Myth one: Poor families are large families.

Herrnstein and Murray imply that low-IQ people are too stupid to avoid having lots of kids and so increase the likelihood of poverty. This belief spawned the myth that poor people either have insatiable sexual appetites or are just trying to milk more money out of the welfare system by having more children. The myth has led some to call for social incentives to keep poor people from reproducing. Others go further and suggest sterilization for certain groups. The underlying logic is the same: prevent the bad genes from spreading like cancer. However, there is absolutely no factual support for this position. According to the census, there is no difference between the average size of a poor family and a non-poor family. The average American family has just under two kids regardless of its income or the number of parents in the household. This fact holds true for families receiving government benefits. Seven out of ten families receiving AFDC have two or fewer children.[132]

Myth two: The poor are too lazy to work.

The myth about poor people's reproductive prowess is complemented by an even more popular individualistic explanation for poverty: that poor people are too lazy to work and would rather just ride the so-called welfare gravy train. Proponents of this view argue that this moral deficiency (laziness) leads to poverty, and that a little more hard work and initiative by these people would insure a less impoverished existence. While this is not a strictly IQ-based argument, Herrnstein and Murray would certainly claim that there is a relationship between IQ and these values—that dumber people are less likely to value hard work.

Once again, though, this individualistic explanation for poverty has no systematic factual support. First, most people who can work, do work. In 1989, for example, of the twenty million poor people in the United States who were at least fifteen years old, about one third were unemployable because they were ill, retired, or full-time students; of the remaining 13.2 million capable of work, about 8.2 million (62 percent) held jobs for at least part of the year. More than half of these workers were employed for the entire year in either a part-time or full-time job.[133] These readily available facts show clearly that having a job is no guarantee that you will not be poor. Structural factors such as wage levels are an immensely important part of the reason for why over 35 million Americans of all ages live in poverty. It is no accident that Herrnstein and Murray ignore these facts, since they would force them to abandon their individualistic explanations that blame the victims of social problems for their own pain and suffering.

Myth three: The poor receive generous assistance.

Another myth is the alleged attractiveness of government assistance programs such as AFDC. This is the so-called welfare gravy train that lazy poor people hop aboard so they can avoid work and sit at home all day watching television, drinking Ripple, and reproducing at will to get larger checks. As we have already noted, contemporary critics of government assistance, including spokespersons for the New Right, argue that such assistance destroys the incentive to work and creates dependence on handouts. As a result the poor do not develop marketable skills and feel badly about themselves.

Once again, however, this argument is based more on rhetoric than reality. In 1993, the average monthly AFDC payment was $377 per family, or $4,524 per year. Add another $290 or so per month in food stamps and you have a whopping annual income of about $8,000 before taxes.[134] The average assistance is about two-thirds of the official poverty level for a family of four ($14,763 in 1993). In real terms, these benefits are smaller than in 1973. Some gravy train! In addition, only about 60 percent of all families eligible for benefits even apply. And despite more rhetoric, these meager programs are hardly the source of fiscal crises and federal deficits, since they amount to less than 3 percent of the overall federal budget. Although the New Right wants us to believe that these assistance programs are a critical source of America's economic and moral decay, the facts tell another story.

Because assistance levels vary greatly from state to state, it is relatively easy to assess if these programs are really causing people to eschew work in favor of this government handout. For example, the average AFDC payment in Connecticut in 1993 was $560 per month, while in Mississippi it is $120 per month. But neither rates of migration nor labor force participation are explained by assistance levels.

Myth four: The poor keep having children to augment their benefits.

Conservative critics make the same mistake by asserting that poor people have additional children in order to get higher benefits, and Herrnstein and Murray rest their basic argument against welfare on its alleged "dysgenic" effects (i.e., causing the birth of low IQ children). Policy-makers implement these mistaken ideas when they pass laws such as the recent one in New Jersey which denies mothers any benefit increase if they have another child while already receiving AFDC. The same factual critiques presented above are applicable here. First, the increase in benefits ($64 per month in New Jersey) seems like a very weak incentive for having another child. Since these recipients already have at least one child, they probably know that $64 a month is not enough to pay for a child's expenses. Readers who are parents know that $64 a month does not even cover a month of a child's formula! Second, the benefit increase for children varies greatly by state, thereby establishing another perfect testing ground for this assumed incentive to reproduce. Just as we saw with benefits in general, illegitimate birth rates are not responsive to differences and changes in assistance.

Myth five: Once poor, always poor.

The argument that poverty is caused by intellectual (or moral) deficiency among poor people is also challenged by the reasons that people enter poverty and how long they stay there. While some families and their descendants will probably always be poor, most poverty spells are for a short period of time. People and families are constantly falling into and out of poverty. For example, of all nonelderly people who completed a poverty spell in 1992, over 60 percent had been poor for two years or less. While these people may fall into poverty again, they are not permanently mired there. The same basic pattern is found among AFDC recipients. About two-thirds of all people who start receiving AFDC in a given year will be off the rolls within one year.[135] Because they are vulnerable, many of these families may receive AFDC in the future, but policies that prohibit people from receiving benefits for more than two years make little sense in view of these facts. Given the small number of families who remain on AFDC for long periods of time, it will probably cost more to crack down on these than it would be to simply ignore them. Table 4-2 presents the more frequent reasons people begin a poverty spell and the average length of time it takes to complete a spell given its origins.

These facts challenge many popular myths about poverty. First, it is clear that the most frequent reason for a poverty spell is the household head's fall in income—most often through the loss of a job. But this causes a relatively brief poverty spell that usually ends when a new job is acquired. Second, having children puts many people into poverty, especially young people, but the duration of poverty is very different for adults and non-adults. For 8 percent of adult-headed families, having another child causes a poverty spell for a little over five years. For non-adult headed families, new children (what some call "children having children") are almost twice as likely to initiate a poverty spell but the spell will last only half the time.

Table 4-2.
Reasons for poverty spells

Reason for Poverty Spell Beginning	Percent of Total	Length (Years)
Falling earnings for household head	38	3
Transfer income falls	8	5
Increased family size	8	5
Child becomes household head	15	2
Born into poverty	9	7.6

Source: Mishel and Bernstein (1993), p. 282.

These facts also illustrate an ironic relationship between poverty and government assistance.[136] They suggest that the surest way to push a family into poverty and keep them there a long time is to lessen any government assistance they may receive. Thus, it is the failure of anti-poverty programs to keep pace with inflation, not the alleged cognitive or moral deficiencies of the poor, that actually increases poverty. Finally, it is clear that the way to stay poor the longest is to be born poor. Herrnstein and Murray play into these myths that promote the view of the poor as personally unworthy—implying, but never stating overtly, that society would be better off without these people altogether.

Structural explanations are, however, more relevant to the question of how many people are in poverty; explanations focusing on individual characteristics address the different question of who is in poverty.

The later chapters of *The Bell Curve* will make calculations such as the estimated increase in the unemployment rate resulting from a fall in tested IQ. Such calculations rest on assumptions that are only implied in the earlier chapters, namely that test performances that affect which persons are in which jobs also determine what jobs are offered. While personal characteristics of intellect and morals may have some explanatory power, we believe that poverty is more importantly caused by factors beyond the control of poor people themselves. We shall focus on two:

employment realities and educational quality. With regard to both, it is important to keep two questions distinct. One kind of theory asks how many people are poor, are unemployed, or are uneducated. Another asks which people are poor, are unemployed or are uneducated. It sometimes (falsely) seems that the answer to the question "who?" automatically also answers the question "how many?" and that if you know what individual traits make one more likely to be unemployed, you also know what determines the unemployment rate. The analysis of *The Bell Curve* depends upon confounding and confusing these two questions.

That they are really distinct questions best answered by distinct kinds of theory is evident from considering what might influence the structure of positions in a society. For instance, a certain number of jobs of a particular kind exists, regardless of whether the number of people qualified to fill them is larger, the same as, or smaller than the number of jobs. A sharp decline in investment that might result from distant financial causes and that has nothing to do with the mixture of people looking for work might sharply decrease the number of jobs. If so, there will be a sharp rise in unemployment, but it is foolish to look for the causes of that rise in the characteristics of the people looking for work. You might just as well try to understand the dynamics of a hurricane by examining the trajectories of rain drops. The Great Depression brought home to most people the danger of fallacious reductionist accounts of unemployment.

What makes the Herrnstein and Murray analysis of social problems reductionist is that they systematically assume that any adequate theory of individual behaviors gives an adequate theory of social structures. While there are some times when social theorists use this kind of explanatory strategy constructively, there are also known limits to it. Specifically, whenever there is competition for a limited number of positions, the outcomes for different people are highly interdependent, and an individualistic model will fail. If a high score on an MCAT (Medical College Admissions Test) assures one a position in medical school, does that mean that if everyone got a high score, everyone could go to medical school? Obviously not. There are only a certain number of structural places to be filled. Conversely, suppose no one got a high score. Does that mean that no one could or would become a doctor? It is more likely that the places would be filled by different people. This is true even if the relationship between individual traits and individual success is not just strong but perfect. Determinants of individual success or failure cannot explain structural changes.

In recent years, structural changes such as high rates of unemployment and declining wages have contributed heavily to increasing poverty rates.

The fact that many poor people *do* work challenges the notion that
some biological or moral deficiency causes their economic difficulties.
The constant call for poor people to work misses two crucial points. First,
there are often fewer jobs than people who want them. For every anecdote about some "welfare queen" who refuses to work there is another
about 5,000 people lining up in the winter cold for 200 available jobs at a
hotel or factory, or about a recent college graduate busing tables at Den-
ny's to stay alive. Beyond anecdotes, there is strong systematic evidence
that the supply of jobs (especially good jobs) is smaller than the demand.
The Bell Curve and most popular political rhetoric ignore these factors.[137]

Second, jobs that do exist increasingly pay starvation wages. You can
work year-round in a full time job and still be poor, even if paid more
than the minimum wage. For instance, a job at the federal minimum
wage ($4.25 an hour) pays about $8,500 a year before taxes; the official
poverty line for a family of four is almost $15,000 (1993). Declining wages
affect more than just minimum-wage jobs. Taking inflation into account,
from 1967 to 1991, a large group of workers found themselves with significantly less purchasing power than they had when purchasing power
peaked. As all wages decline, many people who work long and hard find
themselves suddenly poor through no fault of their own. They still show
up for work and put in their time, but their paychecks buy less and less.
The 1980s were an especially fertile period for the expansion of low-wage
work. In 1979, 25 percent of the work force earned wages at or below the
poverty level. By 1989, 28 percent of the work force earned poverty
wages.[138]

In addition to the failure of wages to keep up with inflation, the actual
types of jobs available is another structural contributor to the growth of
the working poor. In short, positions that disappeared during the 1980s
tended to be high-paying manufacturing jobs with good benefits and union protection. The jobs that appeared during the 1980s tended to be in
the low-paying, no-benefit, non-union service sector.[139] In fact, in the
1980s about 6.3 percent of the work force shifted from these relatively
good jobs to these relatively bad jobs. Undoubtedly, many of these workers found themselves suddenly poor even though they were working. As
with wage levels, the workers have no control over this structural shift. It
is absurd to blame the allegedly low IQs of workers for poverty resulting
from these structural factors.

Of course, not all members of the work force faced declining incomes
in the 1980s. Corporate executives, for example, earned much more in

1989 than they did in 1979, even taking inflation into account. The after-tax earnings of corporate executives increased 60 percent between 1979 and 1989 as production workers' earnings declined 10 percent.[140] Their increase was not due to a sudden burst of intelligence among the cognitive elite. A more structural argument suggests that those executives who set wages gave themselves big raises while slashing their employees' wages or eliminating their jobs. These same people also made decisions to sell, move, or abolish companies, leaving workers without jobs and themselves with comfortable lifetime incomes (often called golden parachutes). A structural analysis maintains that such decisions and shifts have contributed far more to increasing poverty than the alleged individual deficiencies of poor people.

Contrary to the Herrnstein and Murray assumptions, Americans do not have equal access to educational opportunities.

Chapter Six of *The Bell Curve*, assessing the alleged relationship between IQ and educational success, is one of the least persuasive segments of the entire book. Its logic exemplifies the grand leaps of faith and poor methodology that dominate the book. It ignores a plethora of systematic research by psychologists, sociologists, journalists, and educators that paints a much more complex picture of educational attainment. This section will focus on only a few elements that challenge *The Bell Curve*'s simplistic view about intelligence and education.

There are two main structural components to the relationship between educational success and economic success. First, is all education the same, either in actual quality or in how people perceive its quality? Second, do all Americans have equal access to quality education. On both, we believe there is a significant qualitative difference among American schools, and that so-called cognitive ability has very little to do with the quality or quantity of schooling a person obtains. Instead, non-individualistic factors such as social class, social networks, and discrimination lead to unequal educational outcomes that translate into unequal employment prospects. As we noted, Kozol (1992) has recently painted a stunning picture of the "savage inequalities" among U.S. public schools. In one urban school, 110 history students in four different classes must share 26 textbooks; elsewhere, sixth graders share desks with second graders. In contrast, suburban schools (and some urban schools in upscale areas) offer multiple gymnasiums, swimming pools, and driver's education. Although such differences produce high rates of functional illiteracy and poor test performance, they do not stem from the cognitive abilities of students and parents, but from the mechanisms for funding public schools in the U.S. Public schools generate the bulk of their revenues through local property taxes. Thus, schools in wealthier areas can generate higher per-pupil expenditures. In the 1980s, this reliance on local property taxes increased as the federal government scaled back its contributions to public schools. This political agenda has regained popularity recently, and *The Bell Curve* will certainly be used to justify further cuts in federal funding. If, as Herrnstein and Murray argue, cognitive ability is the key dimension to educational success, why continue putting money into schools where the students are biologically prohibited from capitalizing on any educational improvements?

Of course, taking this logic to its next stage, we could argue for the abolishment of all schools—or at least for all expensive schools. Since *The Bell Curve* insists that IQ determines everything and that IQ is set before age of 15, why bother at all with schooling after that? Chances are, however, that people who support the Herrnstein and Murray argument will not take their children out of school. Perhaps they understand the other key structural element of educational opportunity: that certain schools impart prestigious credentials to their members that then open doors for future educational and economic success. These credentials may have nothing to do with educational content, but they have everything to do with opportunities. The argument does not mean what it says, and it does not say what it means. To justify policies that will accentuate the class bias in the schools, it suggests that there is no class bias, and then argues for increasing the importance of ability and ability testing.

Conclusions

We have examined the statistical analyses of Herrnstein and Murray and their conclusion that low intelligence is the primary cause of poverty, school failure, and unemployment, and we have found that they have not been able to sustain it. First, they have failed to meet scientific canons of measurement of variables and statistical usage. Important examples that, by themselves alone, invalidate their findings are serious technical errors in the measurement of their major variables and inadequacies in the model specifications for their logistic regressions. Second, they have not asked the questions a social scientist would ask when supposedly strong explanatory variables were found to provide so little explanation. In this case honest researchers would ask what other variables might more adequately explain the existence of social problems. Herrnstein and Murray, however, have a political rather than an academic purpose. Their political agenda requires that the disadvantaged be blamed for their own condition.

We have pointed to the more important social explanations for social problems, explanations related to social structure and social/economic trends and conditions. Structurally, it is clear that our social stratification system funnels the lion share of opportunities to those in the higher social rankings. Those on the lower rungs of the ladder are relatively, and often absolutely, deprived. One of these disadvantages for the poor is their residential segregation. Herrnstein and Murray, however, argue that this segregation is inevitable and that it is the elite whose actions ensure a successful society. The reader will note that this opinion is antagonistic to the democratic values to which the authors pay lip service.

Economic structures are also related to poverty and other social problems. For example, we have social/economic structures that narrow the job choices and curtail the wages of certain groupings of people, particularly women and members of minority groups. Shifts and changes in the economy result in unemployment or poverty level wages for some people. Without social policies to assist those deprived or to provide a financial floor in the wake of social and economic changes, the disadvantaged have little chance. To ask the frailest in our society to face the greatest number of difficulties is unfair, utterly inhumane, and ultimately ineffective in reducing social problems. We have argued that the social problems would be greatly exacerbated, not decreased, by cutbacks in social services and other social programs. These provisions need to be strengthened, not weakened.

Herrnstein and Murray, on the contrary, argue that the spending of government moneys on social services, and compensatory or financial assistance programs should be halted. Their political agenda here closely matches the agenda of the New Right, which bases its case largely on the value of individual independence. Social programs, it argues, create dependency and in consequence an increasing inability of the individual to overcome problems. While Herrnstein and Murray have developed a new supporting argument—namely, that it is low IQ that causes social problems and because low IQ cannot be remedied, programs for the disadvantaged are wasteful and useless—they revert to the dependency argument when it appears to be politically effective to stress the hidden costs of social programs. The two arguments are loosely tied together by means of the classical eugenic argument that welfare encourages the breeding of the cognitively unfit.[141] Thus they play into our society's myths relating to poverty and other social problems. We must conclude that their arguments have nothing to do with fairness or humanity, little to do with social science, and everything to do with political ideology.

The political ideology is obvious—support of a New Right assault on government initiatives aimed at narrowing the gap between the rich and the poor. To support this ideology they appeal to a analysis of the costs and benefits of social programs. They distort both the benefit side of the equation and the cost side in order to show both a lack of substantial benefit and excessive costs. They develop a personal deficiency argument to explain poverty, in order to cause benefits of programs in education, job training, or child support to disappear. They revert to dependency arguments to inflate the costs, suggesting that besides direct costs, we must worry about undermining the family or the work ethic. They can then argue that all money spent on such programs is not and investment for potential future return, but rather is wasted. In the rational analysis based on economic efficiency, a decision to invest where benefits do not exist and costs produce no tangible returns is simply stupid.

Chapter 5

Family Matters and Moral Values

The analysis of the family and the role of women is central to the connection of *The Bell Curve* to the popular base of the political Right.

A principal goal of the New Right is the destruction of the heritage of the New Deal, especially the consensus that the federal government has a role of ensuring a basic floor, a safety net, for citizens. The assumption of federal responsibility for ensuring a minimal level of living was anathema to the Right when such programs were enacted in the 1930s, and the central social agenda of the New Right has been to undermine it. Sometimes policies can be undermined by indirection. For example, a massive federal deficit, created through the tax cuts and military spending of the Reagan administration, has given the conservatives the political opportunity to reduce the social responsibility of the government.

Nevertheless, to alter this federal role significantly over the long term, the public understanding of social problems must change. The analysis of the situation of women, children, the infirm, and the family is central to that revision. The first programs were designed to protect children from hunger and provide minimal assistance to the elderly. Social Darwinists such as Herbert Spencer waxed eloquent about the processes weeding out the unfit. He argued that the starvation of widows and orphans showed Nature being "a little cruel so that it can be very kind," as, too, did the pneumonia that carried off the elderly and the infirm. Such an analysis was hardly viable as a political platform in the nineteenth century and it is not viable today. Today, the New Right must convince us that no one will really be hurt by the elimination of social programs. In the long run, everyone will be helped. Women will be made more self-reliant and industrious, children will be born only into families that will be able to care for them, and the social pathology of the ghetto will be reduced. We must be convinced that the programs to ameliorate social problems are actually causing them by encouraging immoral behavior and genetic deterioration.

Skillfully making the case that government should not be involved in helping individuals in distress is Murray's specialty. First, problems encountered by people who are hungry and without jobs must be defined as occurring because of individual inadequacy or misbehavior. Second, it is necessary to ignore both eligibility requirements for government assistance and the people actually served—in other words, the facts—to make the case for adult wantonness so that support for such people can then be viewed as support of behavior that undermines the American family. Third, it is important that federal investments in children be seen as costs to the nation, not investments in our capital for the future. Given these premises, conservatives can target welfare for abolition and advocate the return to "old-fashioned morality" by both the reintroduction of informal punishment through guilt and shame and the formal punishment of the courts and prison. This is the social agenda of the *Contract with America* justified and defended by *The Bell Curve*.

The arguments in *The Bell Curve* are distinctly different in tone from those of the *Contract with America*. Herrnstein and Murray make apparently aseptic, objective, social-scientific arguments that various kinds of social breakdown are produced by lack of cognitive capacity. Theorists on the political right make the argument that those problems are a result of moral breakdown, and mobilize moral outrage about them. *The Bell Curve* draws these different arguments together in the view that welfare, and other social services have "dysgenic effects," creating the very incapacity that they are alleged to resolve.

The Bell Curve makes the argument that the cornerstone of American society, legal marriage, is undercut by low rates of marriage and high rates of illegitimacy and divorce. The incidence of all of these, according to this argument, is concentrated differentially in American society, primarily among those of lower IQ. Since IQ is inherited, these illegitimate offspring of low IQ people are themselves of lower IQ. The low IQ is enhanced by poor parenting. Finally, the scenario Herrnstein and Murray have presented is, in their argument, exacerbated by public assistance, which provides financial support that prevents women from experiencing the full disaster of bearing children out of wedlock.

This argument of Herrnstein and Murray misrepresents societal problems, is dishonest, unfair, and based on fallacious assumptions. Let us engage this argument and examine both the premises and conclusions in the light of reality.

The analysis rests on a fallacious interpretation of data that do not support the conclusions of the importance of IQ in determining family structure.

The data included in *The Bell Curve* fail to support the contention that IQ is related to any of the rates considered. Logistic regression analyses are presented as the basis for their argument.[142] By the conventional measure of how much of the variation in some behavior is explained by the regression, R-squared (see Appendix 1), Herrnstein and Murray's analyses explain very small fractions of the behaviors they examine, usually less than 10 percent. Herrnstein and Murray then imply that the analysis supports their conclusions that variations in marriage, divorce, and illegitimacy are explained by IQ. This is simply dishonest. The authors assert a relationship to which they cling even when their data fail to support it. Since the authors want to make this argument, we can assume that they have sought data to support it. This, then, must be the best they can do—data that clearly do not support their conclusion.

Earlier chapters have discussed other ways in which the analysis is dishonest. Here, Herrnstein and Murray have not used education as an independent variable in their regressions, and they use it as a control variable only to distinguish the high school from the college sample. They subdivide the sample into parts. As this is done, sample size diminishes, in some cases to very small numbers. In some cases, the authors draw conclusions for American society based on samples as small as sixteen cases.[143] The relationship between IQ and these measures of family formation exists only in the minds of the authors. Since the data do not support these conclusions, these ideas are unsupported assertions.

The analysis takes legal marriage as the cornerstone of society in order to conjure away widows, orphans, and unrelated individuals.

Central to the argument is the assumption that legal marriage is the cornerstone of society. Most of us would probably agree that the family is a cornerstone of society. Legal marriage rates are, at best, only an indirect measure of familial relationships. Throughout the history of the United States, common law marriage, couples cohabiting as man and wife without legal sanction, has occurred sufficiently often for states to recognize these unions as established family units. Neither is the monogamous legal relationship of the United States the only possible arrangement for the family, nor is a sexual relationship and parenting synonymous in all cultures with marriage.[144]

In *The Bell Curve*, legal marriage is assumed to describe family relations: the legally married woman is assumed to be living in a two-parent household. Despite their own data of a 90 percent marriage rate for all Americans, Herrnstein and Murray assert a differential marriage rate for different sectors of society. They achieve this only by manipulating the ages they are considering. Differential marriage rates disappear over the life-span of the individual; thus these authors are forced into using an early cut-off of ages to demonstrate a difference. At no point do they attempt to describe the actual living conditions of individuals who have been legally married. In the discussion of marriage rates and divorce rates, no attention is given to widowhood, separation, or remarriage.

The reliance on rates to describe societal patterns avoids any discussion of what marriage means to different groups in American society. First of all, Herrnstein and Murray assume that marriage is equally available to all women in society. Here the authors reveal their ignorance of the conditions of life for people in poverty. Those who study health statistics and population trends know well the fragility of the newborn. The conditions of life in the American slum are bad. They are so bad that neonatal and infant mortality rates equal those of the poorest of the developing nations. Further, male babies are more likely to succumb than female babies. This, coupled with a higher accidental death rate for boys than for girls, produces an unfavorable sex ratio by the time adulthood is reached.[145] Women outnumber men in the ghettos of America. In addition, large numbers of poor men are in jail—hardly a location to encourage marriage. (Nor do we provide them with a living wage so that men in jail can adequately support their children.) Poor women do not have the same opportunities for legal marriage or financial support as women who come from better environments.

Why should poor women marry? Among the motivations for marriage, we can list the desire to insure a sound financial basis for the family, a desire for friendship and intimacy, and guaranteed access for fathers to their children. Herrnstein and Murray assert that the smart thing for women to do is marry. But is it equally smart for poor women? Apart from their more limited ability to coerce men into marriage compared with higher-income women, unemployment and underemployment are endemic among the very poor. The likelihood that marriage will improve the finances of a low-income family is slight. Rather, as a steady stream of studies of low-income families has demonstrated, the low-income male when working fails to earn enough to meet the needs of a family.[146] Instead of contributing to an enhanced well-being of the household, a man may use up the resources of the family. Studies argue that it may be rational for low-income women to be more concerned with the needs of children than are their mates, and that they have greater control over the resources of the household when they are not legally married to the man.[147] Totally aside from grosser cases of abuse and addiction, we need to remember the story of one poor woman who saved for months to buy toys for her children for Christmas only to have the money disappear in the week before the holiday. Where it went was made clear when her husband parked his newly-purchased car in front of the house on Christmas Eve.[148]

Coercive regulations designed to keep a woman and her children in a legal marriage, no matter what, ignore the real situation of many poor people. Keeping a woman in a relationship to an abusive, addicted, or violent spouse may save money in the short run, in the sense that it keeps them off the welfare rolls. But it does not represent real support of family values, and it is often a powerful generator of social problems and pathologies in the long run.

As divorce records clearly indicate, legal marriage often fails to provide a personal relationship and comfort for the wife. Men who struggle unsuccessfully to make a living are often less than affable mates. Low-income women face a higher probability than higher-income women of steady abuse and physical injury.[149] The unmarried woman can either move out or refuse entry to the man. It may often be the smart thing for a low-income woman not to marry in the first place and remain in greater control of her life. Yet even Herrnstein and Murray must admit that most women, irrespective of their place in society, do, in fact, marry at some point in their lives.

The Bell Curve gives a simplistic and deceptive analysis of divorce rates.

The interpretation of divorce rates is a complicated matter. For Herrnstein and Murray, it is simple. The rate of divorce has risen dramatically because of willful and unintelligent actions of people, thereby creating an unprecedented level of failure for the family.

First of all, divorce is only one of many causes of family breakup. Prior to World War II, societies experienced a widespread breakdown of families relatively early in the life of partners due to death.[150] Women's death in childbirth was much more common than today, and epidemic diseases including tuberculosis and the widespread summer epidemics of cholera and typhoid killed not only children but also parents.

Nor can divorce be simply equated with marital failure. Divorce has been differentially available in societies over time. The rise in divorce rates coincides with important changes in divorce law and in the financial availability of divorce to all families. The period after 1965, when Herrnstein and Murray show an increase in divorce rates, coincides with two changes. First, no-fault divorce began to become available across the nation. This involved two important changes in law: it was no longer necessary to show fault to provide grounds for divorce, an expensive and possibly humiliating experience. In addition, alimony payments to the divorced wife were no longer automatic. Thus divorce became cheaper for men and more readily available for women.[151] The second major change was expansion of access to legal services for poor Americans as a component of the War on Poverty. Prior to that time, poor women, once legally married, were rarely able to raise the money to pay the lawyer to institute divorce proceedings. Once married, they stayed married although their husbands may have long since departed. In the case above, this is not the breakup of a healthy marriage. The marriage has already broken up. Such divorces clarify the legal situation, protect the woman, and allow her to remarry.

Divorce is presented by these authors as willful and unwise activity. Rather, earlier divorce laws were coercive for marriages, particularly for women, intending to force women to remain in marriages irrespective of the nature of the relationship. Divorce laws were a hangover from the nineteenth century when women and children were considered the property of men. Deprived of equal rights to marital property, unlikely to be equally employed or employable, and required to demonstrate fault if divorce was to be granted, few women had access to a means to formally end a bad marriage. Poor women who had less to lose in divorce had no means to pay the costs of legal divorce. When divorce laws changed there was a rapid increase in divorce rates.

What the unusually high divorce rate in the United States means for the family cannot be answered with the divorce rate alone.[152] Remarriage rates must also be considered and the remarriage rate is high, although it declines for women as they age. Men at all ages will remarry. While many American children will live at some time in a single-parent household, far fewer will remain in a single-parent household throughout their youth. Rather, American society is characterized by complex family relations of his children, her children, and our children and the multiple relations with other relatives that such an arrangement implies. Rather than too little family, many have a rich complexity of families.

Herrnstein and Murray oversimplify and misinterpret the data. With both marriage rates and divorce rates they fail to take into account the changing age profiles of society, especially the impact of a rapidly increasing young adult population.[153] Divorce rates are always particularly high in the early years of marriage. If the age profile of the population has a bulge of people in the young adult years, as ours did in the late 1960s and 1970s, the rate of divorce is expected to rise. In addition, the authors misrepresent the divorce rate. They present it in terms of the likelihood that all marriages will end in divorce. Rather, the rate should be interpreted as the probability that marriages in a given year will end in divorce. People married in different years, therefore, have a different probability of divorce.

All the previous errors converge in the analysis of illegitimacy.

Herrnstein and Murray end their analysis of the American family with a consideration of rates of illegitimacy. By adding illegitimacy to the absence of legal marriage and divorce, they complete the ways in which an undeserving single-parent household can emerge. Illegitimacy is presented as characteristic of families whose mothers have flaunted the traditional and necessary pattern of family formation in which childbearing occurs only after legal marriage. Such an unacceptable pattern, they suggest, occurs mainly among women who are dumb. In this discussion of illegitimacy, the authors deepen their attack on the single-parent family by introducing immorality geared toward a rip-off of society. Ignoring evidence to the contrary, they make the argument essential to labeling these mothers as undeserving. The primary intent of this argument is to destroy the compassion that would hinder the political agenda advocating elimination of all public support for these families.

Herrnstein and Murray's discussion of illegitimacy is even more seriously inadequate than their discussion of marriage and divorce. The United States has a very serious problem of teen pregnancy.[154] Herrnstein and Murray add little light and much obfuscation to this problem. Their proposals would not only not help to solve the problem but would make it worse. Teen pregnancy is a problem irrespective of whether or not the mother is legally married to the father. First of all, it is a medical problem. Young women become physically able to conceive a child before they are sufficiently physically mature to carry the child safely to term. Therefore, young teenagers have a higher probability of serious complications of pregnancy and maternal mortality than older women. In addition, their babies are more likely to be premature, or full-term babies of low birth weight, and to die in the early months of life. Pregnancy among the young is a serious health problem. Secondly young teenagers are still in need of parenting themselves and usually are not ready to assume the responsibilities of parenting.[155]

We can prevent much teen pregnancy, but not by the methods proposed by Herrnstein and Murray. American teenagers are sexually active. Teenagers are risk takers who usually fail to take into account the long-term consequences of their actions. Although Herrnstein and Murray imply that teenagers often have babies either to get welfare or because they can get welfare, teenagers do not plan ahead. Young, urban teenagers become parents usually as a result of opportunistic relationships. Rural teenagers often are propelled into parenting by very early age of marriage, particularly in poverty stricken areas like the southern Appalachians. (Women there have high rates of teenage pregnancy but low rates of illegitimacy because they are married as young teenagers.) Married or not, the consequences for young women are the same. Depriving these young people of support will do little except exacerbate the negative consequences of their situation—increasing mortality rates, decreasing the adequacy of parenting, and increasing poverty and the numbers of women and children who are homeless, a situation that provides the worst possible environment for child rearing.

Higher-income families are more successful at preventing teen pregnancy because they have greater access to resources. Contraception, with abortion as a backup, effectively prevents teen pregnancy or unwanted pregnancy at any age. High income families throughout history have had means of protecting their young from unwanted pregnancy through close supervision and even single-sex private schools. Low-income families have fewer means.[156] Many high-income families confronted with a rebellious and uncontrollable child resort to the pill to ensure against the early arrival of a grandchild. When this fails, the family physician arranges an abortion. It is no surprise that Herrnstein and Murray find a lower illegitimacy rate among those of higher income. Until the late 1960s, doctors were explicitly forbidden by federal law from disseminating contraceptive information to women on welfare. Abortion is not available now since the Helms-Hyde amendment prevents federal money in Medicaid from being used for abortions. Neither contraception, which is expensive, nor abortion is available as freely to low-income families as it is to high-income families.

It is in this section of their book that the most outrageous distortion of data occurs. Herrnstein and Murray argue that illegitimacy has increased dramatically in the United States. They support this by a measure that shows the highest possible increase, the proportion of all births that are illegitimate. From this measure they conclude that illegitimacy has increased. However, the increase in the proportion of births that are illegitimate is not the consequence of a dramatic increase in illegitimate births but because of a decline in the legitimate births. Illegitimacy has increased most for white women, but the contribution of white illegitimate births to the entire illegitimate birth rate remains low. The sharp increase that Herrnstein and Murray find is an artifact of choosing a number that implies an increase in the numerator when it is the denominator that has decreased.[157]

This deliberate distortion is developed further by a series of obfuscations. Herrnstein and Murray next propose a "magic of compound interest" creating an even greater rise in illegitimacy.

> Anyone who is trying to understand social trends must also realize that the magic of compound interest has created an even more explosive rise in the population of unmarried mothers and children. In 1960, for example, there were just 73,000 never-married mothers between the ages of 18 and 34. In 1980, there were 1.0 million. (*The Bell Curve*, p. 179)

Like much of the rhetoric of this book, this sounds good, conveying a dramatic picture of what is happening. But what does it mean? What is the "compound interest?" Are the authors arguing that illegitimate parents have illegitimate children, thereby causing across time a cumulative growth in illegitimacy? Where is the evidence that such a statement is true? There is none. In the next sentence, the numbers of illegitimate children in 1960 and 1980 born to mothers between 18 and 34 are cited as proof of the increase. Why the cut-off age of 34, especially when we know that many women, especially professional women, have postponed childbirth to the later years of fertility? The influence of this postponement on the numbers of illegitimate births is not considered by the authors. More importantly, numbers alone do not give evidence of changing behavior. The population base must also be considered. Herrnstein and Murray use the words "illegitimacy ratio," but they do not calculate the ratio, giving the reader raw numbers only.

The decades they are considering are decades of rapid population growth. Our numbers increased from 181 million in 1960 to 228 million in 1980 and 250 million in 1990. Overall population growth, however, does not give sufficient information on which to evaluate the importance of a change in the numbers of illegitimate births. In the period immediately following World War II, there was an unprecedented rise in the birth rate. Many more babies were born to adult women than had been the case in the previous decades. By the mid 1960s, the first baby-boom babies were just beginning to enter the child-bearing ages. The number of young women began to grow dramatically in relation to the number of older women. Far more women were entering the child-bearing years than were leaving. As the numbers of women increased, the numbers of children being born increased, *even though the birth rate was falling*. As the numbers being born increased, the numbers who were being born outside of marriage increased. Finally, to the extent that illegitimate births are more often first births, younger women can be expected to have more than older women. Herrnstein and Murray artificially inflate illegitimacy by not counting all births to women over 34 years of age.

The central aim of their argument will not become clear for hundreds of pages. Then, Herrnstein and Murray will become very concerned about the "dysgenic" effects of welfare—i.e., that welfare causes less-fit, cognitively disabled people to be born.[158] The classical eugenicists of the United States and of Hitler's Germany used to term it "pollution of the race." Herrnstein and Murray make a great show of pulling back from any "eugenic" policies. They do not advocate the sterilization, expulsion, euthanasia, or extermination of those people.

Instead, they say that they "merely" advocate an end to the "dysgenic" effects of welfare. However, the view that welfare encourages births is a myth. Contradicting the great bulk of theory and existing research, they must convince us by sleight of hand that welfare produces births of the children who are the problem. They must convince us that it is immoral for those children to be born and that welfare is responsible for the very problems it ameliorates.

The section on illegitimacy rates illustrates the many ways in which Herrnstein and Murray abuse and misuse information to make their point and do so with empty phrases that capture the imagination of the reader. With clever rhetoric, statistical distortion, and manipulated data, they try to convince us that welfare is causing illegitimacy to rise.

The analysis is in support of a mythical, demonizing view of welfare recipients.

The United States has engaged in "welfare bashing" since the beginning of public assistance. A favorite stereotype is the image of the woman who deliberately has illegitimate children to obtain welfare money. Despite all evidence to the contrary, this stereotype persists. and Herrnstein and Murray uncritically repeat and reinforce it. Because it is such a prevalent belief, it is difficult to refute with information. We can try.

Most children on welfare are not illegitimate. Families divide into about equal thirds of one-third families with only legitimate children, one-third families with both legitimate and illegitimate children, and one-third families with illegitimate children. Over time the legitimacy status of children changes as more women become legally married, often to the father of her illegitimate children. Women do not have children to get on welfare or remain on welfare.[159] Rather the welfare population has as low a birth rate as any group, fewer than two children per family.[160] Further, most women on welfare are legally married. Most women also remain on welfare a relatively short time, moving onto and off welfare as they gain or lose jobs. Welfare serves as their back-up to cover their needs when they lose their jobs, much as higher-income families use their parents and savings. Finally, women who remain on welfare for long periods are often seriously ill from such diseases as diabetes, heart disease, and hypertension.

The Herrnstein and Murray picture of family support suggests that women on welfare have families to which they can turn, a picture that is untrue (if they have families, the families have no resources). Many have very few relatives. The image of the extensive extended family is another welfare myth.[161] Herrnstein and Murray also suggest that they can find support within their community; again untrue—the community is broke. Further, they suggest they could go to work; again untrue. These women have tried that; they all have work histories. They are on welfare because they have lost their jobs and have not found another.

The relation of women, work, and welfare has been made more complicated by the recent changes in the job market. Welfare women come from the sector of occupations that are at the bottom of our job scale. Historically, older women were part of the domestic-service market, a job market that shrank dramatically after World War II when modern technology replaced the hired girl.[162] Women entering the welfare rolls after 1960 were part of the marginal work force (technically called the secondary labor market), temporary workers who worked the peak seasons in food processing plants or in the clothing industry and were laid off when the season ended.[163] Many of these jobs have now disappeared as the industries have moved south and then out of the United States. There has been a radical transformation of work patterns. One-third of American jobs have been moved from full-time positions to temporary part-time positions.[164] Many of these are exempt from the laws governing conditions of work and of hiring. The jobs are low paid, with no fringe benefits. Together with these changes, poor women face the inadequacy of the minimum wage of $4.25 an hour—a rate that does not yield enough with a full-time job to meet the basic needs of a family, much less with part-time work.[165] A woman on welfare has little opportunity in a job market that will not pay her enough to feed her family if she finds a job.

The values that inform the welfare regulations have done an about-face in recent years. Welfare came into being at a time when this nation believed strongly that women belonged at home and that mothers had an absolute duty to remain at home and raise their children. Historically, black women worked for pay throughout their lives, using grandmothers and older children to help in child-rearing, even sending their children back to southern farms and grandparents when they were small and needed constant supervision. It is not until the 1960s that poor black women begin to enter the welfare rolls in numbers approximately commensurate to their need. The regulations of welfare, however, have forced women to make choices. The "man in the house" rule that precluded welfare everywhere until the late 1960s required that destitute intact families separate if children were to be eligible for financial assistance. Women were expected to be at home caring for these children. To ensure this, the welfare rules required a strict penalty of deductions from the welfare check for any money earned by the mother.[166]

Then American women in the 1970s began to enter the work force in substantial numbers. The return to work of American women has been fueled by financial necessity—most work, not for the reward of work itself, but because their families cannot maintain their quality of life without two incomes. Women compensate for the loss of earning power of their husbands. If there is any single villain in the decline of the family, it is probably the forced increase in labor force participation, which the political Right proposes to strengthen.[167]

The attitudes of Americans toward the woman at home has changed as women have entered the job market in large numbers. It has changed most dramatically toward the welfare mother. Rather than seeing mothering as a critical necessity in welfare families in which the conditions of life for children are most dangerous, the nation has turned against the welfare mother for not attempting to earn her keep. We have dramatically changed our attitude about what women should do and what is important. Thus, we castigate the welfare mother despite the fact that we have provided neither reasonable opportunity to work at wages that would allow her to earn the keep for herself and her children, nor significantly altered the rules and regulations, written for a different time that, with change, might make welfare sufficient to give her a hand up while she worked. The community cannot meet the needs of these children, growing up in a dangerous environment. Daycare opportunities are scarce and usually cost well above what a minimum wage worker will bring home. Our laws still make it a crime to leave children under certain ages alone, and a woman found guilty of doing so faces a term in jail, and her children, foster care. With all of our enthusiasm for moving welfare mothers back to work, we should ask what will they do, how much can they earn, and what will happen to their children. Herrnstein and Murray make very clear that their aim is to make welfare disagreeable enough so that unmarried women will not have children or will give them up for adoption. Aside from the question of who is going to adopt them, it is clear that it is the children who are being punished in order to change the behavior of their mothers. Herrnstein and Murray present no evidence that such a strategy would be successful. Even if they had evidence, punishing children for what parents do is in this society considered to be morally wrong.

An increase in shame is unlikely to reduce illegitimate births, while it would exacerbate their negative consequences.

Finally, Herrnstein and Murray suggest that we must return to an emphasis on values, values that will make unwed motherhood shameful and costly to women. It is already costly because the welfare mother has little to share with her child and increased responsibilities. Welfare is already shameful in this society, sufficiently so that welfare mothers expect to be berated by secretaries and administrators in the services they must use and humiliated by the workers at the public assistance office. One welfare mother regularly carries an old magazine that she pretends to read when in public in order to avoid seeing the looks of other people.[168]

Illegitimacy historically was shameful. The shame did not prevent births. Rather the shame of illegitimacy is a shame we visit upon the child. It is the child who is the bastard. Do we want to return to an earlier time by adding pejorative names to the disadvantage of poverty for a substantial portion of our population? To what end would we do this? The product of such terms is only reduced confidence, a further erosion of the sense of self we know is essential for productive lives as adults.

At this point, Herrnstein and Murray have exaggerated the incidence of single-parent households by incorrectly using the rates of marriage, divorce, and illegitimacy as indicators. They have inflated the estimate of change in these rates by choosing numbers that give the highest possible rate and by failing to correct raw numbers for the increasing population base. By omitting critical information, they portray the incidence of marriage, divorce, and illegitimacy as caused solely by individual will. Disregarding all of the facts about welfare families, they present welfare as a primary cause of the growth of the single-parent household, a problem they attribute exclusively to the behavior of women. Having blamed poor women for their situation, they argue for moral sanction, shame, to force these women to alter their condition.

The argument thus far has been that individuals who are poor and unmarried or divorced are ruining the base of society. Such behavior is solely the fault of the individual, who therefore deserves no support and no compassion. The limited assistance society provides through welfare is misguided and harmful to the rest of us, since it allows these women to continue on their path of destruction.

The alleged poor parenting by poor test-takers then prepares a crucial bolt-hole for the Herrnstein and Murray analysis.

The authors return to eugenics to intensify their attack on the single-parent family through a critique of parenting styles, which, Herrnstein and Murray claim, further increase the inadequacies of their children (already of low IQ, since IQ is inherited). Through poor and inappropriate parenting, the already-limited ability of their children is made yet lower, further weakening the quality of the citizenry.

Poor women, they claim, have poor parenting skills. Unlike the high-income parent whose parenting skills nurture the cognitive abilities of their children, the low-income woman resorts to authoritarian child rearing, ensuring yet more inadequate offspring. The authors blame the woman for the deficits of her environment. Where are the equal resources? The money for toys? The programs that enrich the lives of high-income children? The knowledge that the higher income woman has gained through her own education about the development, needs, and possibilities of children? Rich kids throughout societies and history usually have been raised by the women from lower levels of society, the nursemaids and the household help. Their care has been supplemented by the resources of nursery school, high-quality private school, music, sport and dancing classes, and the opportunities that come with wealth.

Even more importantly, Herrnstein and Murray are presenting the high-income style of parenting as if it were appropriate for all of society. The dangers to life in the ghettos of America are more extensive than the dangers surrounding the high-income child. Poor women will tell you that to survive their children must learn not to question but to obey and to obey immediately. Their child rearing is geared to ensuring this as the first and most fundamental goal they must achieve.

These authors' lack of appreciation of child rearing among the poor reminds us of the persistence of belief that wealthy people can manage poverty better than those who are poor. Extensive studies of nutrition conducted by the United States Department of Agriculture demonstrated conclusively that starvation exists among the poor in this society and that the poor do the best job of getting the most for their food money. (This study also showed that the worst nutrition is practiced by the very rich with their over consumption of steak, ice cream, and alcohol and avoidance of leafy green vegetables and dried beans.)[169]

Given the weakness of the evidence for any linkage between low IQ and poor parenting, why include the analysis at all? The answer depends on understanding the structure of The Bell Curve as a whole and its relation to the programs of the political Right.

On one hand, the pedantic and painstaking analysis of parenting styles, which ignores any of the structures and conditions that constrain them, is partly an exercise in victim-blaming stereotypes. On the other, Herrnstein and Murray are well aware how tenuous are the relationships on which they have built their argument, here and elsewhere. The argument in their Chapter Ten constructs a fail-safe plan for it. Even as they argue for the importance of genetic differences, they are preparing to argue that it does not matter whether the differences are genetic or environmental. They will need the argument. We have seen that their analyses leave more than 90 percent of the variation unaccounted for. This is not surprising. When you ignore the conditions that directly bear on behavior, you cannot explain the behavior well. What Herrnstein and Murray are doing is preparing a crucial counter for the failure of the whole genetic argument. They will say "it doesn't matter." Even if all the problems of poor children are environmental we must prevent children from being raised in those terrible conditions; we must ensure that they are never born (shame) or that if born, they are raised by someone else (adoption, orphanages).

The coercive character of their analysis of the family is mirrored in their analysis of crime.

In the chapters on the family, the solution has been offered of a return to the use of social norms to control the incidence of single-parent households. All the problems of society are viewed as stemming from poor choices made by inadequate people. Therefore the society should institute the controls of the nineteenth century where women were prevented from divorce by marriage law and by laws that deeded all marital property to men. Women leaving a marriage were destitute, had no right to their children, and had to endure the ostracism of the community. Those who bore children out of wedlock were "fallen women" whose children bore the shame of being bastards. For the extreme conservatives, this is a proper way to respond to the single-parent households and thereby curb their destructive spread.

In the section on crime, the authors provide the rationale for a rapid expansion of our prison system. Crime, they argue, is the consequence of the limited intelligence of the offender. To defend this position, the authors must rely primarily on the work of Jensen and Herrnstein. They cite other authors as supporting this limited view of the origins of crime, but they fail to appreciate the complexity of the arguments of social scientists like Hirschi and Selvin, whose work on the complexities of relationships underlying different rates of crime is a well-known example of the role of multiple variables in accounting for social phenomena, and a primary teaching tool for students learning how to separate and integrate multiple variables in social research.[170] Yet Herrnstein and Murray cite Hirschi to make the case of the most simple-minded possible explanation of criminal behavior. To find other support for their position they have to move far afield to small rural communities in Sweden and to New Zealand, both countries with a low crime rate in general and places where informal social control in communities is intense and the overall level of living is high. The extreme poverty and disarray of American center cities is not found in either of these places.

They have no data to support their argument that criminal behavior is the consequence of limited intelligence. They assert that their data support their argument but they have managed to explain only 1 or 2 percent of the variation in who becomes a criminal. No serious social scientist would claim support for their argument from these data. The explanation of criminal behavior is a complex problem and one that has failed to yield simple answers. Correct explanation must involve the opportunity for meaningful employment for the young, the differential distribution of wealth, the way the justice system operates, whom the police arrest and charge, what imprisonment implies and what happens to those who have been incarcerated, the presence or absence of an organized underground economy based on criminal activity, and the extent of drug addiction and the drug trade. The example the authors use to demonstrate the inherited pattern of crime, the higher probability that sons of criminals will be criminals, ignores all the reasons why such children face larger obstacles to meaningful adult life than other children.

Why would anyone argue such a simplistic view of crime when even their own data fail to give any support for the argument? Clearly, the answer must be to set a base for the other major plank in the conservative platform for change—namely the rapid expansion of the prison system and the strengthening of the authoritarian state. Criminal behavior must be seen as a consequence of individual stupidity and waywardness, not a consequence of social problems. However, the United States already has the highest proportion of its citizens behind bars of any country in the developed world. According to this argument from the Right, the United States, therefore, must have more stupid people than any other nation. Does anyone really think this is the case?

Conclusion

We have demonstrated that Herrnstein and Murray have no data supporting their allegation that low rates of marriage, high divorce rates, and high rates of illegitimacy are the result of differences in IQ. We have further discussed why all of this analysis fails to account for or consider the real situations of people. Herrnstein and Murray are using a scare tactic to convince us that we need to introduce an authoritarian attitude in society that legally coerces and morally shames people into dictated patterns of behavior. If these people fail to conform, they must experience the full measure of consequence. No help will be available to ease their burden.

This is a cruel and inhumane response. Given the narrow margins of survival now faced by the very poor, this is tantamount to declaring war on the poor. The analysis on which these conclusions rest is unscientific, an assembly of assertions, of ideas without support from the data. In some cases the data have been deliberately falsified in order to make a point. This is dishonest analysis, unfair interpretation, and ultimately a dangerous argument, for to the extent that it supports a political position it endangers the survival of a substantial portion of American children.

It is also a sexist and a racist argument. Herrnstein and Murray's argument is directed against women and children. Women are at fault for bearing children out of wedlock, causing single parent households, or seeking relief from bad marriages through divorce. The poor in this book are the urban poor, primarily blacks. Sixty percent of welfare recipients, most legally married at an early age and without an illegitimate child, are white and rural, and are not the poor portrayed in this book. Rather the 50 percent of black children on welfare for all or part of their lives are the targets of these authors. Their intent is to establish the single parent household as a threat to society, to place the blame for this on individual choice, to erase compassion for these women and children, and therefore to justify turning off welfare as an option for the poor.

Herrnstein and Murray have linked central American values of individual independence, a traditional view of the American family and its importance, and the desire for law and order with a political agenda. This agenda is designed to enhance the control of the state, diminish the compassionate, supportive role of the state (particularly the redistributive functions of income maintenance programs), and force women back into the narrowly-defined roles of child rearing within legal marriage. To make these links, they have produced "scientific evidence" that social problems derive solely from the willful and misguided acts of individuals and that governmental intervention to ameliorate the distress of the poor results in uncontrollable costs and further enhances the social problems. While the link is drawn between values and political goals, the link is not sustained either by appropriate facts or correct scientific analysis.

This erroneous and misleading analysis is a necessary part of the political argument of *The Bell Curve*. In this chapter the costs of governmental intervention are escalated to include intangible costs to the normative framework of society and to the social order. Government intervention to ease the consequences of poverty result, according to their argument, in undercutting basic social values of independence, individual responsibility and parental obligation. Financial support to single parents, whether this has occurred through divorce or birth out of wedlock, further erodes the social order by undercutting the basic institutions of society, particularly the family. Thus these authors adopt a nineteenth century view of women's roles and ignore the social impact of poverty on human lives in order to present an analysis of governmental support for poor children that inflates the costs and minimizes the benefits of such support. Herrnstein and Murray suggest that the costs include erosion of necessary values and the family. This leads to their argument that a more rational approach is to enforce conformity to social standards now endorsed primarily by the New Right.

To make this structure palatable, Herrnstein and Murray propose an idealized view of the past where all individuals conformed to the norms of the majority, where the state maintained order without crime, and where families remained intact and able to provide for themselves all that they needed. Neither minority populations nor women challenged the social order. With fallacious data and incorrect analysis, they argue that the world has seriously strayed from these roots. Central values are extracted from the larger value frame of society, given a hierarchical supremacy and argued without attention to other critical values. Such values as equal rights for all, independence for women, and the rights of citizenship are ignored. If this argument is accepted at face value, the American belief in the importance of compassion, of responsiveness to those who suffer, is destroyed. In its place is support for the authoritarian state.

Chapter 6

Race Relations

The argument that this is a meritocratic society or that federal interventions are unnecessary must deal with the issue of race.

The New Right views the United States as an open society of equal opportunity, in which people get ahead through drive and native ability. Traditional status barriers, privilege, or group disadvantages have disappeared. Such barriers or disadvantages contradict the values of self-reliance, personal responsibility, and opportunity, and would require government policies and interventions. For the New Right, markets governed by individual self-interest lead people to operate in the public good. Inequalities are an irreducible result of individual differences in ability and motivation.

A defense of this vision of an open society based on equal opportunity must deal with race. Race is an ascriptive group characteristic: individuals are born into a racial category; they do not choose them. Race is associated with the largest single cluster of inequalities in American society. Black income has hovered at about 60 percent of white income for a generation. Black unemployment runs nearly twice that of the rest of the society. Nearly half of black children grow up in poverty. Ghetto communities are poor, dangerous, violent, drug- and crime-infested. Ghetto schools often lack textbooks, skilled teachers, and hope. In 1984, blacks constituted four percent of the nation's managers and three percent of physicians and lawyers, but they constituted over fifty percent of its maids and garbage collectors.[171] These massive inequalities are the single most visible fact in virtually any large American city. They cannot be ignored. To argue that the United States is a society of equal opportunity that makes government programs unnecessary requires an account that blames these conditions on the inferior capacities of blacks.

Any structure of cumulative disadvantage represents a problem if we are committed to equal opportunity or to equal concern. Structures of inequality that affect whole groups, such as women or blacks, from which it is not possible to "pass," represent a more severe problem because every member of the group tends to be held back by stereotypes and disadvantages of the group as a whole. Such ascriptive traits are often the basis of a "master status," in which a black or female lawyer is perceived as black or as female first and as a lawyer second.[172] Responses of employers, insurance companies, schools, Realtors, neighbors, judges, cabdrivers, or police to individuals because of their group membership creates a pervasive system of inequality in sharp violation of ideals of equal treatment, equal concern, and equal opportunity.[173]

Moreover, the principal set of programs the New Right wishes to abolish are deeply involved with race. This is not because the majority of recipients of government aid are black. Even those programs geared to the poorest of the poor such as Aid to Families with Dependent Children, food stamps, or school lunches, have a majority of white recipients. In programs such as government-insured school loans, more than ninety percent of the recipients are white. The largest fraction of people helped by affirmative action programs are women. Nevertheless, race is central to political support of these programs. The civil rights movement encouraged and reinforced movements by women, older people, students, the disabled, and other groups to open up schools and the society. Affirmative action programs led to the expansion of the rights of women, children, students, the unemployed, those with disabilities, and others. Race relations are the key to issues of equality and welfare more generally.[174] The problem of race is an American dilemma.

To deal with race is not only a necessity for the political Right but also an opportunity. Blacks are a minority in the American population. Since voting is higher among more privileged groups, blacks are an even smaller portion of the electorate. Racism is still an immensely powerful political force.[175] Even though in decline, explicitly prejudiced beliefs still represent a powerful minority position.[176]

Under these circumstances, the political outcome of many battles depends on whether the issue is polarized by race.[177] Issues of schooling, health care, aid to cities, aid to the poor, and more generally health, education, and welfare, may be viewed as benefiting racial and ethnic minorities or as matters of general welfare. If they are represented as race issues, they gain the support of only a minority of the population. Thus, it is not only indispensable for the spokespersons of the New Right to address the issue of race inequality, but to the extent that they can make race and affirmative action the central issue of American politics, they can use it to outflank and attack the welfare state as a whole.

The political strategies of the New Right regarding race leads to a highly contradictory set of arguments.

The New Right uses race to make a highly volatile political appeal to its audiences. The basis of this appeal differs with each audience. The differences force the Right to make arguments that are often contradictory. Such contradictions are endemic in politics, in which different positions must be combined and reconciled. The New Right must combine individualism (libertarian limitation of government powers) with traditional conservatism (stressing law and order, assertion of values). Its position is thus particularly contradictory with respect to race. For some purposes, it must stress racial differences, often taking them to be absolute and innate. For others it has to stress an individualism that says that race is an illusion and makes no difference.

These contradictions are embodied in *The Bell Curve*. The authors find their central image in the bell curve itself, which gives the book its title, with its emphasis on means and variation. Their argument relentlessly focuses on the differences between the means of different groups, while constantly stressing that there is a range of individual variation around those means so that groups overlap. Herrnstein and Murray often suggest that their analysis in *The Bell Curve* is not racist because it is individualist, taking account of the immense variation of individuals around the group mean. Yet the individualist character of the analysis is central to ideological positions that fail to see, and therefore fail to rectify, social causes of social problems. A number of recent analyses have demonstrated that the dominant justifications for racist and sexist structures in the United States are individualist.[178] Not only do individualist analyses often legitimate failing to deal with social inequities, but they have further connections to many inegalitarian ideologies.

Herrnstein and Murray say that the assumption of genetic cognitive equality among the races has practical consequences and that it makes no difference whether genes are part of the reason for differences between white and black performance. They say that race is a difficult concept to employ in the American context but that they will still comment on possibly genetic cognitive differences among races

Which do they mean? The contradictions in their argument stem from a political situation and a theoretical task that require contradictory views.

At the center of all those contradictions are those about equality of opportunity. They must both acknowledge the immense inequalities in the society, which seem to prevent equality of opportunity, and argue that those inequalities stem from and are consistent with equality of opportunity. All of the more specific analyses of historical trends or conceptualizations of race and bias stem from this central issue.

The view that predominates in *The Bell Curve* and drives most of the analysis is the assumption that race and ethnic inequalities of opportunity were eliminated in the United States during the 1960s and in the War on Poverty, if not before. Thus, black, Hispanic, and other minorities now have an equal chance at quality education, jobs, and social success. Any disadvantage must be the result of defective ability. However, this view coexists with another one, that says that the immense social inequalities continue to produce inequalities of life chances. Herrnstein and Murray say that when a society makes good on the ideal of letting every youngster have equal access to whatever allows latent cognitive ability to develop, it is in effect driving the environmental component of IQ variation closer and closer to nil. They also say that the United States is still very far from this state of affairs at the extremes. If one thinks of babies growing up in slums with crack-addicted mothers compared to children growing up in affluent, culturally rich homes with parents dedicated to squeezing every last IQ point out of them, then, according to Herrnstein and Murray, even a heritability of 0.6 leaves room for considerable change if the changes in environment are commensurably large (*The Bell Curve*, p. 109).[179]

Which is it? Has the environmental component been driven almost to nil? Or are there still immense inequalities? This passage is one of the few where substantial inequality of opportunity is acknowledged. In it, the contradiction is resolved because the only difference in opportunity that is recognized is in the opportunity to achieve high IQ. Moreover, the passage suggests that only extreme cases are suffering under extreme environmental deprivation. Finally, those extreme cases are treated as the fault of an irresponsible mother. These ways of minimizing the contradiction are not sufficient. Most opportunities are differentially available and resources are unequal; they are unequal not only for extreme cases but for typical ones; and the inequalities are not the fault of irresponsible mothers.

There is a more serious problem here that is papered over. The axiomatic view of the whole political Right is that there exists rough equality of opportunity in the United States: not perfect equality of opportunity, perhaps, but rough equality. That axiom drives the Herrnstein syllogism. Yet, in any American city, whether you look at schools or playgrounds or jobs or social contacts, you do not see equality of opportunity. Many neighborhoods are so dangerous that parents who are able will spend vast amounts of money not to live in them; schools are so inadequate and dangerous that many parents are willing to spend thousands of dollars a year to send their children elsewhere. This inequality of opportunity has always been a serious problem for American values.

Nor is the problem merely one of attitudinal prejudice. Myrdal's concept of cumulative causation shows ways that attitudinal prejudice or conscious racism need not be present for discriminatory, racist inequalities to occur. The issues are commonly analyzed in terms of institutional racism, institutional sexism, and the like.[180] Central to arguments of *The Bell Curve* or *The End of Racism* is that there is no such thing as institutional racism. However, the mutual reinforcement of many disadvantages has exactly the same effect as conscious racism and is bound up with it in any case. For example, Myrdal (1964) noted that black health was much poorer than white health, which in turn led to lesser employability, greater likelihood of calling in sick, lost pay, and other disadvantages. A small fraction of this poorer health was the result of direct discrimination: the refusal of white hospitals or white doctors to treat blacks. But differential access to medical care did not result from direct discrimination. Segregated housing, low black income, and fee-for-service medical care led doctors, black and white, to avoid predominantly black areas. Lower levels of black education led to many fewer black physicians. Even with all these inequalities, access to health care could be equalized as a matter of government policy,[181] but relative black powerlessness resulted in that not happening. In the period since Myrdal's analysis, some progress has been made in equalizing access to health care, although mainly with regard to direct discrimination.

Moreover, the concept of cumulative causation shows why black levels of health would be far below white levels, even if there were equal access to health care. High levels of poverty, low levels of education, and concentration in dirty, dangerous or toxic jobs or residences will lead to lower levels of health, regardless of health care. Restricted contacts, stereotypes, and a subculture will reinforce the cumulative effects of such factors. Myrdal showed that with regard to health, as with political power, ownership of businesses, education, or concentration in backward and insecure jobs, it is usually the cumulative operation of many factors, reinforcing each other, that leads to the inequality. Such inequalities may be intertwined with stereotype, prejudice, or privilege, but separating out the contribution of conscious prejudice is neither possible nor germane. It is not possible to find a prejudiced person and tell them to stop acting in the prejudiced way.[182] It is not germane because the contribution made by one particular element, such as unequal health, does not depend upon the motives of the individuals producing the differential. In such a system of cumulative disadvantage, finding occurrences of conscious prejudice and discrimination is beside the point. It is the net health gap that is unfair and that contributes to the rest of the racist system, and it is the operation of the total health and health care system that produces the gap. Myrdal showed similar structures of cumulative causation in such fields as occupation, black businesses, crime, education, housing, family structure and political involvement.[183]

Forms of racism

In 1942, the central issue of *An American Dilemma*, the dilemma for the white majority, was that the history and position of black Americans was fundamentally inconsistent with any meaningful version of the value that "all men are created equal." For most of American history, chattel slavery created a group well-described as enslaved physically, economically, socially, legally, sexually, and morally, and psychologically subjected not only to the exploitative whim of individual white owners but also to the violent mercy of all whites. Moreover, slavery was replaced by a system of Jim Crow segregation, inequality and political, legal and economic subordination that lasted into the 1960s.

Myrdal showed that the result was not only inconsistent with constitutional guarantees, but fundamentally unstable. At any particular time, the level of racism and discrimination may balance a low standard of black living, the level of racism being sufficient to maintain the black poverty, ignorance, and social disorganization, and the low black standard of living maintaining the level of racism so that each mutually causes the other. For any particular type of inequality, such as levels of health, crime, or political power, the cumulative effect of the whole system may make it difficult to change in isolation. For any particular individual, associations, stereotypes, connections and ties to others may make it difficult to change their situation without changing that of others. These may give the system such an appearance of immobility that it appears biological. Nevertheless, Myrdal argued, this whole appearance is an illusion. The mutually reinforcing effects amplify changes. A decrease in white racism and discrimination or a decrease in black poverty can send the system into a positive spiral, as it leads to further decreases in black poverty or white racism that reinforce the original change. Conversely, an increase in white racism or an increase in black poverty or unemployment can lead to a negative spiral, in which the initial change is amplified.[184]

Within the framework of a structure of cumulative causation, one would expect the passing of the Civil Rights and affirmative action laws of the 1960s to have set in motion a spiral of improvement. The fact that many indices of black segregation and distress are as bad or worse today than they were in 1970 is what occasions and gives plausibility to analyses such as *The Bell Curve* or *The End of Racism*. What those analyses obscure is that many forms of racism and racial inequality were untouched by those laws, and that there were powerful negative forces working to increase black poverty. There was a positive spiral for some blacks, that, in the absence of countervailing forces, would have led to general improvement.[185] At the same time, the higher unemployment rates, stagflation, de-unionization, de-industrialization, and cutbacks of social services in the 1980s created an increase in segregation and misery for other blacks, that, in the absence of countervailing forces, would have led to a negative spiral. The result of the two contradictory forces is the fact that virtually all analysts accept with regard to the condition of black America: increased inequality and differences within the black population.[186]

The changes that have come about are relatively recent and limited. Less than a decade after the Civil Rights Act, the Nixon administration was on record as opposing them.[187] Even had the policies been seriously pursued over the period, two decades is a short time in which to transform powerfully rooted social structures. The environment became even less conducive to substantive change in the 1980s. Moreover, as we showed in Chapter Four, there were substantial benefits for some groups at the same time there was active regression for others. Thus, contemporary studies of the social position and the economic, political, and social resources of African or black Americans, such as those reported in *A Common Destiny*, show a mixed set of outcomes with considerable progress in some areas and regression in others.[188]

Figure 6-1 represents an overview of some of the forces that have affected race inequality in the last two decades. It ignores lags and delays, which, in processes which often involve families and identities and are often considerable, and it makes no effort to represent the real complexity of race relations or of the policy issues which bear upon them. However, in contrast to the analysis of *The Bell Curve*, which sees a conflict between equal opportunity and unequal cognitive endowment, Figure 6-1 shows a conflict between two contradictory social forces, often operating on different segments of the black community.

Herrnstein and Murray's analysis enormously oversimplifies the concept of race and slides illegitimately from the social construct of an ethnic group to the biological concept of race.

Biologically and genetically, differences between races are minuscule. Indeed, the amount of genetic variability within races is huge compared with the genetic variability between them. Specifically, skin color is not correlated with deep or pervasive genetic differences. Classifying world

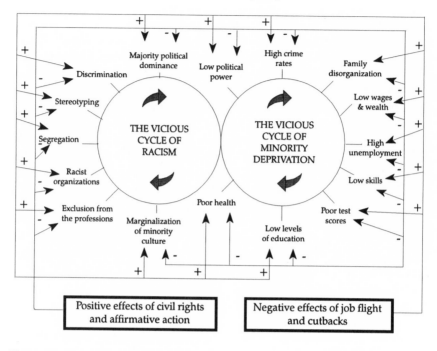

Figure 6-1.
Race and ethnic cumulative causation

populations by their genetic commonalities and differences (including such traits as blood types), does not produce clusters anything like those based on skin color, which racists emphasize.[189] Our ability to categorize people into groups rests on minute genetic differences. Many of the dramatic single-gene substitutions easily split the human species into clearly distinct groups (by hair color, eye color, ability to taste obscure chemical compounds). As soon as there are more than single-gene substitutions it becomes difficult or impossible to identify differences between groups on the basis of genes. Race, as used in political discourse, is a social construction. Furthermore, Herrnstein and Murray confuse the concepts of race and ethnicity, the latter concept normally referring to a group of people sharing a social and cultural tradition.[190]

In their Chapter Thirteen, "Ethnic Differences in Cognitive Ability," Herrnstein and Murray suggest that there are unrestrained and emotional discussions about race differences that need to be restrained by the findings of science. They argue that ethnic differences in cognitive abilities are neither surprising nor in doubt. East Asians and Jews score higher than the United States average; blacks and Hispanics score lower.

The argument for substantial and partly inherited racial/ethnic differences in intelligence plays a crucial role in *The Bell Curve*. However, the argument consists of very weak claims. Herrnstein and Murray claim only that test performance measures a real and enduring ability; that racial differences in that ability are intractable and consequential; and that *some part* of that racial difference (between 0 percent and 100 percent) is genetic. What is important about the claim is not its substance, which is tenuous, but that it is a claim about what is a useful and important scientific question. It forms the groundwork for claims about how racial inequalities are to be explained, how they change, and how they affect or may affect social policy considerations with respect to social problems. The tentative speculations in Chapter Thirteen become transformed into axioms and assumptions in Chapters Fourteen, Fifteen, and Sixteen.

In all of this, Herrnstein and Murray imply that they are not racist in the same sense that the racist, psychometric, and eugenic theorists of the first part of the century were. For one thing, they stress that individual differences are very much larger than the group differences. For another, they don't think that Europeans are the smartest. Asians (and Jews) are even smarter.[191]

However, the big test score differences, and the ones most crucial to the argument, are between blacks and whites. Herrnstein and Murray give a table of studies showing IQ differences ranging from zero to two standard deviations (SD).[192] The earlier and the Southern studies show the greatest differences, and Herrnstein and Murray's estimate of 1.22 standard deviations is in the middle. With a gap of one standard deviation, the average white respondent has a higher test score performance than 84 percent of blacks. This is true at every SES level, but especially at the higher levels. They say that attempts to explain these differences in terms of bias have failed. They estimate that over the last few decades the gap has narrowed by perhaps three IQ points. Since their case that there are immutable racial differences evaporates if the gap is disappearing, they downplay the data from the National Assessment of Educational Progress, the National High School Studies, the College Board Achievement Tests, the American College Tests, and the Graduate Record Examinations, which all show a shrinking gap. Against that, they argue that there has really been a widening gap.[193]

Chapter Fourteen, "Ethnic Inequalities in Relation to IQ," begins an assault on affirmative action. It argues that not only is there not any discrimination against blacks in the United States today, but also there is pervasive discrimination in favor of blacks. The chapter starts by asking to what extent ethnic differences in education, occupation, poverty, unemployment, crime, and illegitimacy can be explained by IQ. Their answer is based on a statistical model that ignores and contradicts all the qualifications and disclaimers that the authors state elsewhere about whether the source of the difference is genetic. Rather, ethnic differences in test performance are now treated as 100 percent genetic and as producing racial levels of unemployment, illegitimacy, and the like. Chapter Fourteen argues that among whites and Latinos, the existing differences are a simple function of IQ; when IQ is controlled, they disappear. On the other hand, once one has controlled IQ, blacks are *more* likely to graduate and become professionals. Controlling IQ in analyzing ethnic wage differentials shrinks the difference from a few thousand to a few hundred dollars, and the ethnic differences in unemployment, illegitimacy, marriage, and the chance of falling below the poverty line get smaller but remain significant.

In Chapter Fifteen, "The Demography of Intelligence," they focus on how IQ scores change as a function of genes. IQ scores have risen powerfully and consistently in every country and every group in the world; the scores of black and white respondents have converged by about one-fifth of the distance separating them a generation ago. In the face of this, Herrnstein and Murray argue that there is a dysgenic tendency causing downward pressure on IQ. Highly-educated women have fewer children. They suggest that the US has experienced dysgenic pressure for most of the century, particularly among blacks, that has expanded the gap between black and white. Current immigration policies are a source of further dysgenic pressure. The IQ of recent immigrants has been about 95.

Finally, their Chapter Sixteen, "Social Behavior and the Prevalence of Low Cognitive Ability," attempts to consolidate their previous analysis by showing the huge causal impact of IQ and IQ changes. Herrnstein and Murray drop their previous qualifications about the causal interpretation of their data and use this causal interpretation to argue that IQ explains the bulk of group differences and trends in social outcomes. They present a table that purports to show huge causal effects of IQ on social problems. When the mean IQ is reduced to 97, there are 15 percent more dropouts, 12 percent more women on welfare, 4 percent more children in poverty. It is hard to square such arguments with their disclaimers, that the chapter is not about whether low cognitive ability causes social problems, because causal relations are complex and hard to establish definitively.[194] They conclude that whether the sources are genetic does not matter; the association is clear enough so that any policy solution must be capable of succeeding with such stupid people.[195]

We shall focus on the argument in Chapter Thirteen. It is the pivot on which Herrnstein and Murray develop their policy orientations towards population, immigration, affirmative action, education, incarceration, and federal interventions. Their argument hinges on what we have called genetic reductionism or biological determinism and on the mistaken identification of heritability with genetic inheritance and immutability. First, we will look at their argument; then we will examine the more general points about heritability and inheritance, building on our earlier analysis in Chapter Two. This in turn will lead us to clarify some issues about environments, which will bring us back to policy recommendations.

The race hypothesis proposed by *The Bell Curve* is that some fraction of the fifteen IQ points separating black and white Americans is caused by genetic differences.

In line with the requirements of the political Right, *The Bell Curve* aims to legitimate a stream of thought that has been academically and politically marginal in the United States since the fall of Hitler. To do so, it does not need to argue that theories of genetic inferiority are correct, but only that they are possibly correct and worth exploring.

The important issue in science and in social policy is not how questions are answered, but what questions are asked and how they are asked. For instance, if someone were to submit an article to an astronomy journal examining the question whether the moon was made of green cheese, that article would be rejected as nonscientific. It would not matter whether the article used sophisticated spectrometry data and concluded that it was most unlikely that the moon was made of green cheese. The question is such a bad question from the standpoint of science, contradicting so much of what we know about planetary bodies, that the whole endeavor could only be some kind of joke. No reviewer would say, "Well, it is *possible*; the question is worth exploring." Further, if the article made weak, cautious claims for green cheese, the reviewer would be even less likely to take it seriously, not more likely.

The Bell Curve attempts to change the definition of what is a worthwhile question to investigate, both for theory and as a reasonable assumption for policy analysis. It takes a number of ideas that now appear only in marginal journals such as *Mankind Quarterly* or the *Journal of Personal and Individual Differences* and proposes to make them mainstream. The race hypothesis proposes that the fifteen IQ points separating black and white performance on IQ type tests is a reflection of real and important genetic differences. The Herrnstein and Murray strategy is not to estimate what that part is, but rather to present evidence and counter-evidence, leaving the matter open. They assert that neither argument can be excluded, and that it is highly likely that both genes and environment contribute (*The Bell Curve*, p. 311). They claim further that the data provide no basis for an estimate of just how much genes and environment contribute[196], and that they remain "agnostic" on that issue.

It will turn out that all this is largely an illusion. The evidence and counter-evidence have been preselected, and they are irrelevant to the question in any case. The arguments that follow the above statement are not as agnostic as Herrnstein and Murray wish to appear. To say that some unknown fraction of the current race differences in IQ is genetic is a peculiarly weak and unclear hypothesis. To say that somewhere between 0 percent and 100 percent of Americans can walk on water is certainly correct, but it would be a fairly large jump from there to the hypothesis that some Americans probably can walk on water. Moreover, we have already seen some reasons why the question of what "fraction" of the black/white difference in test scores is genetic is not a well-framed question, and we will see others shortly. Indeed, hypothesis is probably not the correct term, and it confuses the difference between a scientific hypothesis and a political innuendo. All scientific knowledge is conditional; even the most firmly supported theories are hypotheses in the sense that they are dependent on the present state of knowledge and conceptualization. But, to be science, they must be formulated so as to be as definite and unambiguous as possible. Even the most speculative analysis (say, in astrophysics) will be formulated so that both critics and supporters can agree on what is being claimed.

A politician often proceeds in a very different way, with controlled ambiguity. The idea that some unspecified fraction of the race difference is due to genetics is more like the politician's ambiguity than like a scientific hypothesis. Herrnstein and Murray try to make it seem that the question that they are pursuing is a more definite one, somehow related to the issue of heritability. Their assumption that the heritability of intelligence is somewhere between 0.4 and 0.8 (itself a very indefinite hypothesis) becomes the question, what fraction of the group difference is due to differences in the groups' genes and what fraction to the groups' environments? They state explicitly that it is not possible to infer from the heritability of the trait within groups that group differences are genetic, but then they do precisely that. While purporting to acknowledge (and even emphasize) that heritabilities contain no information about the causes of differences between groups, they misstate and trivialize this fact (The Bell Curve, p. 298). The misstatement begins with a hedge: heritabilities tell us nothing for sure about the cause of differences. They begin with what appears to be an emphasis of the same point, but in the recapitulation heritabilities have suddenly become evidence that traits are genetically transmitted in individuals. The issue is trivialized by a misleading analogy (The Bell Curve, p. 298).

The argument is a good example of the method used throughout The Bell Curve. It presents itself as an even-handed acknowledgment and popularization of a major point made by Richard Lewontin, one of the critics of hereditarianism, not only acknowledging it but stressing it. But in fact, they trivialize the point so that they can continue to make the very arguments that they have said are invalid. As we shall see, in the very next paragraph they will engage in a calculation that takes heritability estimates to show the degree that group differences are genetic in origin. More generally, they will construct the hereditarian arguments about dysgenics and the causes of group differences throughout Chapters Fourteen, Fifteen, and Sixteen.

The paragraph is a disclaimer, involving deft sleight of hand. It is like the magician's gesture of pulling up his sleeves to show that nothing is concealed in them. In the very gesture, the magician conceals something. Herrnstein and Murray could not ignore Lewontin's point unless they first took care to pretend to acknowledge it. The considerations we raised in Chapter Two show some of the reasons that their argument here makes no sense. But the issue is important and so we will review the basic genetic considerations that allow us to evaluate the ideas to which Herrnstein and Murray slide, that a high heritability

- does not tell us that differences between races have a genetic origin
- does tell us that the differences between races are unlikely to be environmental
- tells us that the trait is genetically transmitted in individuals
- depends on the environment at least in the sense that corn dies in the Mojave desert.

Of course, heritability tells us nothing about the origin of race differences, period. It is not a measure of genetic transmission in individuals, which is a nonsense category. The point about environments is not just that you need a viable environment; rather the point is that heritability is utterly blind to the many differences in environment that produce group differences and will treat them as being genetic when they are not.

The exact value of the heritability of a trait is irrelevant to discussions about the causes of differences between groups.

Here, as in many other cases, Herrnstein and Murray construct a highly contradictory argument. On the one hand, they grant that a high heritability of a trait that could be measured by test scores does not imply that the cause of group differences is genetic. On the other, they immediately engage in calculations to show that it does show that the differences could not be environmental. Their arguments move from heritability to inheritance to the notion of biological limits on capacities and changes. We will look at the facts and concepts involving heritability and then examine some of their arguments in more detail.

Much effort has gone into attempts to measure the heritability of IQ. But the exact value is completely irrelevant to the discussion at hand. We can explore why this is so by extending our analysis from Chapter Two. There, we saw that heritability is simply a partitioning of variation within populations and is independent of the average value of a trait. Because it is a statement about the source of *variation within* (both of these two words are critically important) populations, it cannot be used to tell us anything about the source of the difference between two groups.

Lewontin has suggested a thought experiment that neatly illustrates the lack of a relationship between heritability and group differences. Suppose we are interested in the genetics of height in corn. Suppose further that we have two kinds of seed, open-pollinated corn, full of genetic variability, and inbred lines of corn, with no genetic variability. Suppose, further, that we have two different inbred lines, one with genes that cause short plants, the other with genes that cause tall plants. Within either of these collections of inbred seed, there is no genetic variability. Finally assume that we have two different kinds of environments available: greenhouses and fields. Within any specific greenhouse there is no environmental variability; in the field environmental variability causes variation in height. Remember that the heritability of this trait is just the fraction of total variation in height that is caused by variation in genes, measured in a specific population in a specific environment.

The heritability of the height of a single stalk of corn is undefined and meaningless, for heritability does not refer to a genetic mechanism operating within some single case. Without any change in the genetic mechanisms, we can increase or decrease heritability just by mixing seed in different ways, with more or less variation among plants placed in more or less varied environments. In what follows, we shall use the assumptions of *The Bell Curve* that radically simplify the relation between genetic and environmental variation by assuming that there are no interactions.[197]

The scientific issues are clear and well understood,[198] but they continue to be ignored by many of the arguments in and stemming from *The Bell Curve* and so we shall proceed step by step. First, to fix the concept of heritability more clearly, we can take batches of inbred corn and raise them in different circumstances. By definition they have no genetic variability, and the heritability of height, or of any other character, will be zero. And we can take batches of corn and raise them under controlled, identical environments. By definition, when there is no environmental variation, heritability goes to 1.0. It is easy to see that the entire structure of the Herrnstein syllogism and its corollaries depends on such cases.

Experiment 1: Suppose we raise the open-pollinated variety under ideal conditions in the greenhouse. We are very careful to ensure that each plant receives exactly the same treatment. There will be variability in plant height, and since there is no environmental variation in the greenhouse, this variability can be ascribed completely to the action of genes. Hence, $H = 1.00$.

Experiment 2: Now suppose we raise the inbred variety in a field outdoors. In this case, since there is no genetic variability, any variation in plant height is due to the environment. Therefore, $H = 0.00$.

Experiment 3: We can see the effects of this variation if we raise the open pollinated variety outside. Here, variation in height will be due both to genetic and environmental variation. In this case, H will lie somewhere between 0 and 1. The precise value of heritability in this case will depend on the relative amount of variation in the environment: more uniform environmental conditions would lead to larger heritabilities, more varied environmental conditions to smaller heritabilities.

These first three experiments illustrate the way in which heritability depends on variation in genes and variation in environments. Note that in none of the three experiments did we know or need to know anything about the average value of the plant height. Furthermore, the heritabilities we measured depended critically on the precise environment in which we raised the plants. Different environments will clearly change the heritability of the trait.

How might conclusions from these experiments be applied to humans? To what extent are different environments, such as a ghetto or an exclusive suburb, like individual greenhouses with controlled, uniform environments? Such communities contain enormous variation in environments. To specify how similar the environments are, we would have to know what aspects of the environments are important. If it is just a matter of adequate food, then they may be relatively similar; if it is a more complex matter of roles, identities and stimulation, they can be quite varied. Even within a single family, there is an enormous variety of environments with respect to these conditions. A second child is born into a very different environment from the first because he or she is born into a family that already has a child in it. To the extent that the environment relevant to scholastic and intellectual accomplishment involves such roles, identities, labels and relations, there is likely to be a lot of variation within a given family. Thus the social environments we will observe will be nowhere near as uniform as that in a controlled greenhouse.

Are different races or ethnic groups like inbred varieties of corn? Yes and no. The central assumption of anyone who talks about biological races is that groups like blacks or Asians may differ from each other on the average in their genes for most things. Certainly this is an organizing assumption of *The Bell Curve*. On the other hand, everyone recognizes that there has been enormous mixing of the human gene pool throughout human evolution. Even during the last few thousand years, there have been huge migrations and conquests. The Egyptian empire, the spread of Christianity, the Mongol conquests, the Gupta empire, the spread of Islam, the European conquests, the slave trade, and similar events mean that even if we had bags of inbred corn before, we certainly do not now. Areas such as Europe and the Middle East were genetic crossroads. As we noted earlier, any human group variation is dwarfed by the fact that genetically we are a single human race. Genetic differences between races involve a very small number of genes. Most genetic variation in our species can be found within races, not between.[199]

Heritabilities do not and cannot contain any information about the causes of differences between groups.

Let us extend the corn experiments to clarify what heritability can and cannot tell us about the causes of variation when we are dealing with groups that have variation both in environments and in genes.

Experiment 4: Now suppose we raise two different inbred varieties outside. There is environmental variance, but we are careful to see that both varieties are exposed to exactly the same environments. Within both populations, H = 0.00. All variation within populations is due to the environment. But it is reasonable that the two different populations grow to two different mean heights. The difference between the two populations is caused entirely by genetic differences. That is, in this experiment, although the heritability is 0.00 within each population, the cause of the difference between the two populations is entirely genetic.

Experiment 5: Suppose we now plant the open pollinated variety in three different greenhouses: one with full nutrient solution, the second with a nutrient solution a bit deficient in some elements, and the third with a very deficient solution. The height of the plants will be directly related to the adequacy of the three nutrient solutions.

Within any of the three greenhouses, the heritability of plant height will be 1.00, since all the observed variation *within* is caused by genes. Notice, however, that the mean plant height will be different in each environment for reasons that are unrelated to genes. That is, the heritability of height is completely independent of the mean. The different heights observed *within each* of the three greenhouses are caused entirely by genes; the different heights observed *between* the greenhouses are caused entirely by environments. These last two experiments illustrate the central fallacy to which Herrnstein and Murray subscribe. In these cases, populations with heritabilities of 1.00 have differences in average values entirely caused by environment, and populations with heritabilities of 0.00 have differences in average value entirely caused by genes. Indeed, we could easily have constructed examples with any sort of relationship between heritabilities and causes of mean differences precisely because *heritability is a measure that contains absolutely no information about average values or about differences in average values between populations.* No increased sophistication of measurement, no added complexities of models, and no amount of philosophical musing will ever extract this information from heritability.[200]

Thus, as we have repeatedly stressed, Herrnstein and Murray have no basis to argue that high heritability tells us that group differences are probably not environmentally caused. A high heritability of IQ within the white or within the black group does not mean that the differences in average scores of the two groups are caused by differences in genes, nor does it tell us that group differences are caused by environment. It simply tells us nothing about the cause of mean differences.

Even after environmental manipulations, heritabilities are still irrelevant to any discussion of average group differences.

As we discussed in Chapter Two, complex interactions between genes and environments are likely. We will mention, but will not pursue, the striking cases in which the reactions of others is the environment. Imagine that one variety of corn has a beautiful tassel; and imagine that a little boy goes into the greenhouse and picks all those tassels. That corn would be decimated and would never produce. The existence of the different tassel is entirely genetic; but, of course, the cause of the damage is entirely environmental (the boy).[201] If race (skin color) is genetically passed on, then every effect of racism, which is entirely environmental, will be 100 percent heritable. But even in cases that do not involve human perceptions and intentional behavior, what is central to the arguments of Herrnstein's syllogism, or the meritocratic caste corollary, or the race hypothesis, is that environments have become more similar. What does it mean for environments to become more similar?

Experiment 6: We plant two different populations of the open-pollinated variety of corn in a greenhouse. One population receives a standard nutrient solution. The second population receives the same solution lacking the nitrates (needed in substantial quantities) and without any zinc (a trace element required in minuscule quantities for vigorous corn growth). The plants lacking the nitrogen and zinc will grow stunted. Within these two populations $H = 1.00$, since all variability in height within populations is due to the action of genes. However, in this case the difference between the two is completely environmental, caused by the difference in nitrates and zinc. Although the heritability of height is 1.00 within both populations, the cause of the difference between the populations is entirely environmental.

Suppose that we are now disturbed by the observed differences in plant height, and seek to discover the reason for the differences in height. We examine the nutrient solutions and quickly discover that there is a large difference in the amounts of nitrogen present. We correct this problem and repeat the experiment with virtually identical results: once again one population grows to dramatically different heights from the other. At this point, having corrected what appears to be the major difference in environments, are we any more justified in using this collection of information to argue for a genetic cause to group differences? As should be obvious, the answer is no. In corn, tiny differences in quantities of an essential trace element can produce virtually the same differences we observed earlier. Indeed, the amounts of zinc required by corn plants are so small that they are quite difficult to measure.

We would certainly say that the two environments for our corn plants have become more similar. But have they become more similar in the way that was crucial to the difference in phenotype? Indeed, if we were to change the door handles on the two greenhouses to be identical, we could reasonably say that the two environments have become more similar. Nevertheless, neither of these increases in similarity will have a substantive effect on phenotype. Having made these changes and observed no effects on plant height, we have absolutely no new evidence about the cause of differences between the two populations.

Anything as complex as human abilities is certain to be affected by an enormous number of environmental variables, some obvious and many very subtle. A bald assertion that environments have become more similar (especially when there is substantial evidence to the contrary) still does not allow us to conclude that the cause of the differences is genetic. Herrnstein and Murray argue that the combination of high heritability and increasing similarity of environments leads them (reluctantly) to the conclusion that the cause of the observed differences in IQ is genetic or partly genetic. Whatever we might think about the evidence for the premise of this argument, the conclusion is a nonsequitur.

Throughout Chapter Thirteen and indeed throughout Part III of *The Bell Curve*, Herrnstein and Murray present themselves as giving an even-handed summary of the pros and cons of arguments of genetic racial inferiority. It is this summary that enables them to conclude that there are good arguments on both sides, so that the question is entirely open; they will be "agnostic," while using in their further argument the spurious certainty that while we do not know how much of the difference in performance is genetic, we almost certainly know that some is; while we do not know how inferior blacks are genetically, we almost certainly know that they are inferior. Their summary of this scholarship is even more biased and tendentious than their presentation of the genetic considerations.[202]

Conventionally, evidence on the issue is divided into direct evidence, which involves direct measures of the effects of genes or environments with regard to race, and indirect arguments.[203] Herrnstein and Murray devote approximately ten times as much space to the indirect evidence because the direct evidence is almost uniformly unfavorable to their case. The most favored indirect arguments for theorists arguing a genetic difference are those that depend on Charles Spearman's "g" and a one-dimensional conception of intelligence.[204]

The Bell Curve systematically ignores or misrepresents the direct evidence about the presence or absence of racial differences in intelligence.

Direct evidence about systematic changes and effects of environments or genes would ultimately have to be decisive, regardless of any kind of indirect argument whatsoever. We do not randomly raise white children in black families, black children in white families, change infants' skin color, or crossbreed people to measure results. And a good thing, too.[205] Nevertheless, the evidence that has accumulated from the natural observations corresponding to such experiments shows, virtually without exception, no racial effect.

Herrnstein and Murray do deal with direct evidence only after they have spent much space dealing with indirect arguments. When they deal with it, they use the technique we have described as a moon walk, claiming to be forced into an "agnostic" position, that is, a position that is agnostic about how much of the poor test performance of blacks is a result of bad genes. Their treatment of the direct evidence consists of four steps, each of which is deceptive and misleading. First, they summarize the transracial adoption study by Scarr and Weinberg, and give a secondary reference to others, which they say indicate some sort of gene-environment balance. In fact, there have been some seven direct studies of the relation between genes and intelligence.[206] In six of them, the data show unambiguously that there is no relation between race and genes for intelligence.[207] In the guise of a fair-minded summary, they pick the one study that can be interpreted as ambiguous, and they then interpret it that way, censoring the explicit interpretations of the authors while appearing to agree with them.[208]

Second, besides a dismissive footnote about another study, they give a boxed synopsis of the German study of the measured intelligence of illegitimate offspring of black and white American troops in Germany during World War II (Eyferth, 1961). Herrnstein and Murray ignore the fact that the study found no differences. Rather, they say that the study was inconclusive but consistent with the suggestion that the black/white difference was largely environmental (The Bell Curve, p. 311).

Third, they assess the difference between themselves and theorists such as Richard Lewontin, Leon Kamin, and Arnold Rose. In the only place where they cite these authors' work, they say that these authors "although they do not say so in so many words" argue for zero genetic influence, while Herrnstein and Murray argue an agnostic position. In fact, neither characterization is accurate or honest. Theorists such as Lewontin have never denied the possibility of genetic influences; what they have denied is that there is any convincing evidence of any genetic influences. They have also argued that the conceptualization and method that treats heritability as a measure of the fraction of environmental and genetic effect is simplistic, scientifically obsolete and logically flawed. As we have seen, Herrnstein and Murray grant the point, but they then continue treating heritability as a measure of the fraction of variation that is genetically inherited.

Moreover, Herrnstein and Murray's "agnosticism" is a pose. Their question of how much of the group difference is genetic is like the old question "when did you stop beating your wife?" It begs the question; its function is to lead the reader to entertain the race hypothesis, without requiring Herrnstein and Murray to defend it. However, as soon as they turn to the further analysis, their agnosticism and warnings that one cannot infer genetic differences promptly vanish.

Herrnstein and Murray begin their discussion of indirect arguments by suggesting that, given heritability, environmental differences would have to be implausibly large to explain the observed test performances.

Earlier, we noted that Herrnstein and Murray warn that you cannot infer a genetic basis of group differences on the basis of heritability, using the Mojave Desert analogy to convey the point. On page 298, *The Bell Curve* takes 60 percent of group test performance to be due to genes, and asks how big environmental differences would have to be to produce the observed difference in test performance. It suggests that a high heritability of IQ, while it does not exclude the *possibility* that the differences in average scores of the two racial groups are caused by differences in the environment, makes that implausible because the mean environment of whites would have to be 1.58 standard deviations better than the mean environment of blacks to explain the difference in performance (*The Bell Curve*, pp. 298-299).

The calculation is based on a remarkably naive reading of the environmental variance component of heritability. We have seen that the variance being partitioned is variance in *phenotype*. The units of environmental variance will be those of the phenotype, not those of the environment. The statement that might be made from Herrnstein and

Murray's calculation is that the difference in mean environments would have to be whatever would cause 1.58 standard deviations difference in phenotype. Phenotypes may be exquisitely sensitive to small changes in environment or very insensitive, as we saw in our Experiment 6 and in our discussion of norms of reaction in Chapter Two.

The Herrnstein and Murray argument is one that Jensen made at various times. Jensen used an estimate of heritability of 0.8, and so he argued that mean environments had to be more than four standard deviations different. Herrnstein and Murray appear to be giving a more moderate version in which the mean environments have to differ only by 1.58 standard deviations. In considering this argument, Herrnstein and Murray do not bother to show the reader why it is implausible to suppose that mean environments differ by race by 1.58 standard deviations, except to say that would mean that the average black environment would be at the sixth percentile of white environments. We have seen that they systematically refuse to look closely at what environments are. Even if the relevant environment is just the supply of food, basic security, and basic education, it is not clear what is implausible about that. Nearly half of all black children grow up below the poverty line; approximately 90 percent of people living below the poverty line are malnourished. If the environment also involves social dynamics such as isolation, ghettoization, formation of networks of friends, identity formation, or the pervasive use of drugs, we do not see how anyone could plausibly estimate a difference of less than 1.58 standard deviations.

In some ways, to answer the argument empirically is beside the point. The argument is so logically flawed as to be meaningless. Moreover, any estimate of heritability large enough to make the black/white environmental difference implausible will utterly destroy the argument on empirical grounds. In a different place, they describe James Flynn's finding, which is uncontested, that among both whites and blacks, in every society for which we have data, the mean performance on IQ tests has improved about a standard deviation over the last generation—i.e., by about the same fifteen points that separate white from black performance. Mean black performance on IQ tests is about what mean white performance was a generation ago (actually, since black performance has increased faster than whites, the time span is somewhat shorter). From the standpoint of fostering IQ performance, the mean difference between the environment of children today and that of their parents is almost certainly less than that between whites and blacks today. The hopeless vagueness of Herrnstein and Murray about what is a good environment makes it hard to measure, but it is hard to imagine any reasonable estimate (e.g., of nutrition, child care, education, identity, or encouragement) suggests that the generational difference in environment is greater than the racial one.

Herrnstein and Murray do not tell the reader that, in the context of Flynn's findings, Jensen's argument is demolished. The original argument, which said that mean environments must differ by more than four standard deviations to produce a one standard deviation result, is implausible. Using a table of the normal distribution, one finds that the mean environment a generation ago would have to be below the bottom 100th of 1 percent of environments today. That is why Herrnstein and Murray "improve" the argument to the more moderate view of 1.58 standard deviations—i.e., that the mean environment a generation ago must have been worse than 94 percent of environments today.

Herrnstein and Murray mainly stress Jensen's analysis of test profiles.

The Bell Curve most strongly stresses indirect arguments that emphasize the different test profiles of different racial or ethnic groups. Specifically, following Jensen, they argue that those subtests that are most correlated with performance on other tests (i.e., those that are relatively "g-loaded," such as the Raven's Matrices) are the ones that measure biological capacities. Blacks and Hispanics do relatively poorly on those tests. Asians and Ashkenazi Jews do particularly well on them. Indeed, they suggest that American Indians, who do relatively poorly on intelligence tests overall, do relatively well on those "g-loaded" tests. Thus they conclude that the variety of different cultural differences that would have to be explained in a very ad hoc way by cultural explanations are all simply and easily explained by a biogenetic account. They say that cultural or social explanations are "out of the question" given the diversity of experiences of East Asians and that while they are not "so rash as to assert that the environment or the culture is *wholly* irrelevant," the test profiles of American Indians and East Asians suggests a genetic explanation (*The Bell Curve*, p. 301).

The argument is a good example both of the way these authors deal with evidence and of the way they deal with culture. We will postpone discussion of culture until the next section. With regard to evidence, it is worth noting first that the profile of different groups seems to fit the biogenetic account of Jewish/Asian superiority and African/Hispanic inferiority only because of the highly selective account of the evidence. They have constructed a highly selective and theoretically incoherent concept of East Asians, that ignores the different profiles and averages of *poor* East Asian immigrants such as the Cambodians and Vietnamese. They criticize environmental accounts for not being sufficiently tough-minded, but give an entirely uncritical and anecdotal account of those differences that fit their preconceptions. Since there are many different ethnic groups and many different tests, there are literally hundreds of comparisons that they could have made, many of which would not fit their account. Since they have given no systematic conceptualization or presentation of evidence, they can ignore this material.

What one finds on examination is that subcultures and ethnic groups that do better on tests in general are particularly likely to do better on problem solving requiring abstract symbol manipulation. As we will see, the available sociological or cultural explanations would explain such correlations. Herrnstein and Murray have simply failed to tell the reader the single piece of evidence most relevant to that question: James Flynn in plotting the change in test scores over time—a change that everyone views as principally or entirely environmental—finds that scores changed most on tasks such as those in the Raven's Matrices. Therefore, there is no reason to suppose that such tests are a measure of biogenetic capacity—and considerable reason to suppose that they are not.

Moreover, several outstanding studies of East Asians, which were available to Herrnstein and Murray, not only show how the East Asian performance is achieved, but also that it is not genetically determined.[209] There are no or minimal differences between Asian and American performance in very young children. The differences are produced by schooling. The 240-day Asian school year, in contrast to the 180-day American school year, plays a notable role. Asian school processes de-emphasize testing focused on innate ability ("I can't do that," "I'm not good at that," are feelings that every single school child faces at some times) and focus instead on motivation and work.

The Bell Curve dismisses known cultural and environmental factors because its reductionist, individualist model makes those factors irrelevant.

It should come as no surprise that school achievement, identity, and test performance are bound up with identity and psychological orientation, and that these are generated by families, schools, and subcultures that articulate with life expectations. Nor should it be surprising that the effectiveness of Chinese and Japanese schools depends on the articulation of education within these structures. Nearly a century of social science has demonstrated and investigated the importance of such factors, particularly with respect to the mobility of immigrant groups.

When Herrnstein and Murray say that they "are not so rash as to assert that the environment or the culture is wholly irrelevant," it is a little like a theorist of tuberculosis saying that he or she is not so rash as to assert that exposure to the bacillus is wholly irrelevant. One wonders what evidence they have presented that it is irrelevant at all. The proximate and immediate source of various skills and abilities is the groups one is a member of, one's roles in those groups, and the identity one forms in those roles. *The Bell Curve* has not presented any evidence against this but has proposed that we ignore it. The whole of the theory in the social sciences that swept away the biological and racist theories of the last century rests on a simple observation. In anthropology, sociology, political science, social psychology, economics, history, and a host of other fields it is observed that human beings are social animals who get socialized into different cultural patterns. The bodies of data and standpoints that Herrnstein and Murray would call "environmentalist" have outlined the main processes functioning in families, neighborhoods, schools, churches, gangs, jobs, and other organizations and groups to bring about different orientations. Many of these processes are well understood.

In some subcultures, older men commonly sit and play chess; a child who does so or who gives "smart" answers is rewarded both by adults and by peers. In other subcultures, other kinds of abilities are stressed. For instance, what Robert J. Sternberg calls practical intelligence may be stressed. Such subcultures may teach one the maxim that "A friend is a friend for life; the most important thing one can learn is how to make and keep friends; it is much more important than school or solving puzzles." Still other subcultures may stress athletic ability, courage, determination, and the willingness to stand up for oneself. The opportunities and models that the group has experienced in the past and the complex mix of present structures and opportunities all influence this. Herrnstein and Murray claim to be able to cut the Gordian knot of social and cultural complexity by means of a reductionist analysis of biogenetic intelligence. They devote three pages to "cultural explanations" of ethnic group differences, briefly dismissing the analyses of Mercer and John Ogbu.[210] Mercer, in analyzing the school and test performance of different ethnic groups, found that differences in performance were entirely explained by controlling eight sociocultural variables including social status, home language level, and mother's participation in formal organizations. But, Herrnstein and Murray object, perhaps Mercer is just controlling proxies for IQ. If IQ determines SES, then controlling SES does not show that IQ has no effect, but rather it shows how IQ has its effect.

By now some of the problems with this argument are familiar. The argument is inconsistent with the order of magnitude of the effects that Herrnstein and Murray showed in Part II. Even if their models were entirely correct and unbiased, so that the regressions measured the effects of IQ on variables such as SES (which is doubtful), the resulting effects are so weak that they cannot logically or plausibly sustain the argument here.[211] Herrnstein and Murray seem to be hoping that the reader will remember that Part II showed some relation between IQ and a lot of other variables, without remembering how weak those relations are.

Herrnstein and Murray also cavalierly dismiss Ogbu's findings. They do not acknowledge that Ogbu's analysis specifically undercuts and contradicts a biogenetic account of such test score differences. Specifically, as Fischer and his colleagues have pointed out in *Inequality by Design*, there is a whole pattern of differences in test scores that is consistently and parsimoniously explained by social structural factors.[212] A group's occupational and social expectations lead to identities with regard to school and different kinds of achievement, which the relatively slowly-changing structures of schooling, families, and neighborhoods support.

The practical implications of the analysis are an attack on any program to mitigate inequalities.

One of the reasons that it is useful to look at these social and cultural structures producing the educational and test scores is that they give some idea what would have to be changed in order to change outcomes. Such changes are not necessarily easy. Jobs, families, schools, or neighborhood organizations are highly resistant to change. Gunnar Myrdal's concept of cumulative causation enables us to see how some kinds of change can spiral. They can spiral down as well as up; the loss of jobs or other social resources can just as surely precipitate social disorganization as their support can encourage social regeneration. There is no automatic mechanism guaranteeing the convergence of black and white test scores. Herrnstein and Murray, and more generally the New Right, despite their agnostic pose about structural and cultural sources of social problems, have to systematically deny them. One would expect an analysis that stresses the importance of families, churches, neighborhoods, and peers to resonate strongly with many values of American conservatives. The argument, however, is driven by an intent to cut federal funding for programs for the poor. If one is going to advocate doing nothing about a structure that virtually everyone views as problematical, it is useful to argue that the problem is biologically fixed.

We have substantial evidence that intervention programs work. IQ is not fixed from birth and can be dramatically affected by environmental improvements. Herrnstein and Murray argue that since these efforts have not produced complete equality of results they should be abandoned. If this sort of logic were applied to cancer or AIDS, we would today abandon our search for treatments of either of these diseases. Indeed, the efforts at improvement of the environments of the rural poor or inner city blacks have been far more encouraging than our progress in cancer treatment. Our interpretation of these results is that these efforts must be redoubled.

Chapter 7

The Assault on Education and Affirmative Action

Only a portion of the political implications of the earlier analysis is made explicit in Part IV of *The Bell Curve*.

Part IV of *The Bell Curve* lays out the political agenda and policy implications that the authors draw from their analysis. It develops a theoretical rationale for many of the policies of the New Right,[213] mounting an assault on compensatory programs, general education, and affirmative action. Indeed, the political agenda of the book does not begin on page 389 with formal policy-relevant arguments. Since the first page, it has governed the selection, analysis, and interpretation of data, the review of prior analysis, and the basic concepts, models, and foci of discussion.[214]

The political, moral, ethical, and value conclusions of *The Bell Curve* do not follow from its earlier analyses as a simple matter of logical deduction, but neither are they a gratuitous addition to them. Rather, the earlier analyses have systematically built the assumptions, conceptualizations, and understandings that lead to the political and moral conclusions. We have seen that the early chapters of *The Bell Curve* argue that intelligence is in large part genetic, that it is the central component of work productivity and social class, that it is a principal source of social problems such as crime and deviance, that racial and ethnic groups differ substantially in average intelligence, and that trends in births and immigration are increasing the gaps between and within racial/ethnic groups and possibly lowering the mean intelligence of the society as a whole. The last six chapters of *The Bell Curve* derive from that analysis the same implications that have typically been drawn from it: that compensatory programs cannot work and that the society must accommodate to the inevitability of meritocratic caste and inherited unequal position.

Chapters Seventeen through Twenty of *The Bell Curve* state the principal policy orientation necessary to a general defense of inequality and hierarchy in the United States today. Chapters Seventeen and Eighteen criticize compensatory education. Those programs, Herrnstein and Murray suggest, are trying to do the impossible, namely to improve the cognitive performance of students who do not have the cognitive stuff to do well. Chapter Seventeen purports to evaluate compensatory programs such as Head Start. Chapter Eighteen attacks the "leveling of American higher education" and calls for a return to the orientation of education to the gifted and the elite ideal of an educated man. Chapters Nineteen and Twenty attack affirmative action programs in education and in the work force. In each of the chapters, Herrnstein and Murray argue that compensatory programs are trying to do the impossible, that they are cost-ineffective and inherently unjust.

Americans, in general, do not disagree with the desirability of equal opportunity. There is broad agreement that if there are substantial obstacles to equal opportunity, then there must be government intervention to remove those obstacles. However, a fraction of the population (particularly those in privileged positions) adopts the position that there is no problem and that therefore no solution is needed[215]—i.e., that the major inequalities and obstacles to opportunity have been removed and that the major remaining inequalities are not socially produced and therefore are not socially removable. It is this sentiment that Murray and other theorists who wish to roll back the welfare state must encourage and expand. They have to deny or divert attention from social structures of unequal opportunity, racism, and discrimination. Since massive inequalities in housing, education, health care, nutrition, security, and virtually every other resource are perfectly visible in every American city, and since major disparities remain in access to higher education, jobs, and political power, Herrnstein and Murray have to ascribe these inequalities to innate individual differences in ability in order to attack all programs addressing unequal opportunity.

Overt commitment to elite, privatized education conceals a covert opposition to all public education.

In Chapter Seventeen of *The Bell Curve*, Herrnstein and Murray argue that the Great Society programs such as Head Start tried to increase educational performance and IQ scores, but that they have largely failed.

They suggest that while Head Start makes a modest increase in IQ scores over the short run, these gains tend to erode after a few years, and they describe the sphere of compensatory education as a field of extravagant claims and failed promises. More expensive and labor-intensive programs like the Abecedarian program have made larger differences, but they are prohibitive in terms of their expense and demand for skilled manpower. Ultimately, Herrnstein and Murray conclude that while there is a certain promise in nutritional programs for the underprivileged, education is a waste of money.[216] The only truly cost-effective program for disadvantaged children, according to Herrnstein and Murray, is adoption. While they believe "Governments should not be able to force parents to give up their children for any except the most compelling of reasons," they hope that a return to traditional sex roles will obviate the need for compensatory programs by reducing the number of single-parent households which require them. They chose the 1960s as the better time to which we should return—a time, they claim, when most children born out of wedlock were adopted (*The Bell Curve*, p. 416).

Herrnstein and Murray are not explicit about what aspects of the earlier state of affairs they wish to return to. In any case, their analysis misstates the issue. Most of the children who fail to receive care in the United States are not healthy white infants whom many families wish to adopt. They are handicapped, non-white or older children, who now, as in the past, usually do not have families who wish to adopt them. One wonders whether the authors think that their analysis is likely to increase the amount of trans-racial and trans-class adoption. The call for adoption is sleight of hand. Eugenic, genetic theories naturally lead to support for abortion and forced sterilization,[217] but such policy conclusions cannot build a broad right- wing coalition in the United States today. Neither can Herrnstein and Murray just call for Spencer's "stern beneficence," reducing all programs for poor children. They want to eliminate all programs and to do it "compassionately," and so they have to imply what they know is untrue, namely that if only there were no welfare, then disadvantaged children would find middle-class homes.

The attack on compensatory education is then followed by a call to reorient American education toward the needs of gifted students. With respect to education, Herrnstein and Murray adopt the peculiar view that the traditional aim of American education is education for the gifted, and they adopt a particularly narrow conception of these "gifts." Artistic creativity or social and moral awareness do not seem to be the gifts that education should nurture; rather, it should be oriented to cognitive capacity. Herrnstein and Murray argue that compensatory education has led to a "dumbing down" of American education to the speed and capabilities of those less able, particularly minorities. Compensatory education and programs for the poor and for minorities have been "in," and accordingly we have channeled immense amounts of energy and effort into the black hole of such programs. These authors suggest that a focus on poor, disadvantaged, and minority students is responsible for falling SAT scores, and they call for a reorientation of attention to programs meeting the needs of the gifted.

American education, however, is already oriented to the needs of advantaged and affluent students. While we pioneered mass access to education, many other countries have surpassed us in this respect. Herrnstein and Murray argue that educators, as well as government programs, have lost their vision of an "educated man" in the impossible search for social justice. While they express worries about the segregation, elitism, and inequality implied by their earlier positions, they view those outcomes as a realistic acknowledgment of the facts. Their position is unashamedly elitist, but they represent it as bowing to the inevitable. In contradiction to their earlier argument of increasing leveling of American schools, they recognize the increasing segregation of schools by socioeconomic status, coupled to increasing segregation of the gifted. This segregation, they argue, leads to the more privileged students entering leadership positions in the society. Their acceptance of this as inevitable leads them not to challenge it but to plead for more attention to those students. In a truly remarkable argument, they suggest that since the elite will be segregated and isolated, we must give them more resources so that they can be truly wise and lead the nation with humility (*The Bell Curve*, p. 443). The trend toward elitism is inevitable, and it will evidently be moderated by the wisdom which results from encouraging it.

The central focus of the policy recommendations of *The Bell Curve* is an attack on affirmative action, defined narrowly as providing criteria for selection.

The elitist concept of education then leads to an attack on affirmative action programs in education and to a more general attack on affirmative action programs in the society as a whole. Herrnstein and Murray suggest that there has been a shift in the practice of affirmative action programs. While affirmative action programs were set up to open up opportunities for able but underprivileged individuals left out of higher education or without access to elite positions, they argue, those programs were transformed into politically and morally indefensible quota systems, in which more able (often underprivileged) whites or Asians are passed over in favor of less able (often privileged) blacks.

Chapters Nineteen and Twenty, along with Appendix 7 on the development of affirmative action, mount a frontal assault on affirmative action, first in higher education and then in jobs. The attack on affirmative action stems in large part from the premises that we have already discussed: that the main criterion of placement in schools and jobs should be cognitive capacity; that races differ in their cognitive capacity; and that IQ tests and related tests give an unbiased measure of cognitive capacity. Despite a claim to a critical examination of affirmative action, nowhere does *The Bell Curve* provide an examination of the problem they are meant to solve or an examination of their effectiveness in addressing those problems. It proposes a "framework for thinking about such programs," suggesting that they have to be focused on disprivileged groups. In general, they suggest, affirmative action programs opened higher education and elite schools to black or Hispanic applicants qualitatively less able than the majority groups, by excluding Asian, Jewish, or white working-class applicants. They argue that a return to the "traditional understanding" of affirmative action will eliminate these unfortunate aspects of the programs.

Finally, Chapter Twenty of *The Bell Curve* generalizes the argument against affirmative action. Legal restraints on the use of "general ability" tests as culturally biased and irrelevant to much job performance are based, they claim, on premises which are empirically false. Herrnstein and Murray argue that research studies have shown that such general ability tests are the single best predictor of applicants' future job performance. They suggest that hiring minorities, who often do poorly on general ability tests, would be both inefficient and unfair. A one-sided emphasis on the successes of affirmative action has led to neglecting its failures. They suggest that the literature evaluating affirmative action has stressed its role in equalizing the fraction of managers and professionals who are nonwhite, but that a fair balance sheet would equally stress the inefficiency and resentment produced by affirmative action programs.[218] While Herrnstein and Murray's analysis is driven by genetic assumptions, we have seen that D'Sousa, Murray's colleague at the American Enterprise Institute obtains the same conclusions from the view that blacks are culturally deficient. What the arguments have in common are belief in black inferiority (biological or cultural) and denial that there are, any longer, any institutional obstacles to the success of blacks.

More generally, the reductionist and individualist character of their argument makes it extremely difficult for Herrnstein and Murray to draw up any balance sheet for the effect of affirmative action on the whole society. They would have to estimate the costs to the whole society of increasingly segregated and conflict-ridden race relations. But we have seen that the basic premises of their analysis are the counterfactual assumptions that schools and businesses are guided by an invisible hand to seek talent wherever it exists, so that all race or gender discrimination will vanish without the help of public policies, which can only play a mischievous role. From their standpoint, if only people would treat each other as individuals, all race and gender problems would evaporate. Where there is no problem, there does not need to be a solution. Any problems only require affirming the spirit of individual fair play. This is not an adequate analysis of the source and dynamics of race or of ethnic and gender discrimination, in the United States or anywhere else.

The analysis is a self-contradictory denial of the "broken bucket."

Throughout these chapters, Herrnstein and Murray argue that since it is impossible to change abilities, programs oriented to that goal are utopian and unrealistic. They couple that argument with the view that they are unrealistic in another way. We always operate with limited resources and pragmatically limited political commitments. Wasting those resources on the less able or disadvantaged members of the society is cost-ineffective. Finally, they argue that compensatory programs require a federal bureaucracy unjustly interfering with people's lives, often in a race-conscious way, leading to quotas. The aim of these programs is unjust even if mounting them were possible or efficient.

For example, they attack compensatory education as impossible (because one cannot change capacities); as not cost effective (because one gets a higher return for money and effort spent on gifted, rather than on the disadvantaged, students); and as unjust (because other students have more right to limited resources). As they stand, these arguments seem powerfully to reinforce each other. The attempt to change what is biologically fixed would appear to be an ultimate case of beating one's head against a stone wall and futilely wasting scarce resources. The biological determinist view that it is not possible to increase test scores seems to be powerfully reinforced by political pragmatics. Given the amount of commitment and the limited resources of the schools, we have to decide what is effective and fair. Herrnstein and Murray purport to cut through fuzzy, abstract theoretical considerations with a hard nosed analysis of practical considerations of costs, benefits and efficiency.

At first glance, these arguments of impossibility, inefficiency, and injustice seem powerfully to reinforce each other. If we disposed of infinite resources, it might be possible to do more to equalize opportunities, but we do not have infinite resources. If we had no concerns about individual rights and liberties, we could legislate equal opportunities, but we have to have such concerns. However, on closer inspection, the three arguments are radically inconsistent. Herrnstein and Murray slide between them as it suits them. In fact, these three arguments are a form of the argument of the broken bucket. A man borrowed a bucket from his neighbor, who objected when it was returned with a hole. In reply, the man argued that he had never borrowed the bucket; that it already had a hole in it when he borrowed it; and that it was perfectly sound when he returned it. Any one of the arguments would have been adequate. Together they are hopelessly contradictory and show someone willing to make any argument, without believing it, in order to justify a point.

Herrnstein and Murray use test scores as a measure of the effectiveness of education, while assuming that those are biologically fixed. If this is true, then the whole of education is an utterly frivolous waste of money, for, by their assumptions, such scores cannot be altered to any significant degree. If efficiency were the main concern, then returns to individual students and returns and costs to the whole society would be of concern.[219] From that standpoint, the insistence on a skilled work force and on the outcomes for those students who are most likely to become social costs may be more relevant than the marginal returns for those students who are likely to do well in any case. Such an analysis would calculate the costs to the whole society of segregation, of huge pools of unemployment, of race war, and of social pathologies. When it comes time to evaluate these social costs, Herrnstein and Murray shift to arguments about justice which make any calculation of costs irrelevant.

Herrnstein and Murray argue that the intrinsic lack of ability of many students (particularly deprived, poor, or minority students) means that there is nothing they could learn that would repay the cost of teaching it to them. Repay whom? The criteria Herrnstein and Murray are using to evaluate education are not entirely clear. Suppose, to take the case most favorable for their argument, one is considering the education of a Down syndrome student, who will have difficulty learning to tie his shoes for unmodifiable genetic reasons. How do we evaluate the payoff of teaching that student to be relatively self-sufficient? Should it be compared to the cost of institutionalizing him for life? To that of throwing him on the street? What are those costs? The entire cost-benefit analysis is undefined, and the issue is a moral one. The rhetoric of efficient allocation of manpower which has dominated the whole of *The Bell Curve* merely evades these issues.

Now consider the more realistic case of the classroom of disadvantaged students with a mixture of talents and abilities. We do not know what those talents are, and neither do the students themselves. It will take more resources to find and develop such talents than to give the students a short test which implies that most of them are not worth worrying about. But in what sense is such a test cost-effective? There are potential social costs of neglect; there are potential social costs of partitioning the society into unequal, hereditary, segregated divisions. Neither with regard to education nor with regard to occupation do Herrnstein and

Murray consider such costs explicitly. Their individualistic conceptual framework renders many of the social costs of such inequalities invisible, and they devote enormous energy to suggesting, without evidence, that such costs are negligible or inevitable. They define the general ability test as cost-efficient only by ignoring the costs to the society of defining millions of students as not worth anything. In the conclusion of *The Bell Curve* they will return to these problems, after the body of the work has developed an analytical framework within which the problems are insoluble.

Although *The Bell Curve* argues that compensatory education has been tried and has failed, it has not failed when it has been tried.

The pre-eminent ideological and practical implications of the biogenetic account of inequality center on the possibilities of change. To the extent that different scores on IQ, SAT, or equivalent tests are regarded as the result of unequal educational and cultural opportunities, there is a powerful rationale for removing those inequalities. However, if the scores can be portrayed as innate, that rationale can be undermined. In the United States the inequality of resources and conditions in different schools, and especially between center- city ghetto schools and suburban, predominantly white ones, is striking.[220] In comparison with Western Europe and Japan, the poor and ghetto segments of American education, where inequality of resources is conspicuous, does dismally. These inequalities are the conditions which Herrnstein and Murray legitimize and justify by treating them as the result of genetic incapacity.

Of course, the leap from genetic to practically unchangeable and thence to morally legitimate is not logical. There are any number of biological hereditary conditions which can be medically and socially counteracted. The question of how we wish to treat the disadvantages of students is not the same as that of their origin. Myopia, hearing problems, and dyslexia used to consign students to the margins of the school system. Glasses, hearing aids, and other compensations allow many students with such handicaps to perform more than adequately in school. Whether dyslexia is genetic in origin is not fundamental to how we deal with it. Conversely, there are many environmental disadvantages which we do not feel morally or socially impelled to address.

Compensatory education and affirmative action represent normative policy issues about the sorting function of the schools, questions of whether different students are treated fairly. In *The Bell Curve*, these political issues are misrepresented as being causal issues about the origins of differences in test scores. What pretends to be a descriptive and theoretical analysis of the causes of educational success and failure is instead a policy discussion justifying the further erosion of public education and the reduction of funds to education as a whole. Herrnstein and Murray purports to give a tough-minded evaluation of compensatory education programs. Their starting point is Jensen's analysis that compensatory education had been tried but failed because it tried to change immutable hereditary capacities. They supplement this analysis by arguing that even when it is possible to increase children's test scores, it is not practical, given limited school resources.

Herrnstein and Murray move to this argument because the extensive literature in response to Jensen showed that if compensatory education has failed, it is largely because it has never been tried. The most visible and well-known of the compensatory education programs is Project Head Start. Head Start began as a mixed bag of programs. It was rather a humanitarian response to the situation of many poor children.[221] The availability of federal money for Head Start was announced only a few months before the implementation date. Accordingly there was a frantic rush of applications by school boards, churches, colleges, sororities, and local agencies for funds, giving rise to very different kinds of programs. Head Start emphasized local programs meeting locally set goals, rather than one single monolithic program with national standards. The program was carried out under the administrations of Nixon, Carter, Reagan, and Bush, none of whom fully supported it. Under these circumstances, it is remarkable that it had any effect whatsoever. Head Start and other compensatory programs constitute a negligible fraction of the national budget. The amount being spent on compensatory education for deprived children is barely enough for minimally adequate day care. Herrnstein and Murray argue that this little bit should be taken away because it has not managed to compensate for all the other disadvantages the children suffer.

Herrnstein and Murray create the appearance of failure by evaluating the programs by a goal that they were never primarily set up to reach, namely, to increase performance on IQ tests. Most of the programs were set up to promote much more diffuse social and personal adjustment. Because of the artificiality of their criterion of changing IQ scores, Herrnstein and Murray are able to argue that no one has convincingly demonstrated any long-term improvement from such programs, despite an immense literature showing their success.[222] Herrnstein and Murray argue that although such programs yielded a short-run increase in academic performance, much of the gain has been eroded when the students leave the program.[223] But it is notable that the typical gain of six points is one-third to one-half of the black/white difference. Given that nothing about the children's social situation was changed and that they returned to the situation of disadvantage, it is hard to see how this amounts to a criticism of the program.

The crucial policy issues concern how we interpret the "fade out" of early improvement. According to the figures which Herrnstein and Murray accept, Head Start, at the end of a year, produced short term gains of six to ten points; the Perry Preschool and the Abecedarian project produced about 11 points; and the Milwaukee Project produced gains of some 25 points. Note that these are a significant fraction of the mean black-white difference (15 points), and they are produced without changing anything about the family structure or social situation of the students except giving them access to enriched daycare.

Thus, it is evident why Herrnstein and Murray focus on whether the gains are permanent. They highlight a series of studies which suggest that most of the gains were eroded over the next two to five years. This is just what an environmental interpretation would conclude. After attending Head Start, or equivalent programs, children ordinarily go to the same schools and live in the same housing projects and streets as before. When students return to a poor environment, there is a tendency for the improvements to fade. The predominant finding is that such disadvantaged kids still tend to fall behind the advantaged, but they do so to a lesser degree than those who did not attend the program. Any reasonable test would look at the possibility of making a change in the global situation, but Herrnstein and Murray do not use that criterion. Yet, the program still produces changes in adjustment and school performance inconsistent with the underlying model of genetic incapacity. Such changes are hardly evidence for discontinuing the programs in favor of others oriented to "physiological obstacles to learning."

Since many current compensatory programs produce considerable changes, Herrnstein and Murray make a quick shift to the question of whether those programs can, within pragmatic limits of funding, significantly affect the children's total social environment. Characterizing the environment of a child as complex and beyond our ability to comprehend (or alter), they conclude that no existing set of external interventions can be successful in changing any meaningful part of it (*The Bell Curve*, p. 413). In this context, Herrnstein and Murray shift to an admiration for adoption as the compensatory program of choice. Here, justice or possibility move backstage and the ground of criticism shifts to political pragmatics. Programs must operate within pragmatic limits of resources, skilled manpower, and political commitment. The Abecedarian project is much more expensive than Head Start. It is a program that is equivalent to the intensive child care and early education of middle class children. Can anyone suppose, Herrnstein and Murray ask, that it would be politically feasible to supply such care to tens of millions of poor children? What a politically impractical, utopian proposal!

This is sleight of hand. The question has suddenly been shifted to the pragmatic question of what is politically feasible. Ultimately the theoretical question at issue is not what we are able to afford or what political commitment exists, but whether it would make any difference. In the last generation, it has not been possible to provide all children with an equal opportunity, but the theoretical issue here is whether it is likely to make a difference if we did. In the course of arguing that it would not make a difference, Herrnstein and Murray have to deal with contradictory evidence, and so here they shift ground to political pragmatics.

The Herrnstein and Murray argument that the educational system has been oriented to the performance of poor students leads to policy implications likely to undermine the performance of all students.

Chapter Eighteen of *The Bell Curve* argues that American higher education has been consistently damaged by a focus on the needs and abilities of the less able, using the analysis of SAT scores which they published in The Public Interest in 1992. SAT scores seemed to hit a maximum around 1963 and to go into a decline (from 500 to 475 in math and from 475 to 425 in verbal) between 1963 and 1980, with an irregular and partial recovery of the math scores since then. Herrnstein and Murray consider the two main explanations to be inadequate: that there has been an across-the-board decline in education (the explanation favored by conservatives) or that there has been a democratization of higher education with an increasing number of students taking the SAT (the explanation favored by liberals). They suggest that although each explanation contains partial truths, neither is fully adequate, and so they propose their own: the dumbing down of higher education. This leads to their policy solution: the orientation of education to the needs of the gifted in line with elitist ideal of an educated man.

Against the view that the decline of SAT scores is due to a decline in American education as a whole, they assert that there has been level or increasing performance of high school seniors as a whole; it is only those taking the SAT who seem to be doing more poorly. Moreover, they argue that the performance of the top students has also held steady or improved, especially in math. Thus the drop in SAT scores has been localized in the quarter of all high school seniors who take the SAT.

They argue that education functions differently for different groups within it and that any adequate account of the decline in SATs has to focus on the ways education has failed to meet the needs of this group.

Against the argument that the decline of SATs merely reflects a larger and more diverse set of students taking the SAT, they first argue that the increase in the pool of people taking the SAT in the early 1960s did not decrease SAT scores.[224] But, they argue, the college track of American education was "dumbed down" in the 1960s and 1970s. High school texts were rewritten in simpler language and made less challenging. High school curricula were softened, with more electives and fewer requirements. Grade inflation meant that less effort and homework were required to get the same grades, and so less work was done. They interpret this as a neglect of the needs of the gifted in favor of the needs of the inept. They attribute much of this neglect to the Elementary and Secondary Education Act of 1965 and a general priority given to programs for disadvantaged students. They call for a reorientation of education and educational research to the needs of the gifted.

The policy implications of evaluating the effectiveness of education by performance on the SAT, which is then assumed to be a measure of genetic capacity, are all too evident. Money spent on education is wasted. This position links the analysis to the outcomes of the *Contract with America*. However, it is politically impractical. Accordingly, Herrnstein and Murray shuffle together arguments about genetic capacity and about cost-effectiveness to obtain an argument for spending money on brighter (that is, more affluent) students.

From a theoretical standpoint, their policy implications are a natural consequence of their cognitive reductionism. The testing movement and the emphasis on SAT and similar tests leads to a one-sided emphasis on the educational goal of sorting and sifting students rather than such goals as fostering an educated citizenry or promoting each child's self-realization. The Herrnstein and Murray analysis opportunistically shifts from efficiency arguments to impossibility and justice arguments in order to maintain the support of conservative constituencies. They claim that bright kids have been neglected because the liberal programs have directed attention to the disadvantaged. Policy concessions to the biologically unfit have held back the deserving, able children of the cognitive elite.[225]

Herrnstein and Murray have made no convincing case that there has been a decline in the effectiveness of teaching the college-bound student, that policies oriented to the disadvantaged damage the college track, or that policies they propose will help. They present no evidence that there has been a decline in resources for education for the gifted or that this is due to the resources devoted to education for the disadvantaged.[226] American education overwhelmingly directs attention to advantaged students. There is considerable evidence that it is the elitism of American education that is responsible for many of its ills.

Japanese and Chinese education seem to be outstandingly successful, particularly in avoiding the SAT decline which concerns Herrnstein and Murray. Stevenson and Stigler recently completed an extensive comparative study of American, Chinese, and Japanese education, *The Learning Gap*. While there is considerable overlap in the performances of students in different American, Japanese, and Chinese schools in the first grade, by the fifth grade, the performance of students in the Asian schools has pulled away from those in American schools, so that they are virtually non-overlapping. Moreover, performances of students in Asian schools have become more uniform, while those in the American schools have become more diverse.

Part of the difference is the gross amount of time and effort devoted to education—the 180-day American school year does not teach as much as the 240-day Asian school year. Stevenson and Stigler argue that the Asian schools are also characterized by the absence of tracking and by the requirement that every student master the material, treating that mastery as a matter of motivation and work rather than ability. These characteristics are the exact opposite of those which Herrnstein and Murray stress. Care for students at the bottom may be a tide which lifts all boats. Education is partly a race, and the leaders race harder when they are paced by others. Herrnstein and Murray note that students in American high schools are not motivated to study harder or to get better grades, but they fail to analyze why. If suburban school students are competing with students from schools where most students graduate functionally illiterate, then why should the suburban students and parents wish to work harder? In an Asian school, where the floor has been raised, the parents and students at the top of the distribution have powerful incentives to raise the ceiling. Elitist policy proposals are likely to increase the gap between the United States and other countries.

In the United States, innovative programs like that in North Carolina managed to lift the performance of all students by eliminating all tracking and sorting in favor of having all students pursue a systematic set of competencies, each at his or her own pace.[227] The author of that plan argues that low achievement at all levels is a result of the "bell curve fallacy." When a student runs into academic difficulties it is a fallacy to treat those difficulties as deficiencies in innate inability, and doing so leads to the student's giving up. Since *every* student runs into difficulties, whether the problem is perceived as an question of unsurpassable biological ability or as a motivational challenge is the fundamental determinant of how well students will do. The main limits that all students meet are motivational limits, but these take the form of the view "I'm just not good at that"—whether *that* is addition or calculus. The orientation of education to the idea of a bell curve of biological limits insures that motivational limits will hold back all students.

The central policy initiative of *The Bell Curve* is an attack on affirmative action.

Herrnstein and Murray seek to portray affirmative action as a form of race privilege that contradicts the fair and equal treatment of all individuals in accordance with their individual capacities. These authors suppress the main gender consequences of the programs, as well as the social processes and contexts within which affirmative action programs operate. Their simplistic analysis involves mainly two considerations: fair treatment of each individual and efficient allocation of scarce talent. Their model treats these two as essentially identical; the fairest system would be allocation according to cognitive ability. In education, Herrnstein and Murray take the difference between black, Hispanic, white and Asian SAT scores at prestigious universities to be evidence that affirmative action produces reverse racism. The argument is fallacious, since even an entirely "race neutral" procedure will "pass on" differences in mean SAT scores found among the applicants.[228] Their framework for thinking about affirmative action suggests that only underprivileged individuals should gain preference.[229] It sounds fair, but the way they have conceived privilege denies that there are privileged groups or that apparently neutral criteria can operate as a Matthew principle to reinforce group privilege; and thus this analysis leads to policies by which only privileged groups gain preference. There is a dense mass of social structures of preference, information, and support that constitute a kind of affirmative action program for the privileged.

They obscure the fact that affirmative action programs are of many different kinds. The common element of all affirmative action programs is that they require those who make such decisions as school admissions, recruitment, hiring, promotion, or contracting to take characteristics such as race or gender into account to ensure that minorities or women are not unfairly excluded from consideration. Sometimes this involves formalizing policies such as requiring public announcement of a position, open recruitment, and equal consideration of all applications. Other forms of affirmative action may involve consideration of the criteria by which people are admitted, hired, or promoted. Herrnstein and Murray identify affirmative action with preference. Typically battles about affirmative action consist of arguments in which supporters regard it as compensatory or promoting diversity, while opponents argue that it has the effect of reverse discrimination or quotas. Not all affirmative action involves quantitative goals or timetables. Even one which does, usually does not involve a quota or the hiring or admission of the unqualified. The discussion in *The Bell Curve* systematically identifies affirmative action with the weakening of objective ability or productivity criteria of admission, promotion and hiring.

Herrnstein and Murray argue that the disparity in test performance of white and minority respondents is so large that the original intent of affirmative action has been subverted. They argue for what they call the original intent of affirmative action, which they characterize as "to cast a wider net, to give preference to members of disadvantaged groups, whatever their skin color, when qualifications are similar." They suggest that this involves scrapping the whole edifice of job discrimination law.

In contrast to the usual understanding (that affirmative action requires decision makers to take account of race or gender to avoid unfair treatment) their definition scraps affirmative action in the guise of avoiding preference.[230] But what was the original intent of anti-job-discrimination law? For most, it was the elimination of past disadvantages, particularly racism and sexism, identified with the position articulated by President Lyndon Johnson at Howard in 1965:

> You do not take a person who for years has been hobbled by chains and liberate him, bring him up to the starting line of a race and then say, "you are free to compete with the others," and still justly believe that you have been completely fair. Men and women of all races are born with the same range of abilities. But ability is not just the product of birth. Ability is stretched or stunted by the family that you live with and the neighborhood that you live in—by the school you go to and the poverty or richness of your surroundings. (Public Papers of the Presidents, 1966, p. 636)

The assumption of general human equality is fundamental to the legal and political motivation of these laws. Americans oppose privilege. They agree that it is not a fair race if some people start behind because they or their parents were hobbled. Note also that the rationale for affirmative action depends on the social structure. All the crucial questions concern the hobbles that are social structures: that involve the schools, friends, power, contacts and other resources differentially available to different communities. An individualistic framework makes structures invisible by restricting attention to individual biogenetic capacities.

Why might those making decisions have to take race and gender into account in order to ensure fair treatment? Wouldn't the fairest thing be to ignore race, gender, and other group characteristics? The answers to these questions requires an analysis of racism and discrimination that is absent from *The Bell Curve*. Specifically, it requires an analysis of institutional racism and of the ways that ostensibly neutral practices can have a highly unequal and prejudicial impact on different groups.

Social theorists commonly distinguish a continuum of processes leading to discriminatory treatment, extending from individual racial or gender prejudice and discrimination, to institutionalized racism or sexism.[231]
For instance, there is nothing intrinsically racist or sexist about recruitment through networks of friends and family or about promoting people
or protecting them from layoffs according to seniority. There is nothing
intrinsically racist or sexist about admitting people to schools on the basis
of their test scores or grades, or in hiring professors according to their
publications or their compatibility with the existing faculty. However, in
a context of pervasive racism or sexism in the whole society—in which all
people have not had an equal chance to form influential networks or contacts, acquire seniority, or get an education that leads to high test scores
or publications or compatibility—such criteria can have a highly unequal
and discriminatory impact on different groups.[232]

The concept of statistical discrimination, which is intermediate between individual discrimination and institutional racism, combining aspects of each, illuminates the processes they involve and the reasons that
having decision makers ignore race would not always eliminate racist,
discriminatory policies. In statistical discrimination, an employer may not
hire women because women are more likely to need maternity leave. Or
the employer may not hire black workers because the employer believes
that they will have poor work habits. Or an elite university may not recruit at a mainly black high school. Or a taxi driver may not pick up black
fares because he is afraid of being robbed. D'Sousa calls this "rational discrimination;" argues that it is the typical form of discrimination today; ve-
hemently supports the right of cab drivers, employers, or neighbors to
discriminate in this fashion; and on that basis supports the repeal of the
1964 Civil Rights Act, as well as of all affirmative action legislation. If the
beliefs are false, the situation amounts to individual prejudice. The employees are not being hired, the students are not being recruited, or the
passenger is not able to get a taxi because of false beliefs of the employers,
university administrators, or cab drivers.[233] But even if the beliefs are
true, the resulting behavior is discriminatory. Suppose 30 percent of
women will take maternity leave. An employer may not want to take that
risk, but then the 70 percent of women who do not are being refused a
chance because of their group membership. Suppose 1 percent more
black passengers than white passengers would rob a taxi driver. Taxi
drivers may not be willing to take that risk, but then 99 percent of black
passengers will be penalized because of their group membership. The
concept of statistical discrimination shows that even when employers or
university administrators or citizens are not motivated by prejudice, they
may be motivated to act in ways that are discriminatory and unfair to all
or most women or minority group members.

Most forms of racism do not consist of individual acts of discrimination or antagonism in isolation. The concept of institutionalized racism or sexism highlights the fact that the whole interconnected social structure may privilege or disadvantage groups.[234] Herrnstein and Murray emphasize the fact that "life isn't fair,"[235] but often the law has to be fair precisely because life is not fair without it. Affirmative action represents a commitment to create equal chances that would not exist without it.

Herrnstein and Murray give no systematic analysis of the social structures underpinning unequal opportunity, such as those which produce different proportions of skilled applicants for a position. Their general analytical strategy is to assume that there are only two kinds of forces: individual differences in ability of applicants and individual acts of discrimination by employers. Since they believe that in the absence of government regulation the latter is bound to decrease inexorably, within the framework of their analysis it is hard to see how any discrimination, institutional racism or inequities could ever have arisen. Presumably it was because traditional elites did not realize how much they would benefit from using IQ tests. However, almost all discrimination happens by the Matthew principle. Previous training, social connections, role models, social supports, and institutional pressures produce a given cohort of educational or occupational candidates. These form an interconnected, almost a hydraulic, system. The flow of persons from a family or from a community into occupational or educational pools tends to reinforce itself in many different ways. The other face of this hydraulic flow is a kind of Catch 22 that the members of disadvantaged groups meet when they attempt to break into an enclave of privilege. They may be told that they lack credentials and experience, when the only way to get the credentials or experience is to gain the position for which they are being rejected. Most capacities are socially created,[236] and when they have been created unequally and unfairly, we must interfere with those processes to be fair.

The new political Right is not always opposed to special treatment on the basis of gender, religion, or inheritance; it accepts such treatment so long as it is privately controlled and not accountable to anyone. Affirmative action in support of women or racial and ethnic minorities is opposed, but there is a kind of affirmative action which the political Right resolutely supports. Preferences for the children of alumni, scholarships earmarked for male athletes, scholarships whose claimants will be regionally, religiously, or ethnically limited, or recruitment procedures that are channeled through religious, ethnic kinship, or class-biased organizations and networks are all considered unobjectionable. It is only when there is some attempt to counterbalance the biases of private privilege that the political Right becomes concerned about fairness.

Herrnstein and Murray ignore the real structure of support—search, cumulative reinforcement, and motivation—in favor of a reductionist model of fixed initial abilities. They ignore the massive affirmative action programs for the privileged—preferential admission of alumni children, graduates of elite prep schools, and old-boy networks of contacts which make information about a job or school available—both in education and in business. The problem is not so much that these practices can be eliminated or are undesirable or unfair in themselves, but that ignoring them leads to an analysis that is unfair. It leads to allowing such programs for privileged groups but not for less privileged groups.

In the economy, Herrnstein and Murray believe that the bulk of affirmative action law should be scrapped. In the case of jobs, Herrnstein and Murray suggest that IQ-type tests are the best available measure of an applicant's ability to do any job, and therefore such tests should be the exclusive basis of hiring. This denies that there is any valid question about the relevance of a test to job requirements. They suggest that the original intent of affirmative action laws was subverted by a series of administrative guidelines and court decisions which forced or encouraged employers to adopt rigid quotas. As early as Chapter Three of The Bell Curve, Herrnstein and Murray have taken issue with the Supreme Court decision in Griggs v. Duke Power, 1971. They develop the idea that it amounts to a quota system, and Appendix 7 develops the view that legislative, executive, and judicial reinterpretation have made affirmative action programs more extreme, diverting it from its original intent. The reality is the exact opposite. Griggs stated a relatively weak position, which has been cautiously weakened further since then.

No form of affirmative action can eliminate many of the bases of racism in the society. Mass unemployment, segregation, and desperate poverty concentrated in the ghetto will not be eliminated by affirmative action. Gang warfare, ideological racism, and the activities of terrorist groups such as the Ku Klux Klan or the Aryan Nation will not be eliminated by affirmative action. While affirmative action gave many women, blacks, and Hispanics chances to get education or jobs that they had not had before, these chances came at times when other forces were putting particularly heavy strains on the position of other blacks or women. Affirmative action, despite its weaknesses, has worked. It has kept a bad situation from becoming much worse.

The Griggs decision unanimously ratified the guidelines set up by the Equal Employment Opportunity Commission under Title VII of the Civil Rights Act. Duke Power Company had openly discriminated against blacks prior to Title VII, limiting them explicitly to the worst manual jobs. After Title VII, they replaced those rules with a stipulation which, in that social context, had the same effect, requiring a high school diploma or a successful score on two ability tests for progression out of those jobs. Since intent is difficult or impossible to prove in such cases, the question became whether it is justified to have requirements that have the effect of eliminating most members of a disadvantaged group if the requirements have no clear relation to the skills needed for the position. The guidelines ratified by Griggs suggested that requirements that had a powerful adverse impact and that were not necessary for successfully carrying out the tasks of the position were problematic.[237]

> The Touchstone is business necessity. If an employment practice which operates to exclude Negroes cannot be shown to be related to job performance, the practice is prohibited. (Griggs v. Duke Power, 1971, p. 401)

Thus, business practices which do not have significant disparate impact are not prohibited.[238] Some practices such as seniority or religious affiliation in religious schools are not prohibited even if they do have disparate impact; and practices which can be shown to be related to job performance are not prohibited. Moreover, as early as 1975, in Wards' Cove Packing Co. v. Atonio, the court softened the criteria from "business necessity" to "serve(s) in a significant way the legitimate employment goals of the employer." Subsequent cases have weakened the requirement still further, especially in terms of the burden of proof.

Thus, what Herrnstein and Murray object to is the requirement that employers who use criteria which have significant adverse impact on women or minorities investigate or show that the criteria are necessary or serve legitimate employment goals. While they claim to be agnostic about whether blacks are genetically inferior, their policy proposals depend upon the presumption of large differences in innate ability. While they claim to acknowledge the existence of racism, sexism, discrimination, and pervasive differences in opportunity, the whole story that they have told and the interpretation on which they based their analyses have conjured racism, sexism, and discrimination out of sight, partly by denying the very possibility of institutional racism or sexism.[239]

Employers are often not shy at all about saying why they do not hire blacks or how they avoid doing so. A 1991 report of interviews with Chicago area businessmen found a pervasive belief by employers that black workers were unskilled, uneducated, illiterate, dishonest, unmotivated, lacking in initiative, involved with drugs, unstable, undependable, and had bad attitudes.[240] A portion of their view is almost certainly prejudice. Employers distinguished blacks whom they knew (of whom they said the stereotype was not true) from the majority (of whom they believed that it was). This distinction is a central maneuver protecting attitudes from empirical disconfirmation, well-known in studies of prejudiced attitudes.

Employers believed that black workers are not smart, but this belief is just one element in the bad-attitude complex. To avoid hiring black workers, employers would use mechanisms such as locating in white areas, targeting advertising to nonminority areas, or hiring only friends or relatives of present employees.

Besides the component of employer beliefs, which is simple prejudice, there may be components that reflect statistical discrimination (some blacks are refused employment because other blacks have been unsatisfactory employees) and that, in turn, reflects institutional racism. High unemployment combined with segregation can produce a social structure that generates these attitudes.[241] We have noted that the social circumstances producing instability and lack of skills or work motivation are relatively well understood. Affirmative action represents the recognition that a global self-reinforcing and self-compounding process is involved and that this process is a social problem that must be socially addressed. Affirmative action does not require any employer to hire, retain, or promote any particular worker, certainly not a worker who cannot do the job. It does create enforceable procedures for ensuring that whole categories of workers are not prevented from being given a chance. The opposition of Herrnstein and Murray to affirmative action is complemented by their reinforcing the stereotypes about the ghetto poor, their proposal of test scores as a catch-all basis of statistical discrimination, and their insistence that any test score or certificate is always relevant to the performance of any job.

The reductionism of Herrnstein and Murray's analysis produces illusions that support policies whose effect would accentuate the problems.[242] This result is justified by ascription to defective genes. Reductionist and pseudo-scientific analyses are always problematic, but are particularly dangerous when used to create policies that make the problem worse.

Conclusion

It is not very nice to throw a stink bomb into one's neighbor's yard. It is often not very nice to put "No Trespassing" signs around one's own yard. But in a context where white supremacist and right-wing militias have been organized with machine guns pointed at the gate between the yards, throwing a stink bomb can be a provocation to race war. The present political constellation is driven by the political agenda of the Right, characterized by an assault on equality and on policies promoting equal human dignity or opportunity. Herrnstein and Murray develop central policy arguments against compensatory education, universal equal educational opportunity, and affirmative action both in education and in jobs. They point to the social results of poverty, inequality, segregation, discrimination, racism, sexism, and cumulative disadvantage, and then they advocate the elimination of all programs and policies addressing them.

The great slums, from the London of Dickens to the slums of imperial Rome or Egypt, exemplify the consequences of the benign neglect urged by *The Bell Curve*. A social structure consisting of an illiterate and unhealthy population juxtaposed with a tiny privileged elite did not generate healthy and autonomous individuals or communities. Rather, such neglect crippled and destroyed masses of people and produced pockets of social pathology that undermined those societies. Today, such arrangements lead to yet worse consequences. Such a society is not efficient; it is unproductive and unattractive. The concluding section of *The Bell Curve*, which represents neglect as producing a society with "a place for everyone" must make heroic efforts to explain away its unattractive characteristics. On the one hand, these results are falsely treated as inevitable; on the other, they are pictured as the result of a liberal cognitive elite out of touch with the problems of ordinary men and women.

Conceptions of genetic inferiority have powerful political implications. In the context of the policies derived from those conceptions in the past, Herrnstein and Murray sound relatively moderate. In fact, the educational, social, and occupational policies implicit in the first parts of the book are often far more explicitly elitist, racist, sexist, and reactionary than the arguments that the authors are willing to defend explicitly. From the view that IQ tests are an unbiased measure of a virtually unmodifiable ability, others have concluded that ideals of social or political equality and democracy are biologically doomed; Herrnstein and Murray conclude only that compensatory programs should be reexamined as a possible waste of money. From these assumptions and from low black and Hispanic test scores, others have concluded that these groups are inferior and should be segregated or excluded from the society. Herrnstein and Murray conclude only that they may be genetically inferior and, therefore, that affirmative action programs should be radically modified and curtailed and immigration restricted. From the view of biological inferiority and from the high birthrate of low scorers, others concluded in the past that those who score low should be forcibly sterilized. Herrnstein and Murray conclude only that welfare has a "dysgenic" effect and should be cut off; a woman with an illegitimate child should be put in a situation where she will put the child up for adoption; and local communities should take care of their own people.

This argumentative strategy of *The Bell Curve* has been characterized as "academic brinkmanship," i.e., leading the reader to the brink of various conclusions, from which the authors pull back, disavowing any responsibility but allowing the reader to pursue them. However, within the present political context, the implications that Herrnstein and Murray draw explicitly concerning education, welfare, affirmative action, the courts, and the role of the federal government attack compensatory programs that are relatively popular, deeply institutionalized, and that go to groups, such as poor children, widely recognized to have a powerful claim on public compassion. If such programs are vulnerable, it follows that all other programs of health, education, and welfare such as job training or environmental protection are, too. In the face of growing inequalities and segregation, the political dynamics of these attacks represent the cutting edge of an assault on all programs designed to integrate or equalize opportunities within the society.

Moreover, the real political implications of *The Bell Curve* are only apparent in a political context in which there are several groups on the far right vying for influence in the political system. *The Bell Curve* systematically legitimates the theorists and theories most popular among white supremacist groups;[243] and even though it disavows their specific policy conclusions, it defends a conception of a society with greater states' rights and local autonomy, consistent with their politics.

Chapter 8

The Political Philosophy of Elitism

A hidden agenda of the New Right is the protection of the concentration of wealth and power in the upper five percent of our society. The central aim is the limitation of government to those functions deemed necessary to provide essential police and military protection. The New Right intends to reverse the limited pattern of social responsibility that has developed at the national level of government and reverse policies aimed at opening opportunity more widely and easing the burden of poverty on the sick, the disabled, the elderly, and children. The political problem the New Right faces is the justification of increased concentration of wealth in the face of increasing poverty and declining income for most of America. Given this, a platform that advocates tax reductions for the rich and the elimination of safety-net protection for the poor would seem on the surface to be politically suicidal. Even continued protection of existing inequalities would seem difficult to justify. Only masterful rhetoric could convince the voting public to support such a platform. Assuming that current inequalities are a reflection of innate inequalities of ability, and appealing to traditional American values, the New Right weaves its arguments from the principles that have informed free market economics and from appeals to traditional morality.

The last chapters of *The Bell Curve* summarize and develop this argument, providing an inaccurate analysis of social problems and a peculiar interpretation of history in an attempt to complete the link between the values and the political platform of the Right. The final argument moves to a conclusion couched in humanitarian words but that, if enacted, would lead to a permanent isolation of the poor in a cruel authoritarian state.

The last two chapters of *The Bell Curve* outline a political philosophy or vision for the New Right: the new communitarianism of meritocratic elitism.

We have seen that Chapter Seventeen through Twenty of *The Bell Curve* lay out the rationale for the main policy initiatives of the New Right: criticism of compensatory programs as being ineffective; argument for more elitist and stratified education based on more tracking and market strategies such as vouchers; and elimination or radical transformation of affirmative action programs in education, in government, and in the economy. The final two chapters generalize and consolidate this program in a radical vision of the present and the future. The authors lay out a general rationale for social policy in the United States. Chapter 21 consolidates the historical vision of Part I of *The Bell Curve* and of the meritocratic caste corollary of the Herrnstein syllogism. It argues that there are irresistible forces leading to the separation of the cognitive elite from the situation and interests of everyone else in the society. This process makes much of the social egalitarianism in American values a hollow pretense. Unchecked, economic forces ensure that the incomes of the cognitive elite continue to grow, while those of the mass and especially of the cognitively unable underclass stagnate or fall. If this happens, social forces will ensure that the cognitive elite secedes from the rest of the society, living in exclusive suburbs, going to elite schools, intermarrying, and raising the next elite generation.

Herrnstein and Murray maintain a fundamentally contradictory and ambivalent position, shifting between four distinct analyses as suits their argument: that the increased inequality is a product of liberal policies; that it is biologically predetermined; that it is economically efficient; and that it is a moral imperative. No more than for earlier such efforts is it possible for them to combine these contradictory arguments into a seamless whole. While describing the growth of caste-like structures as irresistible, they elsewhere recognize the role of public policy in producing or moderating those tendencies. Thus, they argue that it is economically and morally improper to moderate them and that we can accommodate to them in a society that has a place for everyone and keeps everyone in his or her place.

The closing chapter poses an alternative vision of rugged individualism and restoration of community. It interprets figures such as Jefferson, Madison, and Adams as inegalitarian thinkers, deeply committed to the view that people are intrinsically unequal. The authors suggest that the entire insistence on moral egalitarianism has led to a disastrous proliferation of the welfare state, which is fundamentally in conflict with American values of limited government and individual responsibility. Not only compensatory education, welfare, and affirmative action, but all of the regulatory and political attempts to meet social needs have led to the situation they describe as a human anthill. From the fictional account of the childhood of King Arthur in *The Once and Future King*, Herrnstein and Murray take the episode in which Merlin introduces Arthur to all forms of life by giving him different animal forms. In the form of an ant, Arthur enters a great anthill over the door of which is inscribed, "Everything which is not forbidden is required." They suggest that the outcome of egalitarianism and the welfare state is an oppressive uniformity where we are not only forbidden to injure each other but minutely required to support each other in ways that sap initiative and are fundamentally unjust.[244]

The view that American values are essentially inegalitarian, or at least not egalitarian, is fundamental to the New Right's assault on equality, and it is also fundamentally mistaken. The framers of the Constitution did not recognize many of the implications of their ideals for race, gender, or class relations. However, they certainly recognized enough of those implications to adopt what Orlando Patterson correctly characterizes as a resolutely anti-Aristotelian position.[245] For Aristotle, equal treatment of those who are unlike and unequal treatment of those who are like were both unjust. But the framers saw that there is an essential core of humanity that we share when all differences are ignored, and we have continued to expand that insight. Moreover, they saw that there are many dimensions on the basis of which people might be judged or rewarded, such as beauty, wisdom, quickness, strength, innocence, moral rectitude, or effort. Since there is no criterion to judge between these dimensions, people have to be treated as equal despite, or even because of, their differences. Patterson notes that rural whites in a state such as Georgia score below the mean in IQ tests, but in the interests of justice and a common inclusive moral community, we do not make that the basis of differential treatment for them. We treat it as a problematic, socially created difference in capacities, and we promote equal treatment to reduce the differences. The New Right sometimes attempts to justify such policies as the abolition of affirmative action, of a progressive income tax, and of public education, and the devolution of powers to the states, as the embodiment of equal treatment. The fact is that such policies support, promote, and accommodate to institutional inequalities, and this is illustrated clearly by Herrnstein and Murray's celebration of "meritocratic" caste, by Dinesh

D'Sousa's view that slavery was not racist, and by the character of Gingrich's "opportunity society."

The castigation of the cognitive elite is a pseudo-populism that responds to a fundamental conflict between *The Bell Curve*'s elitism and egalitarianism.

Herrnstein and Murray particularly denounce the paternalistic liberalism of the cognitive elite. Isolated from contact with the bulk of the population, out of contact with its situation and problems, the cognitive elite see the world in terms of their own experience. They tend to elaborate complex legal systems and moral systems, through which they are well-equipped to navigate but that represent a weakening of the simple clear laws and moral values needed by everyone else, especially the cognitively impaired. Above all, the cognitive elite allegedly favor the creation of a vast, paternalistic welfare state in which the resources of the society as a whole are increasingly used to subsidize and control the underclass, keeping it out of the hair of the elite but making an increasingly serious problem for everyone else.

In these closing chapters, the emotional and evaluative tone of *The Bell Curve*'s discussion of the cognitive elite shifts to a kind of populist castigation of elitist separation, segregation, paternalism, and complexity. The celebration of the cognitive elite as able, productive, and meritorious alternates with the criticism of the elite as isolated, self-interested, and "liberal." Herrnstein and Murray adopt a pseudo-populist stance of antagonism to the segregation, isolation, and self-interest of the elite, taking the inequalities of wealth and income as problematic and arguing that the irresponsible elite are abusing their political influence and acting in their parochial self-interest. But Herrnstein and Murray have consistently argued for policies that will promote the inequality and segregation that they deplore. Whether in the case of education, taxation, wage structures, affirmative action, housing, or other social policies, *The Bell Curve* lays out the rationale for policies that attack any counterweight to cycles of enrichment of the privileged and impoverishment of the poor.

Nevertheless, the pseudo-populism of *The Bell Curve* is a brilliant polemical device. Herrnstein and Murray are fully aware of the defeats of the psychometric and hereditarian positions earlier in the century. To the extent that they are correctly perceived as fundamentally contradicting egalitarian social values deeply rooted in the Constitution and in American life, their argument is doomed. Probably the most famous episode of those earlier conflicts was the dispute between Walter Lippmann and Lewis Terman in the pages of *The New Republic*.[246] Terman defended the importance and validity of intelligence tests in a way that laid him open to a devastating anti-elitist counterattack by Lippmann:

> Finally, a word about Mr. Terman's notion that I have an "emotional complex" about this business. Well I have. I admit it. I hate the impudence of the claim that in 50 minutes you can judge and classify a human being's predestined fitness for life. I hate the pretentiousness of the claim. I hate the abuse of scientific method which it involves. I hate the sense of superiority which it creates and the sense of inferiority which it imposes.

The construction of a rationale for intelligence testing that appeals to elite educators, managers, and employers, and only to them wins the battle but loses the war. Ultimately, the tests will be viewed as a defense of privilege and will be attacked. To avoid this outcome, the concluding chapters of *The Bell Curve* engage in vigorous stage managing that is crucial to a popular defense of the idea that fixed inborn differences between persons should be the basis of social position. The last chapters are a kind of newspeak, in which elitist policies are labeled democratic and egalitarian policies are labeled elitist. Test-oriented selection procedures and highly tracked, segregated educational systems, often based on parents' ability to pay, are not elitist but open and democratic. Compensatory or public education is elitist. Those who support public services are creating a plantation system of welfare dependency. It is the cognitive elite, out of touch with the realities of everyday life, who have destroyed urban communities by setting up federal programs.

This stage managing is a central feature of contemporary politics. In fact, the central vision of inherited ability, which ranks people into superior and inferior, and the use of testing to implement such ranking are both obviously elitist and always have been.

The historical analysis on which the rise of the meritocracy argument depends is naive and erroneous.

Herrnstein and Murray recapitulate their argument for the meritorious separation of the "cognitive elite" from the masses in the late twentieth century. They argue that society has become newly segregated, with people at the top of society showing a new differentiation that reflects the new stratification by cognitive ability. Earlier chapters have criticized the contradictory logic and flawed sociology on which their historical vision is based. The underlying fallacy is that of Aristotle: misperceiving socially-created inequality as being, instead, natural and inevitable. Herrnstein's syllogism requires environmental equalities of opportunity at the same time that it predicts and generates increased inequalities and a kind of caste system. In fact, the whole picture of a great social leveling and increased partitioning is based on sleight of hand. The same groups are going into the same positions; only the justifications have changed. The whole analysis is based on systematically blotting out all the elements of community, neighborhood, family, and school that sustain opportunities and relabeling the result of those structures "innate ability."

We have seen that this vision of historical change has no substantiating data. Nor is it consistent with existing research. American society has been sharply segregated by ethnic group and race since its beginning. The data that Herrnstein and Murray use to document the new cognitive segregation are precisely the data used in the early 1950s to establish the boundaries of social classes. These characteristics are not new.

In Chapter Three we saw how Herrnstein's syllogism structures the argument of Part I. It argues that general ability tests have produced an increasingly meritocratic society. These tests allow schools, employers, the army, and other gatekeepers to determine in advance which candidates will be successful. This success is defined as supervisor ratings and employee productivity. An invisible hand leads gatekeepers to choose able candidates. The growth of psychometric science leads to an upbeat celebration of meritocracy viewed as the expansion of opportunity during the twentieth century. But we also saw that the conclusion of Part I links this vision to the meritocratic caste corollary, which says that more meritocratic structures lead to partitioning, segregation, and assortative mating, leading, in Herrnstein and Murray's view, to rising IQ of the children of the elite and falling IQ of all other children. The concluding chapter of Part I, "Steeper Ladders, Narrower Gates" begins analysis of the downside of meritocratic elitism. Informed by the analysis implicit in the examination of poverty, unemployment, illegitimacy, divorce, and crime in Part II, the conclusion emphasizes that downside.

We have waited 400 pages for the other shoe to drop. Having laid out the direct policy implications of a biologically determinist inegalitarian analysis (the end of compensatory education, the stress on elite education, and the abolition of affirmative action), Herrnstein and Murray then turn to the consolidation of the general policy implications of the analysis. Chapter 21, "The Way We Are Headed," takes the coercive, ugly, inegalitarian, violent, and problematic characteristics of the analysis and ascribes them to the policies that respond to them. For Herrnstein and Murray, unless the federal government can somehow get out of the business of dealing with the problems of the underclass, there is an unsavory choice between Latin American conservatism or the custodial state. The call for a kind of return to the small town of "a place for everyone" is, however, intrinsically implausible. There is no evidence that decreasing federal responsibility will revitalize poor communities instead of producing traditional, ascriptive communities and ugly pockets of poverty. Ultimately the increase in inequality and social problems are nothing but the working out of the Matthew principle—processes that give more to those who have much. The flip side of these processes takes away from those with little even what they started with.

Herrnstein and Murray suggest that there are three cardinal trends that must be considered: the isolation of the cognitive elite, its merger with the class of the affluent, and the deterioration of the quality of life of those at the bottom.[247] While median income was relatively stagnant from 1970 to 1993, the percentage of families with incomes over $100,000 more than doubled, from 2 percent to more than 5 percent. This polarization has been the center of considerable commentary for the last twenty years. What is distinctive about *The Bell Curve*, and what its previous 400 pages were designed to make plausible, is an ambivalent combination of two contradictory sets of arguments about the origin of this downside. According to one, the inequality is inevitable and inexorable; there are biological differences that unavoidable economic processes will reinforce. According to their other argument, there is a moral, social, and political choice to be made about these issues. Using concepts of efficiency and freedom, Herrnstein and Murray urge pragmatic and moral reasons why we should make the choice for inequality. They say that the rising proportion of families with incomes of more than $100,000 since the early 1970s does not seem to be a function of any particular political party or policy, except insofar as those policies encourage an expanding economy (*The Bell Curve*, p. 516). Rather, they suggest that it has gone along with gains in real per capita GNP, whether those gains occurred under Richard Nixon, Jimmy Carter, Ronald Reagan, or George Bush, and that, if the economy grows, there is no reason to think that this trend will be much different under Bill Clinton or his successors.

The graph that accompanies this passage, however, shows that the rise in the proportion of rich families was broken by sharp declines during the Carter and Clinton presidencies (as well as in 1973-1975), and so it is not quite true that it "does not seem to be a function of any particular party or policy." The point of their omission is not to prevent the reader from noticing the tendencies of Republican administrations to encourage polarization of income and of Democratic administrations to restrict this trend. Rather, the analysis begins to shift the ground to a second argument, according to which income inequality is not inevitable but desirable because it is tied to the expansion of national income.

Their analysis inflates the cost and minimizes the benefits of social programs directed to addressing social problems.

Normally the framework used to examine the effects of social programs designed to improve the lives of the less privileged is cast in terms of criteria rooted in equity and morality, concern for fairness and justice in society and the importance of preserving compassion for those who suffer. Herrnstein and Murray discard this framework in favor of one whose primary application is in the world of business—the framework of analysis of costs, benefits, and economic efficiency.

Unlike equity considerations that generate considerable conflict in a society with a wide diversity of cultures and religions, efficiency is a value deeply ingrained in American culture and one that all Americans understand—at least in some fashion. Thus generating the questions within the context of efficiency criteria will resonate with popular understanding in ways in which the more complex reasoning invoking equity will not.

Having cast the questions within the context of analysis of costs and benefit, the authors provide us with arguments to force the conclusions in the direction they desire. Insisting that the source of social problems is intransigent to any attempts at change allows Herrnstein and Murray to erase the benefit side of the equation. Then they escalate the costs. Since no benefits can accrue to the expenditure of money this implies a greater financial loss than the loss of the initial expenditure since the potential benefits of alternate use of this money, such as the expansion of police power and prisons, are also lost.

Two other categories are added to the cost side of the equation. First is the cost to basic American values. Individual independence and responsibility and the importance of achievement would all be undercut by governmental programs supporting or easing the burdens of poverty. It does not matter that these values could not function in the environment encountered by the recipients of these programs. Further, they argue, basic social institutions, especially the family, are fundamentally challenged by these programs. Here, the argument merges with those now put forward by D'Sousa and Gingrich, that the existence of social supports encourages pathological and dependent behaviors and undermines American values. To make any of these arguments, it is necessary for them to ignore both social change and a considerable body of knowledge about social problems.

Finally, they erase the possibility of benefits of legislation and programs designed to promote equality among groups by their insistence that group differences reflect biologically based individual differences. Again, they join with D'Sousa in denying the existence of cumulative causation and of institutional racism or sexism. By negating any possibility of benefit, they put all civil rights legislation on the political agenda for abolition. Thus Herrnstein and Murray establish the parameters of an economic analysis to measure the effects of government intervention to reduce the effects of poverty. While the creation of a cost/benefit equation normally leads to a careful attempt to measure each, these authors pursue a conclusion that Americans have refused to consider since the 1930's. And this is their intent. By casting the analysis in this framework they limit the kind of question or position that can be argued. Positions that require justification outside the framework of cost-benefit analysis cannot be examined. Further they are arguing within a framework that Americans (especially in the business community) intuitively understand and are inclined to accept.

In "Confronting the Problems of the Underclass" they evade the discussion of the social policy origins of the underclass.

It is not quite true that the benefits gained by the elite have made everyone else better off. Indeed, *The Bell Curve*'s central construct, meritocracy, is designed to justify the reality that everyone is clearly not better off. The central sections of Chapter 21 consolidate and summarize the earlier victim-blaming analyses and lay the groundwork for the systematic elitism to come. "Facing Reality About the Underclass" argues that in both the white population and the black a major problem for the society is presented by the birth of incompetent children to incompetent mothers. The transformation of the labor market will continue to make the difficulties of those children more serious. The linkage of the problems of this group to segregation, limited education, and job training is blandly ignored. Finally, "The Coming of the Custodial State" argues that the standard ameliorative responses make the problem worse, by adding to the numbers of people in different kinds of custodial care. Specifically, they argue that given current trends and policies:

- Child care in the inner city becomes the responsibility of the state.
- The homeless will be increasingly interred in custodial shelters.
- Increased policing and prisons become more acceptable and widespread.
- The underclass will become more concentrated.
- The underclass will grow.
- Social budgets and measures of social control will become more centralized.
- Racism will emerge in a new and more virulent form.

This analysis poses important and challenging problems. The trends they refer to are quite real. Increasing concentration of wealth, stagnation of incomes of working families, increasing need for governmental support of fragile families, increased social disorder where the poorest of the population is concentrated, and continuing racism have occurred. Moreover, those problems are not solved by policies that do not address the underlying conditions. The failures and limits of social and economic policies during the last four administrations are the principal source of the resurgence of the Right today. It does not follow that those problems are biologically determined. Rather, the environments in which these children are being raised are so dangerous and so brutalizing that middle class theorists such as Murray are ordinarily afraid to enter them, let alone leave their children there. In order, however, to distract attention from the cutbacks of social services and the shifts in jobs and resources during the 1980s, Herrnstein and Murray treat these problems as the result of defective people, rather than from problems of labor markets, segregation, and opportunities in schools and jobs. They do not show the linkages between these problems; they link changes in the workplace and average earnings to neither the fragility of families nor the increasing social problems of the ghetto. Instead they characterize the growing underclass as the result of inherent shortcomings about which little can be done. If present trends are allowed to continue, they argue, the state will take over the functions of the family, the domestic welfare budget will eat up all our resources, and the police state will be upon us. Large sectors of the population will become permanent wards of the state.

For Herrnstein and Murray, "facing the reality of the underclass" is the magical trick of the vanishing box. Most of us have seen the magic trick in which people, animals, or other items placed in an apparently ordinary box vanish. There are several ways the trick can be accomplished. For Herrnstein and Murray, the supposedly empty box is labeled "the cognitive capacities of the underclass." Training, teaching or other resources placed in the box vanish. Ultimately this is what leads to the stark choice between abandonment and the custodial state: either we must leave those defective people to pursue their own destiny or devote ever-increasing resources to creating ever-increasing need and inability. The dominant message is that those people are fundamentally different and that the ideals of having a society of relative social equality and equality of life chances are delusions. But, as earlier chapters have documented, it is all done with mirrors. The illusion is created by a narrow definition of ability and a conceptualization that eliminates consideration of all the social policies, social forces, and brutalizing social conditions that create the social pathology and stunted functioning.

Often one trick conceals another.   The sleight of hand by which Herrnstein and Murray conceal the ways that social policies of the 1980s increased segregation and inequality conceals a further sleight of hand. It is true that there are very powerful forces in the world economy today bringing American workers into competition with those of other countries. It is true that there are powerful forces of cumulative causation tending to make the rich richer and the poor poorer. Without any change in social policy, these forces would have operated through the 1980s. American social programs such as food stamps, AFDC, Medicaid, and affirmative action, while slowing some of these processes, have been powerless to stop them. It is these failures that motivate Herrnstein and Murray's arguments that nothing can be done to change this; intervention efforts always fail. Now they complement their biological determinist arguments with the economic and moral arguments that we must not only bow to the inevitable but we should help it along.

As an alternative to egalitarianism, they consider an obsolete and undocumented functionalist model of income inequality.

Having suggested that people's productivity and accomplishments differ for reasons that are not their fault, Herrnstein and Murray ask what our policy should be with respect to such income inequalities. Given the immense social problems associated with extreme inequalities, they note that some suggest that these inequalities should be reduced. Against such a suggestion, they flirt with a pragmatic, empirical argument about the consequences of inequality before presenting their choice, a moral argument for the justice of maintaining inequalities.

The empirical argument is that the only way to make the economy grow and produce more wealth for everyone is to have large income differences, and so it is a matter of economic pragmatism to maintain large income differences. These authors say that they could respond with a defense of income differences. For example, it is justified to pay the high-IQ businessman and engineer more than the low-IQ ditch digger because that is the only way to make the economy grow and produce more wealth in which the ditch digger can share. They say they could grant that it is a matter not of just desserts, but of economic pragmatism about how to produce compensating benefits for the least advantaged members of the society, and that such arguments make sense as far as they go. After the experience of the twentieth century, they say, it is hard to imagine that anyone still disagrees with them. But then they move on to other issues, "transcending the efficiency of an economy" (*The Bell Curve*, pp. 527-528).

The argument is typical of *The Bell Curve*. Ideas about the increased economic productivity of inequality have driven much of their historical analysis, and provided the essential rhetoric of their policy recommendations. They wish, however, to link arguments about productivity to morality. Herrnstein and Murray first say that they could, if they wished, present a convincing pragmatic argument for economic inequality being efficient (*The Bell Curve*, pp. 527-528). They say that it is hard to imagine that anyone still disagrees that paying some jobs highly is the only way to make the economy grow, benefiting everyone. However, the fact that they cannot imagine that anyone might disagree is hardly evidence that they are correct. There are several things that Herrnstein and Murray do not reveal about the analysis.

First, they do not tell the reader that this is a version of the well-known functionalist theory of stratification, according to which inequality serves as an unconsciously evolved device to allocate the most able people to the most important jobs.[248] There is a considerable literature discussing the theory, which was widely accepted in the social sciences fifty years ago.[249] Herrnstein and Murray's version stresses economic productivity. It fails to deal with the motivation of education and differences in social values, since those aspects would embarrass their argument. The argument that inequality is the price we pay for progress ignores the costs and inflates the benefits of inequality. In *Inequality By Design*, Fischer and his colleagues have reviewed some of the evidence that the net effect of inequality is to retard growth, both by the loss of flexibility and by associated social costs. Conversely periods and societies characterized by rapid economic growth have often been driven by expanded job security, home ownership, access to education and health plans, and greater equality.[250]

Second, they do not tell the reader about problems with the functionalist theory of stratification so serious that few theorists accept it today. The argument, which sounds plausible when one contrasts the highly paid engineer to the low-paid ditch digger, sounds much less reasonable when one contrasts the highly-paid advertising executive to the low-paid teacher. Further, the theory ignores the question of property income that is central to much income inequality. It also ignores questions about how much inequality is optimal. The ratio of top Japanese managers' incomes to those of starting workers is only about one-tenth as large as in the United States. No one believes that we get better managers with more commitment, or a more rapidly expanding economy.

It is always possible that a more careful version of the functionalist theory may solve such problems, but it is characteristic that Herrnstein and Murray do not attempt this. Instead, ignoring the vast literature critical of the functionalist model, they present it as being self-evident and then slide to moral arguments, which "transcend the efficiency of the economy" (*The Bell Curve*, p. 528), mobilizing sentiments in favor of the supposedly self-evident position. A theory that has been discarded may be correct and come back into use. This cannot happen by simply ignoring its problems and pretending that the earlier discussions do not exist. Although Herrnstein and Murray say they agree with this theory, there are good reasons they do not depend on it. They also have good political reasons for deciding not to acknowledge the earlier discussions.

Their fundamental justification of increased inequalities is moral.

Both the argument that increased inequality is inevitable and that it is economically rational turn out to be mainly feints. They move from economic productivity to just desserts, the political philosophy of the book that serves to connect it to the other strands of social theory used by the new political Right. Herrnstein and Murray and the New Right are unable to directly argue for the morality of increased inequality. The level of deprivation and privilege in the society excludes that. Accordingly they must engage in a shell game, in which they attack equality in the name of equality. They suggest genetic arguments to the inevitability of inequality and economic arguments to the efficiency of inequality. However, unable to substantiate any of these, they shift to arguments that equal treatment requires that public policy allow processes producing inequality to run their course, which allows a kind of return to direct moral justifications. They view inequality as merely the realization of individual freedom, and suggest that it is unjust to deprive anyone of the rewards for his or her effort and ability. This will link their argument to D'Sousa's argument that policies oriented to reducing racial or gender inequalities violate equal rights and to Gingrich's argument that limitation of central government is uniquely consistent with American values of autonomy. Herrnstein and Murray must pretend that the arguments to efficiency, to equal rights, and to autonomy are identical.

A large number of political actions encouraged increased inequalities during the Reagan administration. The view that those increases simply reflect individual rewards for effort is implausible. When unions are broken, profits at the top increase while workers become poorer. When there is deregulation, a relatively small number of people are able to make killings on savings and loans, while most others are forced, indirectly, to pay for those killings. When regulations about bankruptcy or control of pension funds are implemented in a way that favors the rich, this hurts the poor. It is simply not true that the stagnation of the median income and the expansion of top incomes have been automatic processes on which social policy has had no effect.

Herrnstein and Murray, however, must represent the increase in inequality as an automatic effect of a growing economy to justify their unstated assumption that the rewards going to the people at the top are rewards for ability, industry, initiative, and productivity, and are unrelated to the poverty of those at the bottom. They use the implicit model of a set of independent producers such as family farms in which the return for one family farm is independent of that of others. If there is plenty of land and if the higher return for one farm comes from diligence and foresight, the higher return takes nothing from neighbors and may even help them. But modern society does not consist of family farms. We are interdependent in a way that creates the need for rules unnecessary in small towns. Milking the pension fund of a large corporation is not like milking their own cows, and is directly related to the losses of those at the bottom.

The final chapter of *The Bell Curve* advocates individual responsibility and local control to reconcile "meritocratic caste" with American values.

The final chapter of *The Bell Curve* must carry out an amazing transformation. Herrnstein and Murray have arrived at a position that is inegalitarian in the extreme, a caste system of enormous segregation, inherited inequality, and limited horizons for the masses. They must now argue that this ugly caste system embodies American values that all men are created equal. For Herrnstein and Murray, the idea of a "place for everyone" is not only the realization of meritocracy, the wave of the future, but also a return to the essential ideas of the founders of the American Constitution. They even identify those views with the ideas that legitimated traditional slaveholding and aristocratic systems in Europe and Asia. They suggest that the great political thinkers, eastern and western—Confucius and the ancient Greek and Roman philosophers—agreed upon a common ideal: society was to be ruled by a virtuous and wise few (*The Bell Curve*, p. 528).

Such a concept of a society ruled by the virtuous few is not usually associated with democratic theory, which rose to counter it. The fundamental tool for bringing about this transformation is, once again, individualism. The consistent reductionism of the earlier analysis allows a return to Herbert Spencer's "survival of the fittest."

Herrnstein and Murray, like Spencer, suggest that individual freedom requires a limited role for government and that such a limited government promotes economic and social progress. However, the great paradox of Spencer and Social Darwinism was that the pursuit of limited government did not lead to limited government but to imperialism, increased inequality, and increased coercion and police powers to keep the lid on escalating class and race war. This is the natural result of the operation of vicious cycles of deprivation and privilege.

In the absence of social policy, the vicious cycle of disadvantage depresses the political influence of subordinate groups at the same time that the cycle of privilege increases the influence and dominance of dominant groups. Both processes increase disparities of power, influence, and participation, which, in turn promote all the policies and ideologies that generated the problem in the first place. Disparities of power and influence, like all the other elements of the vicious cycle, are reinforced by and reinforce the rest, producing increasing disparities and cynicism of subordinate groups.[251] The result is not conducive to democracy, or to the kind of freedom that the New Right purports to defend.

The Bell Curve ends with a proposal for a radical new approach to the problems of the poor. Using a rhetoric of care, the authors propose that society find a way to reintroduce meaning into the lives of the poor. Here the authors believe they understand what is needed. Paternalistic and patronizing, they point to the solution that will solve the problems of the poor and give meaning to their lives. According to their argument, the poor are only marginally employable. Through the strengthening of the police state and a repressive social order that punishes with shame and with withdrawal of support, women who have illegitimate children or who leave a marriage are to be forced back into the subservient status that prevailed in the nineteenth century. How then to make these outcasts' lives enriched? The creative solution of the New Right is to turn all responsibility for their problems back to them—to their neighborhoods and communities—and let them take care of each other. This, claim the authors, will give meaning to their lives. Such reasoning barely deserves a rational response. With neither employment nor other sources of money, how can the poor meet their own needs? This is a policy of isolation and a formula for neglect; even for genocide. Since only the meritocratic cognitive elite are to enter the professions, where would these communities find the resources for medical care, for education, or other requirements of modern life? It is a recommendation that is not infrequently envisioned as the means to deal with those we wish to banish—a solution reminiscent of the leper colonies of the past, of Jewish ghettoes, or even of the concentration camps of the early years of the Holocaust. It is a prescription that will isolate the poor, insulate them from the rest of society, permit total neglect of their needs, and deny any support from others.

This "solution" to the problems of the poor is the best these defenders of the Right can propose as a social program. The Right's cornerstone is a narrow public policy the major concern of which is the protection of economic growth and the concentration of capital. A coherent social policy

requires principles that can direct a nation toward a responsible and consistent course of action. The argument that Herrnstein and Murray have
struggled so hard to make by distorting knowledge, misinterpreting their
own information, incorrectly analyzing data, and ignoring known facts
does not allow the premises essential for responsible social policy.

Their argument rests first on the premise that individuals exist for the
sake of the economy. Individuals are to be rewarded in terms of what
they can contribute to economic growth. What happened to the knowledge of interdependence so richly generated in the social science of the
twentieth century: that human beings are not solitary animals and cannot become human without other people; that humankind are deeply
and necessarily interconnected; that the survival of one is dependent on
survival of the whole? The authors mount a frontal attack on social responsibility, arguing that we should return to the poor the responsibility
for their own survival, offering no resources through which they can
achieve this, but insuring through increased police activity moral conformity and minimal protest.

Our culture transmits powerful counter-arguments to that of the New
Right, including the content of simple Christian morality—the parables of
Christ who said one must stop to help the outcast, one must share one's
loaves and fishes with those who are hungry. Christian ethics is not
founded on the Matthew Principle, but rather upon the Golden Rule.
Richard Titmuss argues passionately for the importance to each of us that
we be "humane," for without it each of us has diminished his or her own
development as a human being.[252] A great discovery of the twentieth century was that dire poverty can be eliminated in society and that society
will flourish only as that happens. Clearly we have not valued that discovery. What kind of humanity is enshrined in the prescriptions of neglect and brutality proposed in *The Bell Curve*?

Herrnstein and Murray's theories recapitulate Herbert Spencer's justi-fications of inequality.

Herrnstein and Murray represent the themes of "a place for everyone," individual autonomy, hereditary inequality, and meritocracy as the
most up-to-date analyses of the most recent trends. In fact, they are
merely another reincarnation of the Social Darwinist view of society,
whose most influential theorist was Herbert Spencer. Spencer's individualism and his doctrine that progress is driven by competition and the
struggle for survival was the basis of an immensely powerful current of
social theory. We noted that if we are to understand its current reincarnation, we must be familiar with some of its history. Specifically, Herrnstein
and Murray view their analysis as nonracist and anti-racist because it

advocates treating each person as an individual, but the history of Social Darwinism shows that, far from being incompatible, individualism and racism have often been closely allied.[253]

It has always proved difficult to defend the ideal of a society based on inheritance of unequal social position in the United States. The most important of these defenses was developed by Herbert Spencer, who saw individualism and competition as the forces driving social progress.[254] Spencer argued against any government policy that pursues "the greatest good for the greatest number." His moral individualism left it up to individuals to pursue the good. Public policy should limit itself to preventing people from interfering with one another by enforcing protection of property and the public peace. Spencer developed the argument that a society of competing, autonomous individuals was also efficient and progressive, linking the ideology of economic efficiency with moral arguments of just desserts. In Chapter One we saw that he believed that social and natural evolution should be driven by a "stern beneficence," the survival of the fittest. He opposed welfare, public education, laws regulating working hours or labor and other policies now associated with the welfare state, arguing that they had disastrously inefficient consequences. He advocated free trade, laissez faire and government non-interference. For the weak ("widows and orphans"), he recommended individual charity, but argued as well that life is hard, and it is necessary that the improvident starve.[255]

Spencer did not invent the ploy of shuffling back and forth between moral celebration of individualism, arguments that inequality is inevitable, arguments that it promotes progress, and arguments that attempts to counter it will make matters worse. But he utilized all these arguments, and his supporters developed them into a systematic celebration of inequality and justification of government inaction. Until World War II, Social Darwinism conducted a rear-guard resistance to policies such as the progressive income tax, Social Security, government regulation of wages, child labor, and working hours. The best way to see the likely consequence of the new individualist theorizing today is to reexamine its earlier outcomes.

Spencerian social thought was dominant in the United States during the Gilded Age of the late nineteenth century. It was elaborated by theorists such as William Sumner. It gained social influence partly from the support of industrialists. John D. Rockefeller argued that the growth of large business is merely the survival of the fittest; Andrew Carnegie became Spencer's intimate friend and showered him with favors. What really drove the popularity of the analysis was a sense of class privilege. Whether viewed as a sum of individuals or as a set of groups, Social Darwinists stressed differences in the abilities of different groups:

On hailing a cab in a London street, it is surprising how frequently the door is officiously opened by one who expects something for his trouble. The surprise lessens after counting the many loungers about tavern doors... "They have no work," you say. Say rather that they either refuse work or quickly turn themselves out of it. They are simply good-for-nothings, who in one way or another live on the good-for-somethings—vagrants and sots, criminals and those on the way to crime, youths who are burdens on hard-worked parents... Is it natural that happiness should be the lot of such? (Spencer, 1994 [1884], p. 80)

Spencer was independently wealthy, and he felt a hard-nosed contempt for the lower class whom he viewed as both intellectually inferior and morally dissolute. Moreover, he combined the view of the poor as good-for-nothings and sots with an analysis that attempts to make things better by government policy will really make them worse. He argued that government programs usually have unanticipated consequences, undermining the outcomes they ostensibly pursue.[256] For example, he argued, requiring property for a marriage license would promote illegitimate births rather than the care and well-being of children; attempts to interdict slavery would merely lead to crueler and faster slaving ships; public welfare would eliminate the beneficial attitudes of benevolence by the rich and gratitude by the poor; and the provision of public education would inhibit parents from educating their children.[257]

Such arguments allowed Social Darwinist theorists to present themselves as concerned, compassionate, but realistic humanitarians. At the center of Spencer's thought was moral individualism—an attack on equality in the name of equality. Given that people are intrinsically unequal, he argued, it is unjust to mandate any equal treatment for them. Rather, the law should merely protect their equal rights to become unequal. Spencer developed a massive evolutionary theory based on the idea that the growth of heterogeneity was the driving force of evolution; that the growth of individualism was the basis of social development; and thus that inequality was necessary and good. The theory is now obsolete; biological evolution, if it has any consistent direction, does not lead to unicellular individuals, but to more organized and centralized structures. In any case, the social theory of the twentieth century has stressed that human evolution is importantly different from biological evolution. Instead of engaging in a wasteful trial-and-error process that takes enormous amounts of time, humans can understand the source of problems and plan arrangements to solve them.[258] Without that ability, societies would not have survived.

Therefore, during the last decades of his life, Spencer seemed a relic, bypassed by social and theoretical developments. Everywhere, there was increased international competition and government regulation. By the

1890s it appeared to most Americans that the beneficent "invisible hand" of unregulated competition had led to economic depression, to slums, to bloody pitched battles between Pinkerton guards and strikers, to explosions of race violence, and to economic collapse. Programs of *laissez faire* competition were politically and intellectually bankrupt. The foundations of the Federal Food and Drug Administration were laid; a constitutional amendment establishing the progressive income tax was passed; and systems of public and higher education were founded. It was widely accepted that it was necessary to plan the solutions to social problems; that it was necessary to have government policies if we are to succeed in international competition; that the vicious cycles, bloody strikes, and race riots generated by "survival of the fittest" were intolerable, and that the nation needs to be held together by something more than individual self-interest. These views were antagonistic to Spencerian individualism.

The eclipse of Spencerian theory was accomplished by its political, economic, and social consequences.

Spencerian individualist assumptions led to economic and political catastrophe. But, unfortunately, they had to be defeated not once, but twice; and now they may need to be defeated a third time. As a result of the growth of Progressivism, Pragmatism, the Social Gospel, socialism, unions, and other strands of ameliorative thought, Social Darwinism was virtually defunct as a mass political force by the early twentieth century. Lack of schooling, lack of housing, lack of medical care or public health produced neither freedom nor progress. Even the upper class, faced with disease-ridden and crime-ridden slums as well as pitched, bloody battles over wages, found Spencer less and less convincing. However, as we have seen, Social Darwinism then underwent a transformation. The individualist form of Social Darwinism went through a kind of mutation, combining with apparently contradictory currents of nativism, racism, and manifest destiny nationalism.[259] The rugged individualism of the late nineteenth century, combined with eugenic and psychometric academic currents, reappeared in the roaring twenties in a form that appeared to be its polar opposite: fear that "Nordic" and Protestant populations were being swamped by immigrants, leading to racist and nativist opposition to blacks, Asians, Indians, Catholics and Jews. Social Darwinism combined with eugenics and psychometrics, and with racism and nativism. The arguments about welfare dependency, today, are largely a recapitulation of the first phase of Spencerian theory, while the arguments about dysgenics are largely a recapitulation of the second phase. The transmutation of individualism into racism resulted from their common inegalitarianism and from the fact that anti-immigrant and racist sentiments were the only political force that could counter Progressivism. The leap from individual competition to group competition was a short one. Academic theorists found it convenient sometimes to stress group differences (means) and sometimes to stress individual differences (variation around the means).[260] Social Darwinism was an alliance of groups united by their opposition to egalitarianism. Now as in the 1920s, political and moral issues, presented in a biological guise, legitimate inegalitarian policies. These sordid theoretical developments of eugenic and Nazi theory are of historical relevance. An unbroken theoretical flow connects these works to *The Bell Curve*.

During the late nineteenth and early twentieth centuries, political conflicts over equality have hinged on the issues of race, not as a matter of logic but of politics. Logically, divisions of gender, religion, ethnicity, language, and regional or political inequalities—which, in complex ways, cross-cut each other—as well as racial divisions and class divisions could generate central political forces. Each has been the center of conflicts over equality at different times and places, and these different forms of affiliation can be politically mobilized in different ways. But practically, racial divisions (defined broadly to include not only skin color but any distinction by which humans are divided into separate "peoples") have displayed the potential to flare into civil war or genocide in a way that the other divisions have not. Spencerian, Social Darwinist, and racist theory led to a society in which the very possibility of common citizenship breaks down. Patterson notes that if "intelligence" connotes an adaptive characteristic, then one must ask what is "intelligent" behavior for a minority that is threatened and cornered like rats in a blocked sewer.[261] Is it "intelligent" to act as a model minority, as the Jews did in pre-Nazi Germany? Or is it "intelligent" to arm oneself to the teeth and behave as murderously threatening and aggressive as possible? We have never been comfortable with arrangements to which class and race war are a natural response. A look at the ways in which racist ideologies have persisted shows why racial inequalities are particularly malignant.

After World War II, Social Darwinist tendencies went into hibernation in elite-funded groups, but they did not disappear.

In the twentieth century, the evidence that Social Darwinism leads to an abyss was even more compelling than in the nineteenth, and its collapse was even more complete. After the Great Depression, World War II, and the Holocaust, the theories of the Social Darwinists were utterly discredited. During and after the war against the Nazis, no one in the United States could successfully champion ideas such as Carl Brigham's defense of Nordic superiority. The Nuremberg trials revealed Nazi war crimes, such as the experimentation with electric shock to carry out instantaneous (and cheap) mass sterilization. Thus, eugenic, psychometric, and racist theories underwent an internal migration.[262] They did not disappear and theorists committed to them did not recant, but they gave their theories a more individualist and academic form.

The internal migration of Social Darwinist theorists was particularly notable in the case of racist theory. A number of institutes and foundations were set up with the explicit aim of maintaining and promoting theories about race and of combating the cultural emphases in the human sciences. Some persons with substantial resources were disappointed by the retreat of Nazi ideas or regretted the discrediting of all segregationist and racist theory through its association with the Nazis. Wycliffe Draper, a textile millionaire, set up the Pioneer Fund to promote racial theorizing, with Harry Laughlin as its original director.[263] The fund was able to give millions of dollars to theorists such as Phillipe Rushton, Arthur Jensen, Thomas Bouchard, and Richard Lynn. The journal *Mankind Quarterly* was set up by the International Association for the Advancement of Ethnology and Eugenics (now the Institute for the Study of Man). Since 1978, the journal has been in the hands of Roger Pearson, who had established the Northern League, dedicated to the interests and solidarity of all Teutonic nations. Pearson was a member of the ultra-Right World Anti-Communist League. He was forced to resign in 1980 because even the members of that organization viewed him as too far to the right and objected to his packing the organization with avowed Nazis. Pearson was active in organizations set up by Jesse Helms, and in the American Security Council, a private group supporting the Contras. He continues to use a letter of thanks from Ronald Reagan in his fundraising. His politics are evident in his argument that "if a nation with a more advanced, more specialized or in any way superior set of genes mingles with, instead of exterminating, an inferior tribe, then it commits racial suicide." These people and groups generated the stock of theory and argument that *The Bell Curve* now seeks to legitimate.

During the second half of the twentieth century, a variety of groups on the extreme have vied for local dominance on the far right wing of American politics, but have been unable to achieve agenda-setting national stature. In the South and California, segregationist and nativist politics achieved temporary dominance in many state legislatures. Racist and nativist groups have combined support for racial segregation with opposition to immigration. In the aftermath of World War II, a network of radical rightist policy organizations, foundations, and intellectuals was able to maintain a national presence. Organizations such as The American Enterprise Institute, the American Heritage Foundation, the Bradley

Foundation, the Olin Foundation, and the Hoover Foundation allowed radical rightist politics to function, even without mass support.

These organizations are central to the genesis and popularization of *The Bell Curve*. The Pioneer Foundation helped to support Jensen, Rushton, Lynn, and many of the theorists showcased in *The Bell Curve*. The Bradley Foundation backed Murray's work, and the Olin Foundation supported the publication of *The Bell Curve* in a way that helped to make it an agenda-setting media event. *The Bell Curve* attempts to introduce into the mainstream the work of a series of theorists of racial inequality (William Shockley, Arthur Jensen, Phillipe Rushton, Roger Pearson, and Richard Lynn). The American Enterprise Institute, where Murray has been a fellow, supported the preparation of the book over a ten year period, and co-sponsored the conference that helped to make the book a media event. Other organizations, such as *The New Republic*, either because they opposed affirmative action or because they wanted to take advantage of the media blitz, expanded the debate, treating the importance of IQ and the possibility of race differences in IQ as an important, legitimate question that needed discussion.

Historically, in the United States, race has been the politically decisive structuring issue in the equality debate.

Racism represents the most vulnerable spot in the New Deal coalition. Programs that raise the standard of living of the society, such as unemployment compensation, public education, or health care, benefit everyone. Nevertheless, there must be a scapegoat for the failure of the cutbacks of the Nixon-Reagan era; and if such programs can be portrayed as benefiting a small group, they lose their mass support. The process by which race and taxes have been combined with a series of social issues (such as criminal rights, homosexuality, and abortion) to separate Southern fundamentalists and Northern ethnics from the New Deal coalition has been often described. Thus—even though the position of women, of children, of blue collar workers, of the middle class, of students, and of many other groups are all deeply threatened—if the issues are perceived in racial terms, inegalitarian positions can dominate. Paradoxically, if the issues are perceived in more explicitly racial terms, the dominant anti-racial consensus of American values will predominate. There has been a fairly sharp decline in explicitly racist attitudes. The fraction of the population opposing intermarriage of blacks and whites declined from 96 percent in the 1940s to 60 percent in the 1980s, while the percentage opposing integration at work declined from 30 percent in the 1940s to 3 percent in the 1980s. But such attitudes still represent a substantial minority that can be organized on a single-issue basis.

The fundamental fact of any campaign against equality in the United States is its dependence on racial divisions for political muscle. In the United States, the legal segregation and subordination of the black population was sustained by racial ideology, nativism, and ethnic theories that proved to be malignant but powerful forces. Their power to unite inegalitarian positions and to gain mass support makes them an irresistible temptation to the political Right. We have noted that racial/ethnic conflict is the principal force destroying societies in the world today; and history has demonstrated that no society is so educated, so industrialized, or so homogeneous that it cannot be torn apart by it.

When people are separated by skin color, religion, language, custom, or other ethnic signs into distinct "peoples," and when, moreover, one of those peoples holds an advantage with regard to land, jobs, political power, or other resources, a situation of great malignant potential is created. It is a nearly irresistible temptation for the dominant members of the privileged group to appeal to the solidarity of the whole group for support, just as the Bourbon landholders in the South were able to dominate the white lower class by appealing to racism.[264] The result is usually against the interest of the mass of the dominant group. While racism in the South may have ensured that southern white workers had higher wages than southern black workers, it also ensured that those wages were lower than those of Northern workers or farmers, white or black.[265] Dominant groups can usually determine the dominant ideology. When groups characterized by some cultural, religious, or skin-color difference engage in conflict, justified by ideologies of superiority, a dynamic of escalation, retaliation, and conflict is set in motion that can take on a life of its own. In such a conflict, there are often groups and individuals that stress individual variation, but that position does not reduce the main dynamic of polarization and conflict. Indeed, such individualistic positions may aid the creation of disparities.

While the dynamics of such situations are far from fully understood, it is clear that the social dynamic makes individuals sensitive to slights or attacks on any member of his or her group by any member of the other group. Anything perceived as an attack on "my group," "my family," "my culture" or "my people" is perceived as grounds for retaliation on any member of the other group. Further, since the perceptions of all will be filtered through their contacts with members of their own group, conflict escalates. Arguably a central dynamic of social development is toward more inclusive conceptions of citizenship and community (Knapp, 1994), but "primordial" ties still have immense power. When the signs that distinguish a group are clearly visible, so that members of one group cannot "pass," this dynamic becomes even more powerful, and such conflicts can escalate indefinitely to the point of genocide. Thus, those who summon this genie cannot be fully aware of what they are doing, for the genie is not easily put back in the bottle. Nevertheless, the temptation is often irresistible because of the powerful political forces unleashed. Race is one of very few forces capable of directly mobilizing people to attack each other. Thus, racism has commonly produced the shock troops or black shirts for an assault on equality. If social services are perceived as benefiting an ethnic minority, support for them dries up among the majority. This perception is encouraged by myths such as that of the predominantly black welfare recipient, but the mere fact that a minority is disadvantaged will promote the myth. Race then becomes the Achilles heel of the New Deal coalition.[266] Politicians are tempted to exploit the force of racism as a single issue, while maintaining the forms of common citizenship. Thus, in contemporary cases of racial mobilization, it is disguised as something else, as religion, as family values, as states rights, as efficient educational or occupational allocation, as reaffirming American culture, or as scientific bad news about human inequality.

Academic racism and social theory play a role in the transformation of passively racist sentiments into escalating race war.

Thus, it appears that racism takes different forms, governed by different dynamics, and that academic racism can play a crucial role in the transformation from one to the other. There is a mass form of racism, an endemic, chronic set of cultural orientations, rooted in social structures of inequality, competition, segregation, and domination. This form appears to change slowly because it is deeply rooted in slowly-changing social structures and in childhood socialization. But there is also another form of racism—consisting of the active mobilization of racial and ethnic groups around explicit racial ideologies. Due to processes of escalation and conflict, this is volcanic and discontinuous. The degree of cultural and social anti-Semitism in Germany was not qualitatively different in the Germany of 1920, 1935, 1950 and 1965, but the actual social policies and political mobilization were qualitatively different.

Academic racism in the United States over the last generation has tended to be individualistic. Academic theory of all kinds probably has had little effect on the passive mass of sentiments and beliefs, although some theorists suggest that academic anti-racist thought may have helped the decline of explicitly prejudiced attitudes over the last generation, in conjunction with larger political and social forces. On the other hand, academic thought on racism almost certainly has a very important role in the emergence of the second, overt, politically-mobilized form. Although it does not change people's feelings, it does affect whether they get expressed in newspaper editorials and public speeches, and thus, their active mobilization. If David Duke or others like him are to move from the margins into the political mainstream, if they are to form the shock troops of a new assault on equality, it is necessary that theorists with respectable scientific and scholarly credentials argue the legitimacy of the positions, questions, and issues of race inferiority. However, to achieve that, it is not necessary that writers such as Phillipe Rushton or Richard Lynn be accepted as representing scientific truth. Academic theory does not lead; it legitimizes. Indeed, given the unstable and mixed character of the alliances on the political Right, it might be a disadvantage to be too closely tied to any particular racist analyst. Rather, it is necessary only that such theorists be accepted as raising an important and legitimate question and a plausible point of view. Politicians and newspaper columnists can then elaborate and build such theories. *The Bell Curve* represents a qualitative change, opening the door to the legitimation of racist theories.

Racial stereotypes are a main support for views that people are intrinsically unequal and that social policies such as public education, public housing or public health are utopian because they cast pearls before swine. Herrnstein and Murray maintain that their individualist analysis is nonracist because it stresses variation within groups as well as between them. The fact of the matter is that almost every page of *The Bell Curve* utilizes and reinforces racial stereotypes, and attempts to legitimize the work of other theorists who do so.

The ideological uses of racism should not distract us from even more dangerous aspects of this game. The incorporation into the mainstream of the body of theorists justifying the elimination or expulsion of the black population, coupled with the present increased activity of extremist groups acting on the basis of those ideas, changes the whole balance of forces within the Right and within American politics. It is a malignant change.

A comparison of *The Bell Curve* with Dinesh D'Sousa's *The End of Racism* and Gingrich's *Contract with America* shows the essential basis of the contemporary assault on equality.

The Bell Curve binds together a reductionist analysis of social problems with moral individualism, but it operates within the larger structure of theoretical arguments on the right wing of the Republican party. While *The Bell Curve* defends a biogenetic argument predicated on economic efficiency, D'Sousa pursues a moral argument against cultural relativism. The arguments agree that illegitimate sources of racial inequality have disappeared. They disagree as to whether to ascribe the remaining inequalities to biological or cultural deficits. They appeal to different groups.

Herrnstein and Murray appeal to the orienting assumptions of most business people and economists, as well as to the elitist assumptions of some psychometricians, educators and personnel management theorists. D'Sousa appeals to academics, intellectuals, and media spokespersons concerned with defending western values against multiculturalism. Newt Gingrich, in the Republican mainstream, maintains some distance from either position and utilizes the analysis politically.

The Congress of 1995 replaced the loose coalition of conservative groups operating on pragmatic grounds with a highly disciplined and ideologically motivated group and program. Specifically, values of liberty, limited government, opportunity and self-reliance were used to justify massive cutbacks in social programs in order to enable tax cuts for the wealthy. Values of accountability and local autonomy were used to justify procedural changes, making it harder for the poor to obtain social services and easier for the wealthy to cut back such services.

The tone and rhetoric of *The Bell Curve*, with its aseptic graphs and ostensibly neutral tone, is very different from that of the *Contract with America*, with its rhetorical appeals to liberty, limited government, opportunity, self-reliance, accountability, and local autonomy. The analytical individualism (or reductionism) of *The Bell Curve* is not identical to the moral individualism that appears in its final chapters and in the *Contract with America*. Neither implies the other. But they have an elective affinity and they complement each other. The central structures of *The Bell Curve* mount a five-step argument that is indispensable to the program of the political Right. The link between values, argument, and program is forged, and the program then takes on a life and direction of its own. Let us examine what is used to what effect. It is a path into an abyss. Along that path, more overtly racist theorists and groups, whom Herrnstein and Murray or Gingrich would disavow, come to the fore. The connection between these more overtly racist theorists and those under review here is not some subtle nuance of tone or implication of logic. Rather, what connects them is the natural consequences of the actions that they advocate and the groups that they activate.

Step One: The final argument presents the meritocratic cognitive elite not only as the economically viable part of society—those who can contribute to the modern economy—but as the carriers of the superior culture of the nation. These are the totally "good" citizens. Others are by definition unworthy both as producers and consumers in the modern economy. In this analysis, the age-old superiority of the higher social class is supported and upheld. But the argument goes further. The position of individuals in the class structure is necessary and just because it represents the triumph of the American ideal of equal opportunity. Obscuring all the informal structures that maintain family position in the class hierarchy over time, the New Right enshrines (unequal) individual achievement based on ability as the determinants of class position. Thus a fundamental value is linked to observed outcomes in society. For those who cannot achieve, the failure lies within themselves.

Step Two: Because individual failure is a consequence of different genes, inferior individual makeup, government intervention to improve individual chances in life is misguided. The view that inequalities, and all the social problems known to be related to them, are biogenetic serves to minimize the benefit of social programs designed to address those inequalities. All such programs—Head Start, remedial education, affirmative action—fail to improve the chances of the more limited, and further take resources from those who properly deserve them.

Step Three: Morality and the sanctity of the family are invoked to oppose the new freedoms of women to marry only if they wish, and to divorce if marital life becomes insupportable. Illegitimacy and divorce, the result of dumb actions of dumb women, are presented as undercutting both the family and moral order. Women must be punished, not rewarded, for such actions. Rather than daycare, nutritional programs, and child allowances, shame and hardship must be visited upon such women. Having minimized the benefit of any social programs, the analysis proceeds to inflate their costs by arguing that their indirect effect is to undermine the family, as well as the biological integrity of the society, by encouraging unmarried and unfit individuals to reproduce.

Step Four: Should society seek to ease the burdens of those less successful in life, it is characterized as undercutting individual independence, creating "permanent wards of the state." Thus other American values, equal opportunity, and limited government are woven together in a fabric of values opposing social programs. The specter of the custodial state is raised to suggest that attempts to ameliorate the condition of the poor will merely generate an increasing, voracious mass characterized by insoluble social problems. The analysis then merged with D'Sousa's view that racism is no longer a problem and that attempts to deal with the nonexistent problem undermines legal protection of equal rights and the cultural integrity of the society. While D'Sousa and Gingrich stress the alleged cultural and value deterioration, Herrnstein and Murray raise the specter of dysgenic cognitive deterioration to explain increases in inequality and social problems.

Step Five: In case the public is not yet convinced, the argument trades on the fears generated by the economic insecurity of most Americans to portray a need for ever-increasing taxation to support an ever-expanding federal budget for expanding social programs. The arguments suggests that racial inequalities are natural and self-limiting. Enclaves without jobs, resources, or power, functioning like Indian reservations, are justified as the revival of community and the end of welfare dependency. This final step invokes a spurious compassion to argue that the poor will find their lives enriched if they are left to themselves in a concerted program to return to the ghetto all responsibility for the lives within it.

From the history of the 1890s and the 1930s, as well as the internal logic of racial or class polarization, we have seen that these steps take us to a place where other steps become necessary. A structure of polarization promotes escalating conflicts, both economic and racial. The violence of private groups spurs increased demands for police powers that destroy economic production and stimulate other social problems. *The Bell Curve* not only takes the agenda of the *Contract with America* and provides the underpinnings to connect the values to the program but goes beyond the contract to the basic intent of the New Right. Herrnstein and Murray open up a channel and begin the process of legitimizing the work of theorists committed to programs of race superiority, race war, and race extermination.

Chapter 9

The Assault on Equality

There is a radical assault now occurring on the basic assumptions concerning social equality that have been consensual during the twentieth century.

Until the 1990s, David Duke, former Grand Dragon and public spokesman of the Ku Klux Klan, lived on the margins of the American political system. But in 1990 he mounted a credible campaign for the Louisiana senate, securing 44 percent of the vote, and in 1991 forced a gubernatorial runoff. Although both campaigns were ultimately unsuccessful, they resemble the considerable periods of time when terrorist and racist groups dominated the politics of many states. Are these times about to recur? The Klan is illustrative of many rightist groups waiting in the wings, hoping for a mass legitimacy that will enable them to operate within the political mainstream.

The relationship between the Far Right and the political mainstream is well illustrated by Duke. Besides being a former officer of the Klan, Duke was deeply involved with the anti-Semitic and apocalyptic Christian Identity movement and was the Populist party presidential candidate in 1988.[267] Though the presidential campaign attracted only about 50,000 votes, this movement represented a powerful local presence in some areas. There has been increased mobilization of such political tendencies. Groups on the right wing of the Republican party have been able to affect local politics despite the fact that there has been little or no shift in Americans' stated political opinions. Suitably transformed and legitimated, such groups could have a national presence. That conservative Republicans captured the House of Representatives in 1995 is less significant than the fact that the *Contract with America* represented the single most disciplined, ideologically cohesive position within the government. There has been a proliferation of highly organized, well-funded political initiatives on the far political Right. This growth establishes the context within which Herrnstein and Murray are important. Among the campaigns demonstrating a new political mobilization of right-wing sentiments are California's Proposition 184, the revived multimillion dollar violence initiative stressing biochemical treatment of "violence-prone" urban youth, and the California initiative in opposition to affirmative action. There will be more.

There is disagreement among social theorists as to why a particularly powerful thrust by the Right is occurring at this time, and so any account of it must be speculative. However, a number of interesting and plausible suggestions have been made. One set of explanations centers on structural shifts in the economy that have resulted in lowered mobility chances and rates of growth as well as increased inequality. Structural shifts in the composition of jobs have always been the main source of mobility. By the mid-twentieth century, that had changed. Less than 5 percent of the population now remain on farms, and the main expansion of jobs has not been at the top, but in poorly-paid and insecure service jobs (McDonald's) at the bottom, generating downward rather than upward mobility. For two decades, unemployment has been double the rate previously assumed normal; and full-time jobs have been harder to find. Productivity growth in the new service jobs is low, and so their growth along with that of other jobs at the top reinforces other trends toward inequality, such as the increasing divergence of salaries and wages. Large numbers of people have been losing ground. The structural situation of downward mobility and polarization creates a politically unstable situation, vulnerable to the politics of resentment.[268]

A second set of explanations focuses on the international situation. The present shift visible in the United States has also characterized a number of other countries. The dissolution of the Soviet Union and the relative absence of political activity on the political left has eliminated some of the main focus for groups on the political Right. Groups that had devoted their energy to fighting the Cold War have not disbanded but have been able to direct their attention to domestic politics. At the same time, the expansion of international transportation and communication has increased economic competition. During the post-World War II period, some theorists have suggested, the relative absence of international competition made it possible, and the political competition with the Soviet Union made it necessary, to grant various concessions to organized labor, minorities, and the poor. With the sharpening head-to-head economic competition with Japan, a united Europe, and the elimination of political competition, there is a move to eliminate concessions to workers.[269] The growth of multinational corporations has undermined workers' benefits that had been obtained politically. Multinationals can move their productive facilities to locations where there are the cheapest wages, and they dispose of more resources than most national governments, vastly more resources than the potential political opposition. This enables them to use political action committees, lobbies, foundations, and other means to attract political support for whatever policies they require.

While some aspects of these changes and their political correlates are new, others recapitulate a familiar historical pattern. Extending back to the 1970s, most incomes have been stagnating. Periods of downward mobility, stagnation, and polarization have always encouraged the political growth of both the Left and the Right.[270] At the present time, it is the political Right that is most visibly mobilizing. Several theorists have suggested that politics at the present time recapitulate many elements from the Gilded Age and the Roaring Twenties.

The New Right consists of a number of distinct and conflicting groups.

At the present time, the assault on equality has entered a phase that is qualitatively more radical than anything we have seen for more than a generation. Overtly, one finds debates dominated by the issues of local autonomy, individualism, and opposition to affirmative action, the progressive income tax, or public health and education. Behind these conflicts, one finds the mobilization of groups who believe that races are intrinsically unequal and that social policy must be directed toward the elimination of threatening populations.

Periods of downward mobility and polarization have traditionally encouraged the growth of racial violence and a general sharpening of political conflicts. The conception of a political Left, pushing for greater equality, and a political Right, defending existing privilege, simplifies a very complex structure. Often, the fundamental disagreement in politics appears to focus on the issue of equality, with a political Left urging greater equality and a political Right supporting inequality. The issue of big government vs. a minimal government often results from the Left-Right dichotomy, inasmuch as the economic system intrinsically produces inequality while there is more acceptance of the principle of equality in other spheres such as the family. But it is not really correct to say that the disagreement between Left and Right is over the issue of equality; rather, the disagreement has to do with the kind of equality. In contrast to earlier times, when inequality was taken to be part of the natural order, most political positions today call for some type of equality.[271]   In the United States, values of equality are widely accepted, but equality of what? Equality of resources, equality of rights, equality of opportunity, equality of utilities, social equality, equal moral value, or equalizing capacity to act as a member of the society all have different political and social implications. Equalizing any one of those ensures the inequality of others. The New Right often uses the notion that each person should be treated exactly the same to attack programs oriented to equal opportunity, equal moral concern, social equality, or the assurance of equal capacities. If a child living in the street or in a housing project is not getting enough to eat, then these latter criteria will require that the government treat him or her differently from the child in an affluent suburb—that it give him or her something to eat. But it is always possible for the New Right to revert to a kind of Spencerian argument that it is not fair (it is not equal treatment) to give that child something we don't give to others. Since we are committed to many kinds of equality there is a balance between two opposed tendencies, which can have a complex dynamic.

On the far right of the Republican party, there are contradictory tendencies. The enterprise of taking away benefits and programs that already exist is a far more radical one than that of resisting the institutionalization and expansion of programs. If such an enterprise is to be accomplished, at least five distinct right-wing groups have to be coordinated. The central split in the right has been described in different ways.[272] It is a deep contradiction between modernist and anti-modernist positions; between individualist and anti-individualist positions; between libertarian and authoritarian positions; between those wanting fewer government controls and those wanting more government controls; between freedom and order. Each of these has very diverse tendencies, and so very diverse groups have to be coordinated if the Right is to have a cohesive political presence. Some of the particular groups that coalesced with Social Darwinism early in the century do not have a mass presence today.[273] Nevertheless, as earlier, the New Right consists of a coalition between distinct, often conflicting groups.

While Europe and Latin America had an aristocratic Right that defended patrician (i.e., upper class) values and privileges in explicitly anti-individualist and inegalitarian terms, the United States has always defended inequality mainly on the basis of equal natural rights and equal opportunity. The core of the libertarian Right is nineteenth century liberalism, the view that the core accomplishment of the rise of capitalism was the replacement of hierarchy by markets, allowing free choice. This free-market, laissez-faire emphasis was originally articulated by theorists such as Adam Smith, Herbert Spencer, and, more recently, Ludwig Von Mises,

Frederick Hayek, Milton Friedman, and Charles Murray. Many of the central cutbacks and other policies producing greater inequality during the Reagan era were justified in terms of allowing the free market to operate, and the essential thrust of *The Bell Curve* is consistent with this emphasis. It views the capitalist market as governed by an invisible hand which, in the absence of any government controls, eliminates all racial, ethnic, religious, gender, or other privilege.

The free-market Right overlaps with theorists developing a political philosophy of limited government and specifically with legal theorists stressing the original intent of constitutional founders. By the end of the Bush administration, the great majority of members of the Supreme Court were appointees of the Reagan-Bush administrations with extremely conservative views on legal and social issues. This body of legal interpretation represents an essential link between free-market individualists and the concerns of the fundamentalist Christian right on abortion, education, affirmative action, and traditional values. An important strand of American political theory associates liberty with the defense of individual property rights. This theme found one of its classic expressions in Spencer, and is central to the assault on equality. The goal of a return to a kind of small-town social structure featuring local autonomy, individual independence, and strong families is understandably attractive. In that structure, most people could leave their doors unlocked, and they were not exposed to the violence, crime, and drugs that dominate most cities today. Pictures of that social structure are often nostalgic, forgetting the other violence, inequality, and intolerance that existed, and they often ignore the irreversible social changes since then. We cannot go back to family farms, and we would not want to. This ideal of local autonomy drives a number of different agendas on the right seeking moral homogeneity, and it links the modernist, individualist, and libertarian branches of the Right to tendencies that are anti-modernist, anti-individualist, and authoritarian, namely, religious traditionalism, anti-communist nationalism, and racism. The individualist framework of free market and constitutionalist conservatives conflicts with the aims of fundamentalist Christians, nationalists, and segregationists. If those groups are to cooperate in an assault on equality, their disagreements have to be reconciled.

By far the most numerous and important backing of the Far Right has come from traditional religious groups: fundamentalist, evangelical, and Pentecostal Protestants; the conservative branches of the Roman Catholic church; and the Mormon church.[274] Throughout most of the last two centuries, such groups have attacked the immorality of cities. Traditionalist values are offended by urban religious and moral heterogeneity, the breakdown of families and sexual morals, urban crime, and violence. In the twentieth century, social issues such as women's rights, family values, abortion, homosexuality, and prayer in schools have mobilized tradition-alistic religious groups.[275] While the libertarian Right is often modernist and individualist, wishing to reduce the role of government, the tradi-tional religious Right often wishes to expand government support of tra-ditional values. These contradictory tendencies can be reconciled by advocating the expansion of the coercive functions of government but a contraction of social services.

In advocating expansion of police powers, the traditionalistic Right has often been able to join hands with a fourth branch of the Right, anti-communist and patriotic nationalist groups. At times such as the red scare of the 1920s or the McCarthy movement of the 1950s, these groups have been able to dominate the national agenda, and they have always been a powerful force. Like the religious Right, the nationalist Right ad-vocates an affirmative role for government, coupled with a specific con-ception of what distinctive American values are or should be. The collapse of the Soviet Union would seem to many to leave this group without an antagonist—but for a nationalist the world is filled with an-tagonists, and so is the domestic society.

Finally, all four of these positions on the right have very complex rela-tions to a fifth cluster of movements and views, namely, to racist move-ments of many different kinds. It has been less than a generation since the abolition of de jure segregation and Jim Crow in the South. Explicitly segregationist groups have never lost their dominance in many areas. Ra-cial and ethnic bigotry is an immensely powerful political force. In American history, racial conflicts have repeatedly escalated to national mass violence as in the 1860s, during World War I, the 1940s, and the 1960s. The complex linkage of racist movements with some forms of evangelical, Pentecostal, and fundamentalist Christianity is well illus-trated by the case of David Duke.

To say that these five politically powerful groups constitute the politi-cal Right is not to say that they are identical. They have contradictions with each other. For instance, a racist program of segregation and as-sumed biological inferiority of blacks contradicts some positions of each of the other four groups, which, in turn, have other powerful contradictions with each other. Because of the sharp political conflicts between different elements on the right, the task of uniting them has been insoluble for the last generation. *The Bell Curve's* proposal of a place for everyone repre-sents an attempt to unite them on the basis of genetic differences in ability.

Elitist assumptions, which have become entrenched among some psy-chometricians and personnel management theorists, loosely connect them to racist views, and package the whole in the language of economic productivity and efficiency designed to appeal to business people.

D'Sousa's *The End of Racism* links other conservative intellectuals with other publics. D'Sousa takes the concerns of intellectuals in the "culture wars," who defend that idea of an authoritative interpretation of the Constitution and an authoritative cannon of high Western culture, and packages them in language designed to appeal to the Christian Coalition. Since Herrnstein and Murray and D'Sousa develop analyses that trace social problems to defective individuals, they provide crucial ideological supports for the general opposition to federal programs and redistributive policies. The core of this mainspring of conservative policies is well illustrated by Newt Gingrich. His book, *To Renew America*,[276] is a political counterpart to mobilizing the politics of virtue and nostalgia for the small town in a high-tech suburban era. Together, they represent a radical transformation in American politics.

Gingrich represents the coordination of the groups of the traditionalist right and its alliance with the modernist Right represented by Murray.

To Renew America is a synthetic work analogous to *The Bell Curve*, consolidating positions on the traditionalist right that reaffirm traditional values. Gingrich's central concern is to reaffirm traditional values. Central to this reaffirmation and renewal is the belief that some behavior ought not to be tolerated:

> I believe that we are at the end of the era of tolerating alcoholism, addiction, spouse and child abuse, parental indifference, and adult irresponsibility... There is no reason that views on acceptable standards of behavior for the poor cannot change as well. (*To Renew America*, p. 77)

Gingrich does not specify the respects in which we have been overly tolerant of alcoholism, addiction, abuse, parental indifference, smoking, or drunk driving—or what ceasing to tolerate them would look like. The central assumption that Gingrich shares with Herrnstein and Murray is that defective individuals (similar to Spencer's good-for-nothings, vagrants, and sots) are the source of social problems.[277] Few people advocate alcoholism, addiction, abuse, and the like. Racism is a somewhat different case that depends on how it is defined. In any case, there are very serious questions about what Gingrich means by not tolerating these behaviors, and there are other questions about how effective criminal penalties are for enforcing this refusal to tolerate such behaviors. Prohibition was a striking demonstration of the ineffectiveness of criminalization with respect to alcohol. While Gingrich advocates tougher criminal penalties, he expects that the renewal of American values will make criminal enforcement less necessary. More important, Gingrich believes that the renewal will bring about an opportunity society that will obviate the need for welfare and social programs through an increased value of individual responsibility and free enterprise.[278] This opportunity society turns out to be a different form of the Herrnstein and Murray meritocracy.

Since it is mainly a condensed, edited, programmatic summary of Gingrich's twenty hours of lectures on American civilization, *To Renew America* is organized in sets of pigeon-holing, programmatic lists: five core American values; six major challenges; eight major changes to eliminate the welfare state; four main points of W. Edwards Deming's management; five major distinctions between Second Wave and Third Wave education, and so on. Gingrich does not refer to *The Bell Curve*. There are sharp contradictions between the views of the traditionalist Right, who believe that we need to enforce traditional values, and the views of the free-market Right, who advocate individual autonomy. For example, Murray believes that an unmarried biological father should have no responsibilities or rights with regard to a child and that paternity suits should be abolished, while Gingrich believes that paternal responsibilities should be more strictly enforced.

Yet, behind all the specific divergences between *To Renew America* and *The Bell Curve*, there are deep commonalities and instructive linkages. The two works depend upon each other and are actually Siamese twins. They each define individual autonomy and collective values in such as way as to try to bring about a union between the different positions. Only with the rise of the traditional Right does *The Bell Curve* have a readership and political force. Only with the backing of ostensibly social-scientific analyses in *The Bell Curve* do Gingrich's policy recommendations connect to his value statements. The linkage and the contradictions between the two works show the basic logic and the main dimensions of the assault on equality today.

Gingrich's definition of American values is unusual, and he ignores the social science literature on contemporary political opinion and on how and why norms and values change with social development. Gingrich presents an idiosyncratic view of core American values ("basic principles that form the heart of our civilization"): (1) the Judeo-Christian ethic, (2) individual responsibility, (3) the spirit of free enterprise, (4) the spirit of invention and discovery, and (5) the total quality management of W. Edwards Deming.

There are problems with many of these. For example, the first point seems to suggest that Buddhist, Islamic, or atheistic persons are not real Americans, just as many groups on the right believe that Jews are not real Americans, or that Catholics are not. Many people would maintain that the fourth point, the spirit of invention and discovery, is not a basic principle. Gingrich's list naturally omits basic equality. However, the most idiosyncratic definition of core values is in Gingrich's elevation of the thought of the management specialist Deming to a core American value.[279] To take Deming's approach to management as a core American value is strange. We would describe Deming's approach as a set of techniques now faddishly popular among some businessmen. The elevation of Deming's thought serves to associate Gingrich's position with progress. It also illustrates the ways that Gingrich is willing to elaborate on American values in the interests of his political agenda. In any case, it is hard to see how reaffirming such values will obviate the need for social programs and eliminate alcoholism, addiction, abuse, parental indifference, smoking, drunk driving, or racism, without other social changes.

One is left with the idea that tougher enforcement and shame will eliminate deviance. Most social scientists would say that it is naive to believe that tougher enforcement of rules, accompanied by emphasis on shame, always leads to reduction of deviance. Reduction of tolerance does not always strengthen compliance with the norms. When enforcement or shame leads to stigmatization and ghettoization (i.e., formation of a segregated counterculture), it will often increase the sanctioned behavior. Prisons and reformatories can become schools of crime, and so the effect of affirmation and enforcement of norms is more complex than Gingrich makes it seem. If the norms run against the structure of the situation, enforcement may lead to contempt for the law, as in the case of Prohibition in the 1920s. We have noted that increasing pressure on mothers with young children to enter the work force, while failing to provide subsidized daycare or job training, can only increase "parental indifference" and may result in children left at home alone.

The idea is central to the various forces that form the traditionalist Right that Gingrich aims to unite and consolidate. He is particularly concerned to represent himself as anti-racist, in opposition to the old southern Democrats. The maintenance of Republican domination in the South requires that it unite with a segment of black voters, and this is one of the reasons that Gingrich maintains considerable distance from *The Bell Curve*, arguing that values, rather than genes, produce dependence. We have seen that Herrnstein and Murray also represent themselves as anti-racist. While appealing to theorists such as Roger Pearson and Phillipe Rushton, they argue that there exist genetic group differences but that each individual should be treated as an individual. This opposes individualist racism, while legitimating institutional racism. Gingrich claims that racist views have declined, but whether this is true depends on one's definition of racism. For example, the activity of racist movements (measured by the number of reported hate crimes) has increased.

Gingrich, like Herrnstein and Murray, conceives of racism as a set of individual attitudes, ideas, and sentiments, rather than mutually reinforcing structures of segregation, inequality, and deprivation. Yet the analysis of cumulative causation shows that attitudes, ideas, and sentiments are always connected with such social structures, including structures of wealth and power. To deplore the attitudes, while leaving intact the inequalities on which they feed, is to express a set of pious hopes.

While Gingrich is opposed to multiculturalism, his conception of American values leads him to avoid conceptions of biological difference and inferiority. Nevertheless, as with Herrnstein and Murray, the essential point is not what he says but what he advocates doing. Gingrich's aim of reducing the Federal Government's involvement in social policy and returning programs to the states will increase racial inequalities. During the heyday of Jim Crow it was not what the government did that established institutional racism, but rather what it failed to do.

Gingrich's concept of an "opportunity society" synthesizes inegalitarian themes from the New Right.

In place of the loose, opportunistic, and highly pragmatic coalition of conservative and right-wing groups, we now have a disciplined and ideologically coherent, agenda-setting right, which Gingrich describes as a "new American Revolution". To unite the scattered forces of the Far Right and minimize conflicts between the modernist and the traditionalist Right, Gingrich stresses values of independence, entrepreneurship, and limited government. Unlike "a place for everyone," the concept of an "opportunity society" emphasizes the up side of unregulated competition, opportunity and development, while Herrnstein and Murray emphasize the down side, the inevitable poverty and failure of millions at the bottom. The two arguments require each other. Gingrich uses the popular theories of the Tofflers[280] to produce a vision of the high-tech future to be unleashed by government cutbacks. He asks the reader to imagine waking up to a wall-sized high-definition television showing the surf off Maui, and then doing Stairmaster while catching up on the home office via communications devices, avoiding traffic and reducing air pollution (*To Renew America*, p. 55).

This image gives a fair picture of Gingrich's "opportunity society," which is another version of an inegalitarian meritocracy. It is consistent with American values of fairness, equity and equal moral concern only if Herrnstein and Murray are right and the invisible hand of economic efficiency forces employers to give everyone their "just desserts." Not everyone will have wall-sized TVs, Stairmasters, and telecommuting work arrangements, and so Gingrich's analysis needs that of Herrnstein and Murray to account for the Americans who will not have these amenities.

The argument that abilities are inherited is crucial to justifying inherited social position. When Herrnstein and Murray claim that it does not matter whether intellectual ability is genetically inherited or socially transmitted from parents to children, this provides both a disclaimer for their genetic theories and a nonaggression pact between different groups on the right. Stress on family socialization allows a synthesis of the concerns of traditional patrician conservatives and fundamentalists.

Gingrich, D'Sousa, Herrnstein, and Murray all represent their analyses as being anti-racist. They affirm that there is a central choice that has to be faced today between bureaucratic federal programs and the revival of local and private initiatives. For Gingrich, this is mainly to be accomplished by giving powers back to states and voluntary programs. Historically, racism, sexism, and other discriminatory practices are often justified in terms of giving power to states, communities, families, or individuals. Institutional racism, sexism, or other inegalitarian processes that depend on the Matthew principle thrive on the program of decentralization and elimination of government regulation. They are naturally consistent with individualism, which is why these theorists systematically ignore and deny such processes. Gingrich's opposition to group rights, like D'Sousa's and like Herrnstein and Murray's stress on individual variation around different group means not only is consistent with institutional racism but also is the main justification for it.

With regard to welfare, Gingrich proposes eight steps to eliminate the welfare state and replace it with an "opportunity society." The first of these, and the most important, is to adopt Olasky's[281] use of the distinction between the deserving and the undeserving poor, and its corollary, the distinction between "caretaking" (which merely gives people money) and "true caring" (which transforms the recipient). He argues that true caring requires detailed knowledge impossible for government bureaucracies, and that government caretakers can do nothing more than provide indiscriminate handouts (*To Renew America*, p. 75). But will the absence of federal programs lead to private ones? Is it possible for private charity to reach the bulk of the poor? Is private charity more effective because it involves true caring? Do private programs meet social needs more effectively? The year 1995 saw the largest of the programs of private philanthropy, the Foundation for New Era Philanthropy, squander $500 million that people had painstakingly accumulated and contributed to churches and charities. Some of the money was siphoned off on huge consulting fees and illegal skimming by those who controlled the fund, while the rest evaporated in what was essentially a Ponzi scheme. Like the reduction of regulation that produced the savings and loan catastrophe, losing hundreds of billions of dollars that the public now has to repay, privatization of social services does not provide efficiency but a complete lack of accountability. Moreover, private charities, even when they are not grossly inefficient as in this case, are inherently and essentially unequal and uneven in their coverage. This is a consequence of their being more discriminating and selective, but it is also a function of accidents of regional, religious, or group coverage. While it is true that the emotional context of receiving charity is different from that of obtaining a right to which one is entitled, the difference is not that charity produces the attitude of independence. On the contrary, it produces the attitude of dependence.

Ultimately Gingrich's "true caring" is driven by cost-cutting, rationalized by an individualist model of social outcomes as a simple product of individual actions and values:

> People can create jobs as well as find jobs. It is just as important to convince the poor that they can create their own jobs, as it is to help them find jobs. (*To Renew America*, p. 80)

The core of his social theory lies in this idea: if people have the correct (entrepreneurial) values, they will create remunerative jobs for themselves. It ignores the larger social and economic forces that have reduced the proportion of the work force self-employed or employed in small businesses. It is a vision of the frontier, neatly cleared of Indians, but the vision includes no provision to give people the resources that are the equivalent of land. For many communities, the proposal "Let them create their own jobs" is like the proposal for Indians during the last century, "Let them eat grass."

Gingrich's solution to social problems of poverty is the belief that reassertion of American values will bring a burst of growth giving opportunities to all. This is the rationale for abolishing the progressive income tax and corporate taxes in favor of a flat tax or regressive consumption taxes, which would further increase inequality. The belief in that burst of growth is a fantasy. There is no evidence that it would occur, and substantial evidence that it would not. Even if it did, poverty would not be eliminated.[282] During the last decades, substantial growth has coexisted with intractable poverty at the bottom. A central role of *The Bell Curve* is to abandon the expectation that a rising tide can or should lift all boats. In practice, Gingrich's stress on values merges with Herrnstein and Murray's stress on biogenetic intelligence. Poverty is blamed on the poor. The pictures gain their plausibility only from nostalgia for a return to the idealized small town and local community.

For all groups on the Right, inherited inequality represents a central problem.

Despite their many theoretical disagreements, all groups on the right must appeal to establishment, middle-class, and upper-class groups for support, against minority, poor, and working-class groups. Yet, for any of these groups a direct defense of inherited property and social position is politically suicidal. Therefore, as we saw in Chapter Eight, they must demonize the poor to destroy public compassion, while representing their own position as true caring. Gingrich asserts that there are, or will be, opportunities for everyone with good values (i.e., everyone not addicted, abusive, irresponsible), while Herrnstein and Murray are waiting in the wings to explain away the inevitable failure of the man or woman who works hard and plays by the rules but whose below-minimum-wage jobs leave him or her in poverty, vulnerable to illness or to a company's move to Brazil. Herrnstein and Murray do not say that a society with a place for everyone is a society organized to keep everyone in his or her place, but the meritocratic caste corollary ensures that that is the case.

While the view of inherited caste position is one that appeals to some privileged groups, it runs counter to basic American values. Not only have those American values not been directed by a vision of society ruled by a virtuous few, but their central thrust has been motivated by the ideal of equal moral concern and directed squarely against those visions. Essential appeals of Christianity and of our constitution have been directed against established power and inherited inequality of social position. A series of often bloody struggles have reduced the extent of inherited social position.

In theory, the question of inheritance and the question of inequality are distinct. It is logically possible to have a society in which there are relatively small differences in wealth and power but in which social position is inherited. Many farming and peasant communities seem to embody this model of ascribed egalitarianism. Similarly, an inegalitarian society could logically exist in the absence of inherited social position, producing a meritocracy. Unequal positions could, in the abstract, be allocated by lottery, by religious devotion, by political commitment, or by economic productivity. However, in fact, in all societies inheritance and inequality are tightly linked. Parents always wish to pass their advantages on to their children, and so great inequalities produce inequalities of opportunity and inheritance of social position.

American public opinion is uncomfortable with privilege, which leads to ambivalent views about the effects of advantaged backgrounds. The educational system has long been the main place where the society has tried to give some opportunity to all children. It is unable to compensate for family disadvantages and equalize opportunity, and even within the educational system there is a Matthew principle that rewards those who already have other resources. Universal free public education was a major concession won for all. It not only allowed some level of opportunity for all, but a literate, educated population had many benefits for the whole society. The radical character of the present assault on equality is demonstrated partly by its attacks on this principle. We have seen that Herrnstein and Murray stress innate, biologically determined, insuperable obstacles to educational success for disadvantaged students, and they represent the structures of education and employment as already meritocratic. If employers need mainly intelligence and if education has little effect on intelligence, then most expenditure on education is wasted.

Gingrich proposes a different but related attack. He believes that "the greatest single misallocation of taxpayers' money has been the unionized monopolies of inner city education" (*To Renew America*, p. 82). One implication of this belief is his support of the shift to private education using voucher systems. The funding constraints on such proposals always ensure that they are give-backs to the parents who already use private schools, allowing only a few to flee the public schools while reducing the resources of the public schools even further for those who remain. Moreover, in his concept of "Third Wave Education" oriented to learning rather than education, Gingrich also proposes a more general attack, rationalized as a shift to high-tech, lifetime, achievement oriented, learner-focused learning. While his proposals are somewhat impressionistic, it is possible to see their thrust.

His principal example of an alternative to bureaucratic education is the Earning by Learning program, in which volunteers visit housing projects and pay children to read books. It is, indeed, relatively inexpensive to pay children to read and to develop a list of questions by which volunteers can check whether the children have really read the books. It is possible that such a learning program could supplement education. The program assumes that the only problems the children have is that they are unmotivated, and that the way to create motivation is to pay them. However, the education, which Gingrich opposes, does and must do a great deal more than hand children books and pay them to read them. Gingrich aims to replace education, not to give the children an education. His other options to "replace education with learning" are similar. In a learner-focused society, you would have other options, such as calling upon the services of a learning counselor. With his or her guidance, you could consider a variety of learning tracks: traditional classroom, apprenticeship with a "true master," computer bulletin boards. It would resemble a library more than a traditional school (*To Renew America*, p. 145).

The programs seem to abolish any curricula whatsoever, in favor of a kind of learning supermarket. Such a supermarket would give absolutely free play to the Matthew principle. Whether one would be able to use such resources effectively would depend on the previous resources that one had been given, including resources such as knowing what materials are important. Gingrich is particularly opposed to the idea that the content of higher education should be influenced by educators rather than by the marketplace. He describes education as out of control:

> First, campuses are run for the benefit of the faculty, not the students. Second, tenured faculty have become increasingly out of touch with the rest of America, rejecting the culture of the people who pay their salaries. Third, there is an acceptance of higher costs without effective management by administrators. (*To Renew America*, p. 219)

Gingrich is quite correct that structures of professionalism, expertise, or tenure conflict with simple market principles. Gingrich proposes a kind of educational supermarket, in which buyers obtain whatever they want, with administrations assuring that the most marketable items (courses, degrees) are produced at the lowest cost. Gingrich ignores the ineffective and degraded character of such education. There are reasons that educators are assured some independence, both from students and from administrators, to decide the requirements of degrees. Whether in physics, history, medicine, law, English, economics, or any other field, there are all kinds of requirements necessary for a mastery of the field but unpopular with students. In a "learning" supermarket, all such education would be eliminated.

Countries such as Japan, whose educational systems appear to be notably successful, are not characterized by "learning supermarkets." When the market will not provide the outcomes needed by the whole society, course requirements, faculty autonomy, tenure, accreditation, and a host of other restrictions on market principles are necessary. To bring education under control in the sense that Gingrich seems to suggest—to eliminate tenure, to insist that faculty mirror the culture of the rest of America, and to make administrative decisions rest upon the bottom line—is likely to degrade education as a whole.

Gingrich, like Herrnstein and Murray, is a master at packaging radical proposals in such a way as to make them seem moderate. The ugly and violent character of the actions that can flow from his assumptions are covered with a silken handkerchief of rhetoric about American values. The rise of hate groups and right-wing militias all over the country shows the practical implications of many of these views of genetics and politics. Herrnstein and Murray argue that there is a qualitative difference in the cognitive abilities of minorities; hate groups express the view that minorities are subhuman and should be excluded or eliminated. Both Gingrich and Herrnstein and Murray argue that the federal government has no business doing most of the things that it does; the bombing of the federal building in Oklahoma City in April of 1995 shows the way that many people perceive this message. The practical implications drawn from these ideas often are not moderate.

Conclusion: 1. We are at a time of choice.

Both *The Bell Curve* and Gingrich's *To Renew America* describe the present time as a time of choice, a fork in the road. At a fork, everything depends on the question of which paths lead where. We agree that the present time is one of choice, but we think that these authors have given a distorted and misleading map of the paths and options. For Gingrich, the choice is between a rosy path, that reasserts the values of American civilization, family, independence, and entrepreneurship, and a dark path to dependence, bureaucracy, and stagnation:

> The choice between these two futures is stark and decisive. Either we will pull ourselves together for the effort or we will continue to decay. There is virtually no middle ground." (*To Renew America*, p. 5)

For Gingrich, federal programs weigh down the society, and when that dead weight is lifted by slashing federal programs, devolving powers to the states, eliminating professional monopolies, and encouraging private voluntarism, the society will take off.

As we have seen, the "place for everyone" in *The Bell Curve* ascribes social problems to biologically defective people and gives two branches to Gingrich's dark path of dependency, one leading to the custodial state and the other to a "Latin American" structure of privilege. Herrnstein and Murray and Gingrich propose decentralization and ignore or deny the Matthew principle processes that, in the absence of checks, automatically produce polarization and reinforcement of inequalities. They argue that voluntarism, private charity, and the states will produce effective programs to solve social problems, although it has been repeatedly demonstrated that they do not and cannot. They suggest that the poor are poor or are brutalized because we have given them too much and made life too easy for them.

Gingrich, Herrnstein and Murray, and D'Sousa cooperate on an assault against the main programs that limit inequalities of opportunity, life chances, or resources for children of different groups. In each case, the assault is carried out in the name of equality. In the United States, a commitment to social equality, equal life chances, and equal moral concern is deeply rooted. As Sen (1992) has pointed out, virtually all moral and political writings call for equalizing something. Equalizing any one thing will tend to increase inequality among other things. While the dangers of allowing the Matthew principle and cumulative causation free play are widely understood, there is less agreement on specific cases. Therefore equality is always attacked in the name of equality. For Gingrich, an "opportunity society" aims to produce equal opportunity for those with the correct values; for Herrnstein and Murray, a society with "a place for everyone" will give equal rewards to those with good cognitive abilities; for D'Sousa, to those with the appropriate culture. The alleged inequality of the distribution of those values, abilities or culture is a kind of act of Providence, used to legitimate gross inequalities in food, pay, jobs, health, education and welfare. Exactly as in Aristotle's justification of slavery, the inequalities are reinforced by the very inequalities they are used to legitimate. It is the classic case of blaming the victim.

In contrast to these authors, we think that our society faces a fundamental choice today, but we think they misrepresent the choices. The modern world shows increased competition in which the basic literacy, productivity, and societal inclusion of those at the bottom determines many other options of the society.[283] Ideals of societal inclusion and social equality become more important, not less.[284] The unfettered operation of the market will not lead to an "opportunity society" where everyone has Stairmasters and wall-sized videos. Nor will it lead to a return to a kind of small town America with "a place for everyone." Rather, in the absence of effective governmental policies to limit privilege and distribute opportunities, vicious cycles of cumulative causation operate, taking from the poor and giving to the rich. In the absence of social controls, competition in a capitalist economy leads to increased inequality and growing pockets of social pathology. Gingrich is certainly right that a fundamental problem of our time is the budget deficit. However, the Nixon and the Reagan years not only produced a budget deficit, but also social deficits. The savings and loan collapse, pollution by toxic wastes, millions of people dying of AIDS, and the collapse of center city schools are examples of the social deficits. Many of these deficits are associated with vicious cycles of cumulative causation. Individualistic analyses of social deficit and social problems obscure their causes and prevent us from addressing them. The increased inequality, segregation, and concentration of poverty that we face today were the consequence of the programs of favoritism for those with wealth and power, which the Right wishes to expand. If a society does not meet the needs of all its citizens, then it has to devote more and more resources to coercion in order to control the escalating conflict that results. If a society does not work to lift its floor—to help its poorer members—then it unleashes social problems for all its members. Both the eugenic elimination of problematic populations and the authoritarian enforcement of dominant norms are illusory solutions.

Conclusion: 2. The central choice concerns the level of inequality we are willing to accept.

Among all the policy arguments that have appeared in the modern world, the linkage of racism, individualism, and elitism is particularly malignant because it turns inequality into an active good. The increased mobilization of the Right, including the publication of works such as *The Bell Curve* and *To Renew America*, signals and aids a decisive shift in the strategy and dynamic of the Right. This is not mainly because of the arguments that they contain explicitly, nor even because of the shift in the point of view that the books espouse. Rather, one must look at the implications of the arguments they contain, the implications of the works that they legitimize, the groups they mobilize, and the objective dynamic that will obtain should their policies be enacted.

To take only one example, Herrnstein and Murray and Gingrich recommend their policy suggestions as democratic. Their analysis defines the presence of federal programs as anti-democratic (for example, that is the basis of Murray's parable of the anthill, where everything not forbidden is required) and also as undermining democracy by the interests of a large bureaucracy. They believe that enforced equality is undemocratic, and "natural" inequality ("opportunity society" or "meritocracy") is democratic. However, the whole notion of natural inequalities is inapplicable to social differences in wealth, income, power, influence, and the like. Those social inequalities are qualitatively larger than natural inequalities such as size or strength, and they take a fundamentally different form. Moreover, there are historical and social variations in social inequality. The degree to which we take from the poor and give to the rich is a social choice. We think that the unchecked operation of General Motors, DuPont, or state governments is not particularly democratic; it is even less democratic than national policies enacted by Congress. The more important point stems from considering the consequences of a large increase in inequality in conjunction with the radical cutback of social services and the increase in the social problems of epidemic TB, AIDS, or virulent racism. We know a fair amount about what causes a complete breakdown of democratic forms. All such breakdowns in the twentieth century have been associated with large and growing inequalities and with the social conflicts that result.[285] Mass revolt, internment, and expulsion of racial minorities have occurred in the American past.

To take another example, the devolution of policies to the states is not a search for better ideas or administration that is closer to the people. It is not only inherently inegalitarian, denying to citizens in some states the rights and services enjoyed in others, but it is also inherently unable to address many problems of inequality. When policies such as tax laws or regulation of pollution vary from state to state, a company can move to areas that give them the most profitable deal, and citizens find themselves unable to exert democratic controls. In the United States, we already put up with high levels of inequality, inequality of schooling, and inequality of citizenship rights. We lead the developed world in rates of poverty of children. Huge burned-out areas of our central cities, immense police forces, and a higher proportion of our citizens in prisons than any other advanced industrialized society are consequences.

It is easy to speak of a fork in the road or a social choice. To demonstrate a diverging dynamic is another matter; and so our analysis must be somewhat tentative and speculative. We think that it is possible to show three things: that there are alternate possible structures; that there is a dynamic propelling each in a different direction; and that choices today determine which track we take. Often, talk about a critical choice or a new revolution is nothing but hype, like advertisements for a revolutionary new toothbrush. But we agree with *To Renew America* and *The Bell Curve* that the United States now faces a critical choice. We think that these books have described the choices and the nature of the diverging paths wrongly, but we think that there is, indeed, a choice to be made.

Alternate possible social structures are defined by the amount of inequality they permit and require. In the United States today there are increasing numbers of people homeless, begging on the street, and dying, neglected, of tuberculosis and AIDS. Changes in the international economy have driven profound changes in America. There are different ways of pursuing international competitiveness.[286] A lean-and-mean strategy requires enormous inequality; but a skilled and flexible work force requires a high social floor. Benetton, Toyota, or Ikea compete in the international economy with a highly educated, skilled work force utilizing technologically advanced equipment; many Third World counties compete by a lean-and-mean structure of low wages and coercive controls. The two do not combine. Education and social infrastructures as they presently exist in the United States do not allow most American workers to even read the instructions needed to use work processes such as those of Benetton, Toyota, or Ikea. The analyses of *The Bell Curve* or *To Renew America* inhibit us from making the investments in infrastructure we need for the high tech route to competitiveness. On the other hand, we can never be as lean-and-mean as Third World countries, characterized by starvation wages of a few dollars a day.

When countervailing forces oppose each other, a situation of great tension is often produced, whose dynamic is often counterintuitive. When each of the forces is governed by a kind of Matthew principle, so that a gain will lead to further power, permitting further gains, one faces a choice between two diverging paths. Compounding social processes almost certainly will drive us in diverging directions, depending on the path we choose today. Social problems of poverty and inequality compound themselves. The presence of extreme inequalities not only generates social problems and social conflicts but it also generates coercive police controls. The dilemmas of equality and equal opportunity are the basis of much of the tension in Western politics. We have seen that a commitment to equal opportunity involves a commitment both to relative equality (since otherwise unequal parents give their children unequal opportunities) and also to inequality (which results from exploiting the opportunities). Over the last two generations, the contradiction has been resolved by moderating private inequalities through public programs of health, education, and welfare to give all children basic opportunities. However the boundaries were drawn, that essential structure has been accepted. Now it is being radically contested by views that all public programs are inefficient, illegitimate, and counterproductive. It is true that such programs cannot and have not counteracted the inequalities generated by the cumulation of advantage. It is even true that, as Murray argues, such programs tend to help most those who need help least. However, the tendency to help those who already have resources is even more characteristic of market strategies in the absence of public programs.

The rhetoric of the New Right is designed to obscure the fact that there is a level of inequality beyond which basic ideals of equal opportunity, social equality, and inclusive community become a hollow pretense. The United States has almost surely passed that level. What is at stake is not merely a disappearance of a "safety net," since that concept often assumes that social arrangements work well for the great bulk of the population. A "safety net" is designed to provide temporary aid to a small number of persons who have experienced some catastrophic problem. However, the social arrangements and public policies reinforcing or countering structures of inequality are far more pervasive than is implied by that analysis.[287] The social theories of *The End of Racism* and *The Bell Curve* embrace an inegalitarian, discriminatory, coercive cast system and try to disguise it as the embodiment of American values and Christian ideals. In the absence of government interference, however, processes operate that ensure that those who have much get more, while those who have little lose even what they have. This means that additional advantages given to those on the top generate still further advantages, leading to polarization. Unless the process is checked, it can only lead to catastrophic breakdown as in the Great Depression and the rise of fascism.

The present time is one in which the mobilization and countermobilization of groups create considerable ambiguity. Because both the Left and the Right consist of heterogeneous coalitions, certain kinds of theories can powerfully influence the power ranking of groups in the coalitions and the path each coalition takes. The conflicting pressures operating within each coalition and within American politics as a whole lead to a dynamic in which small differences today can lead to great divergence later. The political mobilization of groups outside the political system (unions, racial groups, churches, and academic groups) is at least as important as the mobilization within it. The Right is consolidating the action of single-issue and direct-action groups, at the same time that it is trying to remove many decisions from the possibility of influence of the federal government. Programs of the Right implicitly—and increasingly explicitly—formulated in racist terms mount a frontal attack on central structures of opportunity. Vulnerable groups including industrial workers, women, the poor, blacks, Hispanics, Asians, Jews, and other minorities, who together form the overwhelming bulk of the population, are split against each other, and the Spencerian ideal of moral individualism is used to promote their conflict with each other. With a weak response the entire political spectrum will shift to the right, leading to a path of increasing inequality, increasing coercion, segregation, and racism. If there is a strong response, the fundamental issues of equal opportunity and equal human dignity can be posed anew.

Under these circumstances, many advocate a strategy of bending with the wind. "Pragmatic" theorists advocate operating within an increasingly inegalitarian framework of choices and assumptions, usually on the grounds that rebuilding the New Deal coalition requires conforming to the views of white southern fundamentalists and the northern ethnic middle class. One by one, basic principles of civil rights, affirmative action, public education, progressive taxation, or a basic floor of health, education, and welfare are to be abandoned in a search for middle ground. This ignores the processes from outside the political system that generated that "wind" in the first place. It activates and encourages still further assaults from the right and the increasing shift of the whole spectrum of debate. The changed debate of the present era does not result from any change in people's underlying attitudes. Rather, it results from changes in organization, funding, alliances, and actions, often outside the political system.

Many people feel that a strong response is impossible. The immense funding, the political power, the extensive media coverage, and the economic and social resources of the Right give it considerable power.

Academics are tempted to ignore books such as *The Bell Curve* or *To Renew America*. This leaves opponents of the assault feeling increasingly isolated, demoralized, and driven from the public arena, thus setting in motion new attacks. The rise of fascism early in the twentieth century provides case histories of the process. Each group was tempted to keep its head down, and by the time its members were personally attacked, it found it had no allies. The idea that the move to the right is self-limiting is a dangerous myth; political mobilization around ideologies of biological inferiority sets us on a dangerous path. It involves matters of basic principle. The dominance of racist, sexist, inegalitarian, and coercive structures is not predestined. With a strong response from the public, it becomes impossible for such structures to be used in legitimating the policies of the Right. The social sciences can help by exposing the weakness of the arguments used to justify those policies. Humans are social beings: the bulk of scientific analyses of problems such as discrimination, divorce, education, ethnicity, genetic change, illegitimacy, poverty, race relations, racism, sexism, social mobility, or stratification is not consistent with the simplistic reductionism of the new assault on equality. The fact is that the foundations on which the two works (both Gingrich's and Herrnstein and Murray's) are built is insubstantial, the outcome of their policies is evident from history, and the values on which they are based are offensive to most Americans. It takes people aware of the vacuity of these theories to announce that the emperor has no clothes and to prevent these books from being used to legitimate an assault on equality.

Postscript

By the Spring of 1996, new developments had occurred in American politics. The star of Newt Gingrich has dimmed and the Contract with America was all but forgotten. The Congress of the new Republicans had become one of the most do-nothing Congresses in history, with very few of the proposed legislative changes becoming reality. Nevertheless, the agenda of the New Right continues to shape the American political scene.

Nineteen ninety-six saw a budget impasse without historical equivalence. In the middle of the second session of Congress, a budget had yet to be passed. Major social programs remained unfunded, and local communities did not receive the expected federal money in such vital areas as education. This alone has given reality to many of the goals of the New Right.

Beyond the federal government, the vision articulated by Herrnstein, Murray, and Gingrich proceeds toward reality throughout this nation. Concepts like "bloated bureaucracy" and "job-erasing federal regulation" have become part of American common vocabulary. Conservative state governments are racing to implement the actions advocated by these authors. In advance of federal action, states have set work requirements and term limits on public welfare and some states have moved to eliminate General Assistance for the able-bodied adult, and to modify AFDC, the program that supports children in need. Meanwhile, states have moved to reintroduce capital punishment, to make sentencing more punitive, to remove social services and programs aimed at rehabilitation from the prisons, and to place juvenile offenders under the rule of adult courts. Both state and local governments are returning an increasing share of responsibility for the aged, the infirm, and the disturbed to their families as social services confront severe under funding and Medicaid is cut. Rights long fought for by women and minorities are being whittled away as institutions, communities, and states refute affirmative action and no-fault divorce is questioned.

We are now engaged in another national electoral campaign to determine not only the Presidency but the representation in the House and one-third of the Senate. Significant numbers of senior, highly respected, members of Congress who have represented a more liberal view have resigned or refused to run again. Patrick Buchanan has emerged as an important voice of the New Right, running for office of President in Republican primaries.

Combining veiled appeals to ethnocentrism and racist attitudes with a voice of concern for the American working population and the American family (Buchanan, 1971), he captured a small but important part of the primary vote. He has stated his intention of remaining in the Presidential race, not to win but to influence the course of events. Newt Gingrich has announced his role as secondary support to the probable candidate, Bob Dole. Dole himself, while a staunch Republican, seems to have little ideological commitment. He has pursued the course of a pragmatic politician, sensing what is politically expedient and shifting his position on issues. He is not, however, a defender of most social programs and voted against Medicare when it was introduced and again when it was expanded. As chairman of the Senate Finance Committee, he engineered the tax revisions that included major concessions to corporate interests and increased military expenditures while cutting social programs (see Hilton (1995), pp. 155, 168-171, 177-178, 195-198). Even the opposing political party has felt the influence of the conservatives. The President, while vetoing the extreme measures of the new Republicans, has softened his message of opposition, supporting legislation to curb affirmative action, giving voice to concern for the future of the American family, promising stricter action against crime, and mandating a work requirement and a limit to welfare. As we move to the elections, all parties can be expected to court the right within each party in the attempt to hold together a winning coalition of voters.

The *Contract with America*, *The Bell Curve* and *The End of Racism* will fade from consciousness among the American people. The message of the New Right that these books promote will not.

Appendix 1

Statistical Methods and Issues

The Bell Curve includes a fifteen page appendix on statistical methods that concentrates on two concepts: the normal distribution and regression. It does not describe many of the issues indispensable for understanding the argument or evaluating the conclusions of the book. While there are limits to what can be described in a short appendix, the basic principles and methods can be briefly presented. Although a thorough understanding of the methods of *The Bell Curve* presupposes graduate training in statistical methods, this appendix will summarize the statistical issues necessary to understanding its arguments, and thus it will lay out the basis for some of the criticisms that have appeared in the text. We first look at concepts that Herrnstein and Murray describe: means, variances, normal distributions, and regression. Then we look at further concepts, central to their argument, that they do not deal with at all, namely spurious relationships, measurement error and model specification.

We have replicated the analyses from Herrnstein and Murray's Part II. While the book attempts to give the impression of a careful, objective demonstration, that allows the facts to speak for themselves, it actually confines the data within a strait jacket of implausible and unacknowledged *assumptions*. *The Bell Curve* argues that people who are less intelligent have many social problems, particularly lack of economic or social success; that blacks and Hispanics are less intelligent; and that their stupidity is the reason they have those problems. We think that an acquaintance with the basic issues and methods of data analysis dispels the illusions of Herrnstein and Murray's analysis.

The magician, Harry Houdini, spent the last years of his life uncovering the tricks of fake mediums, who preyed on the recently bereaved. What people don't know can hurt them, if it leads to their being robbed by an illusionist. People who have no interest in stage magic, and who have no wish to become magicians, may need to recognize illusions. In the face of the rise of social theory driven by an ideological agenda, it is wise to become familiar with the techniques such as those used by *The Bell Curve* to manipulate its data.

Means and Variances

Herrnstein and Murray pose most of their arguments in terms of "standard deviations" and "standardized variables," so familiarity with these concepts is indispensable to following their argument. For example, all of the analyses in part II of *The Bell Curve* rest on comparison of effects of standardized Armed Forces Qualifications Test scores (zAFQT) with those of a standardized index of socioeconomic status (zSES). Herrnstein and Murray go to great lengths to "normalize" AFQT, forcing the scores to assume the form of a normal distribution. They center their racial argument on the standard deviation or 15 IQ points which separate mean black and white IQ scores; and they make such arguments as the one that for environmental differences to explain the black/white difference in scores, the mean black environment would have to be 1.58 standard deviations worse than the mean white environment.[288] All such arguments require some familiarity with standardization, standard deviations and means.

A standard deviation is a measure of variability. Specifically, it is the square root of the variance, which is the average of squared deviations from the mean. In any analysis of the quantitative distribution of some characteristic in a population, we refer both to the typical characteristic of the population, called its "central tendency," and the amount of variability or spread in the population, called its dispersion. While there are many different measures of a central tendency, the most common is the average, or mean. This measure is in common use in our society. It is the average learned in elementary school—that is the sum of the numbers, divided by the number of numbers. In statistics, this average is given the formal name of the mean. This is a central point around which observations (or numbers) are grouped. It is a good measure of individual numbers only when the numbers cluster closely around the center. Sometimes they do, but often they don't. A group with a lot of variation, consisting of some very rich people and some very poor people, would be very different from a group in which each person was moderately wealthy. Thus, in addition to the central tendency, we need to know about dispersion, or variation around the mean.

While there are many ways that dispersion can be measured, the most important is the variance. The standard deviation is its square root. Some examples will make it easier to understand these concepts. In Figure A-1 are pictured three groups of nine persons each. For each of the three groups, we have calculated the mean and the variance. You will see

Figure A-1.
Sample calculations of means and variances.

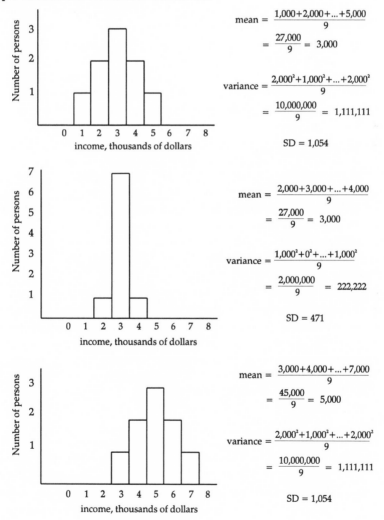

differences in both the value of the mean and the variance or standard deviation. For example, in the first group, someone with an income of $1,000 would have a standardized score of -1.90,[289] conventionally referred to as a z-score, because he is 1.90 standard deviations below the mean.

The fact that they standardize all their analyses allows Herrnstein and Murray to smuggle some questionable assumptions into their data analysis and to massage the data so as to exaggerate the apparent relation of AFQT to other variables. Moreover, Herrnstein and Murray often concentrate on differences between means, ignoring variation. At other times, they slide to a discussion of variation and imply that they are looking at differences between means. This is particularly evident in their discussion of heritability. Heritability is a measure that has to do only with variation; it is the fraction of the variance of a group that is associated with differences in genes. Heritability is about variation. The group differences about which Herrnstein and Murray are concerned are differences in means. Variances do not tell us anything about means and, therefore, cannot tell us anything about group differences in mean.

The Normal Distribution

All three of these groups are approximations of normal distributions or "bell curves" in which the bulk of cases are clustered at the center and their frequency trails off rapidly (and symmetrically) as we move away from the mean. Much of the discipline of statistics is based on mathematical properties of normal distributions. For example, when there is a normal distribution, if we know the value of the mean and the variance, we can describe the whole distribution. About two-thirds of the population is within one standard deviation of the mean, and about 95 percent of the population is within two standard deviations of the mean. Therefore, differences in the size of or value of the standard deviation are measures of differences in the amount of variation around the center of the distribution.

However, to picture these three groups of incomes as normal distributions neglects an important point. Wealth, income, and other social distributions of goods almost never take the form of a normal distribution. While many characteristics that we think of as "natural," such as size, strength, or speed usually are distributed approximately normally, and while IQ is forced to be so distributed by the way it is measured, social rewards and resources usually are not. Most distributions of social rewards such as wealth, income, or power are very different from normal distributions. They take a very different form (such as a Pareto, or a log-normal distribution) with a large group at the bottom, and an elite at the top, many standard deviations above the mean.

Thus, in a population of 250 million, if height is distributed normally (as is approximately the case), if the mean is about 5'6", and if the standard deviation is about 6', then about two-thirds of the population will be between 5' and 6'; about 95 percent of the population will be between 4'6" and 6'6"; less than half of 1 percent will be above 7'; no one will be greater than, say, 12'. But we know that income is very different from this. The mean family income in 1993 was about $37,000, and about two-thirds of all families were between $17,000 and $57,000. But unlike height, where the tallest heights are less than ten standard deviations above the mean, in the case of income we find incomes over $100 million, 5,000 standard deviations above the mean. This is equivalent to finding people taller than a skyscraper. Such distributions, often generated by processes of cumulative causation, are qualitatively different from distributions of natural ability. The fact that distributions of ability and of social rewards are so different is a major problem for any theory that social inequality results from natural differences of ability.

Regression

The main empirical analyses in *The Bell Curve* are logistic regression analyses. Specifically, nearly 200 pages, a book in itself, is structured around 22 graphs similar to that in Figure A-2, our replication of Herrnstein and Murray's result on poverty. However Herrnstein and Murray devote less than two pages (566-567) to these methods, and they give the reader neither the information needed to understand or evaluate them nor references to the literature dealing with the issues.[290]

Regression, multiple regression and other techniques of data analysis, only answer questions within a framework of assumptions. If those assumptions are not met, the analysis can be misleading. Disraeli's statement, "There are three kinds of lies: lies, damned lies, and statistics," is sometimes used to express the fact that statistical analysis can be misleading. The only antidote to such misleading analyses is understanding the technical issues. Houdini, as a stage magician, was able to see through the tricks of fake mediums. The reason that most social scientists have been highly critical of *The Bell Curve* is not that they are "liberals" but that they can see through its tricks.

In order to understand the issues involved in a multiple logistic regression such as that represented in Figure A-2, we must first understand the methods of simple regression and logistic regression. The relationship between two quantitative variables such as height and weight is often characterized by a regression analysis, which is represented by a line

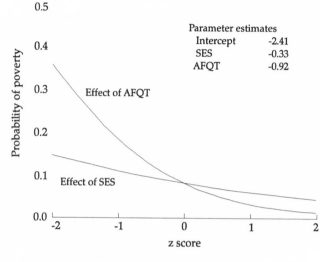

Figure A-2.
Replication of Herrnstein and Murray's result for poverty.

through the center of the values. Like means and variances, there is usually a spread of observations around this line and the greater the spread, the less informative the line. Herrnstein and Murray are correct that the easiest entry into regression is a scattergram. However, if they had presented scattergrams of their data, few people would be inclined to believe the arguments which they make about them. Figure A-3 gives a scattergram of the relation between subjects' Armed Forces Qualification Test scores and their income, from data that Herrnstein and Murray used. Horizontally, people are arranged according to their AFQT test score in 1979 (rescaled by the scaling system of 1989), and vertically by their income. One can see that although there is a tendency for those with higher test scores to have higher incomes, at every level of the test scores, there is substantial variation in income.[291]

A quantitative relationship such as that between AFQT score and income, can be mathematically characterized by a regression. This technique draws a line or simple curve, such as that shown in Figure A-3, through the cluster of points in such a way as to describe their relationship. Regression expresses the "tendency" visible in Figure A-3 as a single number (the slope of the regression line) that expresses the strength of the relationship between AFQT and income. If certain assumptions are met, the slope of such a line measures the effect of one variable on the other. For example, in the above case, if the slope were zero, then those with higher AFQT scores would have neither higher nor lower incomes

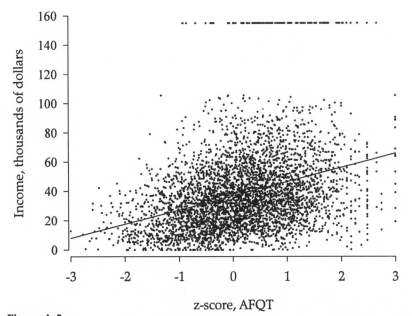

Figure A-3.
Scattergram and regression of income on z score for Armed Forces Qualification Test score.

on average than those with lower AFQT scores. Since those with higher AFQT scores had higher incomes, that is prima facie evidence either that AFQT affects income, or that income affects AFQT, or that other variables affect both of them. If one is willing to assume that income has no effect on AFQT score and that nothing affects them both, then the size of the relationship between AFQT score and income would be a measure of the effect of AFQT score on income.[292] The regression line that best fits the scatter (corresponding to a correlation of about .22) is superimposed on the scattergram of the relation between AFQT score and income. You can see that there is a significant amount of variation from the predicted regression line at any level of AFQT. There is a simple interpretation of the amount of variation from the regression line, compared to the original variation from the mean. The amount that variation from the mean is greater than that from the predicted regression line can be interpreted as the amount of variation explained by regression, and it is equal to the square of the correlation coefficient. In this case $(.22)^2 = .048$. That is, a set of people all of whom had the same AFQT score in 1979 had 95.2 percent as much variation in 1989 incomes as a set of people with varying AFQT scores.[293] However, it obviously makes no sense to say that AFQT "explains" income inequality if that inequality would be almost the same even if everyone had identical AFQT scores.[294]

This elementary fact about the data analysis has more general implications for the arguments of *The Bell Curve*. This is the approximate strength of the relation of AFQT to most of the social behaviors such as illegitimacy, poverty, unemployment or failure in school. While such variables are usually viewed as part of an interdependent system, the reductionist logic of the Herrnstein and Murray analysis is to analyze such variables only one at a time and to treat them only as effects (dependent variables), never as causes (independent variables). They justify the failure to control for those variables partly because they assume that variation in those variables result from variation in intelligence.[295] Then they suggest that the results of the analysis show that intelligence causes the variation in those variables. The logic is circular, and, in any case, even if one grants Herrnstein and Murray's assumptions about them, it is evident that only a tiny fraction of the variation in those structural variables is "explained" by AFQT.

Logistic Regression

In Figure A-2, as in most of Herrnstein and Murray's analyses the dependent variables (the effect) is treated as a qualitative state, such as having been divorced. The kind of regression relevant for analyzing such a relation is called a logistic regression, and it predicts the probability of the qualitative states. Since the probability can only go down to zero or up to 100 percent, in these cases we fit an S-shaped curve rather than a straight line. The simplest way to understand a logistic regression is to see it as fitting a logarithmic function to data such as those in Figure A-4, which shows the proportions of people with different AFQT scores or SES index scores who are in poverty. The dependent variable (poverty) is treated as a qualitative state, ignoring the fact that poverty is just a certain level of income. At every level of the independent variables, Figure A-4 shows the fraction of the respondents who are in poverty.

Herrnstein and Murray always use logistic regressions, even when the dependent variable does not have to be a simple yes/no category. There is a good deal of difference between those at the poverty line and those way below it; there is a good deal of difference between those with one illegitimate child and those with many; there is a good deal of difference between those unemployed for one day and those chronically unemployed. Because it is a non-linear function, logistic regression will accentuate some of the other problems in Herrnstein and Murray's analysis.

In the text of *The Bell Curve*, Herrnstein and Murray present graphs of the fitted regression lines only, plotting predicted values of dependent

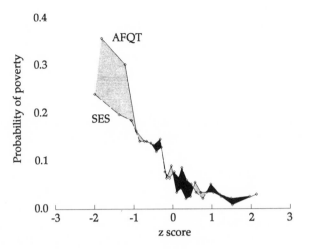

Figure A-4.
Frequency polygons for the data fitted by Herrnstein and Murray's logistic regressions for poverty. Light fill marks areas in which AFQT seems to have a larger effect; dark fill for areas in which SES seems more important.

variables such as poverty as functions of standardized AFQT and SES. This presentation prevents the reader from making any assessment of the effectiveness of Herrnstein and Murray's regression model. Their treatments throughout violate Tufte's (1983) dictum, "above all else, show the data." The graphs Herrnstein and Murray present, such as those in Figure A-2, not only fail to show any of the scatter, but also do not show the data about the relation of SES or of AFQT to the dependent variables. They show only a theoretical prediction of what they would be if the other variable and age were "controlled." To understand what this means, we must review some of the issues associated with multiple regression and causal models. Herrnstein and Murray present graphs of the predicted regression coefficients of AFQT (controlling age and SES) and of SES (controlling age and AFQT). Such graphs are an atypical and opaque way of presenting data. Herrnstein and Murray use this method to give the impression that IQ has a much more powerful relation to poverty than SES. Only about 10 percent of those with the lowest SES appear to be in poverty, while nearly three times that many of those with the lowest IQ are in poverty. However, this impression is mainly due to the idiosyncratic methods and the unrealistic assumptions Herrnstein and Murray make. To clarify the reality underneath these statistical manipulations the first thing to do is to construct an analogue to the scattergram for regression. A scattergram would not be informative since the dependent variable would only have two values, but Figure A-4 shows an analogue, a frequency polygon. Specifically it superimposes the frequency polygons for the effect of SES and AFQT on poverty. It breaks the population into equal sized groups of five percent of the respondents, according to SES and AFQT score. For example, it takes the five percent of respondents with the lowest AFQT scores and calculates the fraction of them in poverty, the next five percent, and so on, and then carries out the same procedure for Herrnstein and Murray's SES index. To maximize comparability with Herrnstein and Murray's result, Figure A-4 plots the points on standardized measures of SES and AFQT. Thus, in the same manner as the multiple regressions in *The Bell Curve*, it magnifies the visual importance of the small number of cases nearly two standard deviations above or below the mean.[296]

At the extreme left of Figure A-4, the lightly shaded area represents the fact that those in the lowest ten percent of AFQT are more likely to be in poverty than those in the lowest ten percent of SES.[297] This area is sensitive to measurement error in SES[298] and AFQT.[299] In this and other respects, logistic regression magnifies other problems of Herrnstein and Murray's multivariate analysis.

Multiple Regression

To compare the effects of environmental variables with effects of native ability, Herrnstein and Murray carry out multiple regressions. Multiple regression extends the technique of simple regression to cases where several variables are interrelated. The slopes of a multivariate regression can then be interpreted as the effect of one variable when controlling for others.[300] To explain the regression procedure, Herrnstein and Murray give a whimsical account of less than one page, in which height and weight are used to predict waist size of boys in a gym: the boys are arranged by height and weight and then levitated to a height corresponding to their waist size. They ask what is the "tilt" of the plane by height and by weight. Unfortunately, their account will be incomprehensible to anyone who has not studied multiple regression, and it does not give any of the information needed to understand their analysis. Part of the difficulty is that the concepts are genuinely difficult to explain briefly, but since these authors have chosen to spend hundreds of pages in the analysis of such regressions, we shall try to do a better job than they do in explaining the basic issues.

A multiple regression, instead of constructing a regression line representing the relation between the dependent variable and one independent variable, constructs a plane which represents the relation between the dependent variable and two or more independent variables. The fact that it is a plane represents the assumption that at every level of one variable, the effect of the other is the same;[301] in this sense, the slope of the plane gives the effect of one variable controlling the other. Figure A-5 gives an example. It differs from Herrnstein and Murray's in that those authors independent variables are SES, age, and AFQT rather than education and AFQT. Moreover, Herrnstein and Murray compare standardized logistic coefficients, so that the relationships are represented as curves rather than as a plane. Nevertheless, the two curves superimposed in Herrnstein and Murray's graphs, replicated in Figure A-2, are cross-sections of the regression plane in Figure A-5, ostensibly showing the effect of AFQT (holding constant SES) and the effect of SES (holding constant AFQT). Given certain theoretical assumptions, the slopes of the plane can be interpreted as additive effects of independent variables. Herrnstein and Murray's discussion of those assumptions is very brief.[302]

In Figure A-5, AFQT has no effect on income. The plane in which the points lie has a zero slope with regard to AFQT. But in the bivariate regression of AFQT and income at the upper left, AFQT appears to be

Figure A-5.
Hypothetical multiple regression of income by education and AFQT.

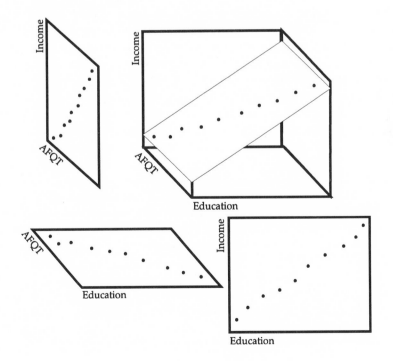

causally related to income. The other two bivariate projections at the bottom show why: AFQT is related to education and education is related to income.

If there are two causal forces that are additive and independent, and if a number of other assumptions are met,[303] the multiple regression coefficient of each can be interpreted as its causal effect on a third variable, such as the chance of being in poverty. Herrnstein and Murray treat AFQT as a measure of native ability and their socioeconomic status index (SES) as a measure of environment. They then regress each of the dependent variables, such as poverty, on AFQT and SES, and they interpret the relative size of the regression coefficients as a measure of the relative importance of (genetic) intelligence and of environment. They interpret the substantial coefficients of AFQT to mean that intelligence has powerful effects, even controlling the environment.[304] Since the effect of AFQT is usually larger than that of SES, they interpret this to mean that the effect of "native ability" is greater than that of the social environment.

Models and Causal Assumptions of the Analysis

We noted that if we are willing to make assumptions that no other causal forces are at work, it is possible to interpret regression coefficients as measures of the effect of the independent variable on the dependent variable. However, in a structure of cumulative causation, that assumption will be extremely implausible. Different processes might also produce a statistical relation between the variables. In the case of AFQT score and income, a relation could result from an effect of AFQT on income, but the same statistical relation would appear if income affected AFQT or if some other variable or variables affected both of them. It is Herrnstein and Murray's assumptions which lead to their interpreting the statistical coefficients of AFQT (controlling SES and age) as measures of the effect of intelligence. The essential point is that the facts do not speak for themselves. More specifically, it is not possible to make causal inferences from statistical analyses except on the basis of theoretical assumptions. These assumptions are summarized in a causal model.

Despite their disclaimers about the difficulty of making causal inferences, Herrnstein and Murray clearly wish to make causal inferences about the relative importance of native ability (IQ) and social, environmental influences (SES). In Part II of *The Bell Curve*, they use a slippery, colloquial and shifting language to imply that the coefficients of AFQT in the regressions show the effects of native ability for predicting which individuals will be in poverty, dropouts, divorced, criminals, etc. They ask whether IQ or SES is a "stronger precursor" (*The Bell Curve*, p.127) or a "more important cause" of poverty (*The Bell Curve*, pp. 129, 135), whether an unborn child would be worse off being disadvantaged in SES or in IQ (*The Bell Curve*, p. 135); whether the disadvantage of low IQ "outweighs" that of low SES in schooling (*The Bell Curve*, p. 143); the "primary risk factor" for unemployment; the "predisposing factor" for illegitimacy (*The Bell Curve*, p. 167); or what is the "most significant" relationship (*The Bell Curve*, p. 265).[305] But in Part III and IV they interpret the data as showing the relative importance of intelligence levels and inequality in groups and in the society as a whole in generating social problems.[306] To make those inferences on the basis of the data they present requires fairly drastic assumptions. They are not explicit about the assumptions they make and they do not report what happens when they relax those assumptions.

They must assume that native ability and SES are individual characteristics; that both of them are essentially stable, independent of each other, and independent of other characteristics of the social situation of the respondents; that they have independent effects on dependent variables such as the probability of being in poverty; and that they are well measured by AFQT and by the SES index. These are heroic but implausible assumptions. We shall focus on four problematic assumptions of the analysis. The next section of this appendix will discuss the assumption that IQ and SES are stable individual traits. The following section will discuss the assumption that AFQT and SES are unbiased measures of the effects of native ability and social environment. Then we shall discuss the assumption that no other forces, systematically interconnected with both of them, are at work. We shall see that in any structure of cumulative causation, each of these problems is accentuated by an analysis that compares a childhood measure of socioeconomic status to an adult measure of IQ. Furthermore, when this peculiar asymmetrical treatment of the time of measurement is not used to inflate the apparent effect of AFQT, Herrnstein and Murray's findings vanish. Not only have they not given us reason to believe that AFQT scores play a greater role than environment; they have given us no reason to believe that AFQT scores play any role in creating the behaviors and conditions they examine.

The Individualistic Bias of *The Bell Curve*

The notion that conditions such as poverty, unemployment, school failure, family breakdown, or crime are individual traits which should be explained by other individual traits such as IQ or socioeconomic status may seem nonproblematic, and for some purposes it is a reasonable approach. For others, it is highly questionable. One of the most important ways that one can "lie with statistics" is to present an answer to one question and then to treat it as the answer to a different question. It is well known that questions such as "What causes unemployment?" actually

involve many different questions.[307] The question of what characteristics
of an individual tend to make that individual more likely to be unemployed probably has very little to do with the question what characteristics of the present period are producing a high rate of unemployment.
Neither of them has very much to do with the question of what social and
economic policies affect the unemployment rate. Herrnstein and Murray
look at the individual characteristics of those who are unemployed, on
welfare, or involved with the police. They find that many of those people
came from poor backgrounds and do poorly at paper and pencil tests
such as the Armed Forces Qualification Test. They conclude that "lack of
cognitive capacity" is an important cause of unemployment, welfare dependency, or crime and that it is more important than environment.
They slide to the conclusion that the different rates of different groups
and the changes in rates in the society as a whole are a consequence of
shifts or differences in cognitive ability.[308] The argument and inference is
fallacious because one concept of cause of unemployment, welfare or
crime (who) has been substituted for a different, unrelated one (how
many).

Herrnstein and Murray are quite explicit that they wish to refute the
structural approach to such problems, discussed above in terms of the
theory of cumulative causation or the vicious cycle. That theory says that
lack of resources leads to a whole complex of stigmatization, lack of opportunity and other deprivations, which reinforce each other, producing
the poor prospects in school, work, family, and criminal justice system, as
well as the poor test scores. Poor children are located in families, neighborhoods, and schools with hazards of crime, drugs, neglect, and exposure to destructive habits. Their networks of friends and role models are
less likely to support the identities, aspirations, and habits required for
the skills and practice that will lead to good performance on a paper and
pencil test such as the AFQT, and those networks and models also produce a host of pathological behaviors and destructive conditions, which
we can call the complex of deprivation. Functional illiteracy and inability
to do well on any test such as the Armed Forces Qualification Test are often analyzed as part of this complex, and they are strongly related to the
other conditions of the complex. Herrnstein and Murray purport to test
this theory by comparing the effects of socioeconomic status to the effects
of AFQT. However, their measure of SES is defective, and socioeconomic
status, however measured, will not measure the effects of the complex of
deprivation very well.

Part of the problem is that Herrnstein and Murray's conceptualization
of the causes and determinants of such conditions has already set up a
Procrustean bed, in which only individual traits are allowed to serve as
causes. They only look at individual characteristics of the unemployed,

divorced, or criminal. Analytically isolated from their situation, the cause of poverty, unemployment, divorce, school failure, or the like appears to hang in mid air as some defect of the people involved. People living in brutalizing situations are often brutalized, but Herrnstein and Murray have not presented any evidence that some cognitive incapacity, tested by low AFQT scores, leads to divorce, rather than that many of the structures that depress school performance also stress families. Rather than investigating or testing the effects of individual and environmental conditions in causing the problems, they assume that the causes are individual characteristics. Such an individualistic analysis of social problems often tend to "blame the victim."

Even if the characteristics of those people perfectly predicted their engaging in socially problematic behaviors, that would not necessarily explain anything about the social rates of those behaviors. Even if their analysis were entirely correct as an answer to the question of what individual traits make someone more likely to be unemployed, that is irrelevant for the different question of why the society has a high rate. If there are many more people than there are jobs, then there will be a large number of unemployed, regardless of the criteria employers use to fill jobs. If the pay of many jobs leaves one below the poverty line, then there will be many working poor, regardless of scores on tests used to allocate people to those jobs. If many schools leave most of their graduates functionally illiterate, many people will be functionally illiterate. Herrnstein and Murray are quite explicit that they wish to redirect social explanations, which have concentrated upon social structural origins of social problems, toward individual characteristics.[309] But their data analysis does not show this, it assumes it.[310] Since they only examine individual traits, they can only find individual causes. Even if test scores were perfectly correlated with such conditions as poverty or unemployment, that would say nothing about the social causes of those conditions. But Part III and Part IV of *The Bell Curve* fallaciously infers that the data show that tiny changes in IQ could produce enormous changes in school or occupational failure, poverty, unemployment, crime, and welfare both in different racial and ethnic groups and in the society at large.[311]

Measurement, Indices, and Bias

Besides the problems of conceptualization, there are problems of measurement. Even if one accepts the notion that ability and social disadvantage are independent, individual traits, the questions how well native ability is measured by AFQT and how well social environment is measured by SES are important. Herrnstein and Murray spend considerable effort to justify the treatment of AFQT as a measure of native ability, but this is an assumption which they bring to the data, and they ignore the data most relevant to it. The fact that AFQT is measured late, contemporaneous with the dependent variables that are being explained, makes it subject to contamination by the social circumstances of the respondents. In the following sections, we shall see that when you eliminate this contamination, the relation of test scores to the dependent variables disappears altogether. In contrast to their careful normalization of the AFQT scores, Herrnstein and Murray are extremely casual about their index of SES. They averaged mother's education, father's education, parental occupation, and family income.[312] There were missing data in about one third of the cases, and in those cases they used the normalized average of the variables they had.[313] The variables which had the fewest missing cases and which therefore played the strongest role in their index, were mothers' and fathers' education. However, these variables also had relatively weak relations to many of the variables that Herrnstein and Murray purported to explain.[314]

This index of four items of different kinds from different periods of time probably has a great deal more measurement error than the AFQT scores. Someone who grew up a millionaire might not show up high in SES if his or her family income was missing; someone who grew up homeless on the streets would not show up low, if their mother was a well-educated drug addict or abused spouse. Therefore, we must ask how measurement error affects the apparent strength of the relation between variables. Usually, measurement error attenuates the relationship. What this means is that any variable with measurement error will appear to have a weaker relation to any other variable than it really does. Thus, if SES and AFQT really have relationships with the dependent variable, those relationships will appear stronger, the more carefully they are measured and they will appear weaker, the more poorly they are measured.[315] Moreover, it is not clear that their SES index measures the appropriate environmental conditions or that it is well conceived as a stable individual characteristic. Socioeconomic status changes over time. In the text we note that contrary to the stereotype of welfare dependency, people move into and out of poverty as plants close down, marriages break up, or illnesses occur. This variation also weakens its apparent effect. Moreover, if people falling into poverty are falling into a situation that will reduce the test scores of their children, while people rising from it are entering a supportive environment, Herrnstein and Murray's estimates of effects will be grossly biased. To see why this is true, we must discuss further the assumptions on which their statistical analysis is based, the issues ordinarily discussed in terms of model specification error.

Model Specification Error, and Spurious Relationships

Both the problems of the individualist character of the analysis and the measurement problems of their indices are accentuated by their failure to look at the effects of any conditions other than SES. We have noted that Herrnstein and Murray fail to examine the effects of illegitimacy, poverty, or any other social condition of the respondents other than their socioeconomic status index. However, existing theory, including the very theory that Herrnstein and Murray say they wish to contest, suggests that many conditions concerning the identity, aspirations, opportunities, friends, and situations of the respondents will affect both test scores and the dependent variables. In a multivariate analysis, what you don't look at can hurt you. Herrnstein and Murray radically reduce the number of variables they include in the regressions, saying that other variables such as education are so bound up with test scores that including them would lead to problems of multicolinearity. They include only three variables, age, SES, and AFQT. But of course, this is an ostrich strategy. By failing to look at a possibly confounding variable, we do not reduce its effect; we merely make it impossible to see whether it is having an effect.

In a simple (bivariate) regression, there is one and only one measure of the relationship between two variables. But in multiple regression, there are different measures of a relationship, depending on what other things are controlled. Therefore, in multiple regression analysis, a great deal depends the choice of variables to include in the analysis. In the social sciences, this is usually discussed in terms of the nature of one's "model" of the data. A model, in this sense, consists of a set of assumptions about what variables are acting on what other variables, and how. If a model fails to include variables which affect both the independent and dependent variable, it will produce a spurious estimate of the relationship.[316] More generally a spurious relationship is one form of "model specification error." This error occurs whenever the actual causal processes do not correspond to those that are explicit in the model.[317]

In Chapter Four, above, we discussed an example of a spurious relationship due to failure to include important relevant variables in the analysis. If we fail to consider the size of fires, it would appear that fire engines produce, rather than prevent, damage, since there is more damage at (large) fires where many engines are present. Whenever one is dealing with a process of cumulative causation, the possibility of a spurious result is particularly acute, because the large number of variables that mutually reinforce each other will produce an inflated impression of the effect of any one on the others. It is characteristic of sociology, and especially of the sociology of stratification that most processes involve a large number of interrelated variables. Herrnstein and Murray present a deceptive oversimplification of a situation that is intrinsically complex. The complex of deprivation involves nutrition, housing, peer group contacts, crime, drugs, self-esteem, labeling, school resources, occupational expectations, and a host of other factors, all of which affect or may affect ,test scores as well as other variables such as the chance of being unemployed. This means that the apparent relation between test scores and variables such as unemployment will be spuriously inflated by the effects of any and all variables in the complex of deprivation.

The existence of mutually reinforcing elements of advantage and disadvantage creates a complex that is difficult to disentangle. Certainly the main assumptions of multivariate causal analysis (especially the assumption that error terms will be uncorrelated) will not be met in a cross sectional analysis such as that of Murray and Herrnstein. Most useful for sorting out the reciprocal causal relations in that kind of a complex are panel data, in which there are repeated measures of the same respondents. One of the reasons that the NLSY is important is that it is a panel, but Herrnstein and Murray ignore this aspect of the data set. They also ignore the principal existing panel analysis of intelligence, the analyses of cognitive flexibility by Kohn and his collaborators (e.g. Kohn, Slomczynski, and Schoenback, 1984; 1990; Miller, Kohn, and Schooler, 1986). That analysis suggests that cognitive flexibility is more an effect than a cause of differences in environmental constraint, and it analyzes how individual orientations and their social situation mutually reinforce each other at work, in school, and in families.

It will be easiest to see how this operates in a multiple regression if we take a single variable, education, to stand for the whole complex. While receiving a large amount of good education is only one aspect of advantage, and while receiving a smaller amount of a poorer education is only one aspect of disadvantage, it can illustrate the problems of omitted variables. We have noted that Herrnstein and Murray make radically contradictory assumptions about education, sometimes viewing it as having only marginal effects on a test such as the SAT or AFQT, and at other times assuming that SAT scores are a sensitive measure of the effectiveness of education. While they recognize an effect of education on test scores and sometimes control for education in their analysis, they are irregular and inconsistent in their controls.[318] Therefore, let us consider what we would find if "native intelligence" had no effect whatsoever on a dependent variable such as poverty, but if education affected test scores and also affected the chance of being in poverty. Moreover, since the situation is simpler in the case of an ordinary continuous dependent variable such as income, we will consider the case of an effect of education on test scores and on income.

Taking education as a proxy for a great mass of other advantage or disadvantage faced by different children, Figure A-5 shows the hypothetical relations we would observe if education affected IQ scores and also affected income, but if IQ scores had no effect on income. It shows the plane in or near which all of the cases would lie, with regard to education, test scores and income. It also shows the three projections which are what one would observe if one only looked at income and test scores, at income and education or at education and test scores. If we fail to look at education, it will appear that test scores have an effect on income, even if test scores have no effect at all.

Figure A-5 portrays a situation in which there is no effect of test scores on income but that there is a spurious apparent effect of test scores due to their relationship to education. The plane in which the data lie is one in which there is no correlation between test scores and income. At every level of education, the slope of the relation between test scores and income is zero. Nevertheless, if we neglected to analyze education, it would appear that test scores affect income. The three projections, showing the bivariate relations, show why. On the lower right, we see that education and test scores have a powerful correlation. Since, on the lower left, education and income also have a powerful correlation, the result, on the upper left, is a strong spurious correlation between test scores and income. This would give the appearance of an effect of test scores which resulted from the effect of education.[319]

Many social conditions that are not well measured by their SES index almost certainly have an effect both on test scores and on conditions such as poverty or having an illegitimate child. Herrnstein and Murray treat such conditions only as effects, never as causes, and they justify their failure to control such conditions by the assumption that nothing affects test scores, which are genetically fixed. We shall examine this implausible assumption shortly, but it is evident that if their analyses assume this, then they do not provide any evidence for it. Moreover, as we have noted, even if education and other conditions of advantage or disadvantage were affected by IQ and had no effect on test scores, that would not mean that changing those conditions would not affect poverty, illegitimacy, crime and the like.[320]

Years of education is a very crude measure of educational quality. The total education received in formal schooling is only a part of total education. And all forms of education are only one aspect of the many conditions of deprivation that influence both test scores and Herrnstein and Murray's dependent variables. In Figure A-5 education is as a proxy for the complex of deprivation, a great mass of variables, none of which are controlled or analyzed either as prior or intervening variables. This example illustrates the way that failing to look at other conditions spuriously inflates the apparent effect of AFQT test scores. Actually, there is no single simple variable that accounts for all of the correlation between text scores and conditions such as dropping out of school, unemployment, crime, or having illegitimate children. To look for some individual measure that will account for the correlations, analogous to education in Figure A-5, is almost certainly a search for a philosopher's stone. Rather than some single condition, there are a very large number of conditions of deprivation or privilege that have been whosn to affect identities, school performance, and social position. It remains to show that they are responsible for the correlation between AFQT and conditions such as illegitimacy.

Cumulative Causation and Time of Measurement

We have suggested that AFQT does not measure native ability and that SES does not measure environment. Test scores of respondents when they were between the ages of 14 and 23 are arguably affected by a wide range of influences from the respondents' childhood and adolescence. Specifically, they are arguably influenced by the whole complex of advantage and disadvantage, that is also having an impact on the variables and conditions that Herrnstein and Murray purport to explain. It remains to demonstrate that this influence occurs and that it explains Herrnstein and Murray's results. Herrnstein and Murray oversimplify this structure and treat these late test scores as a measure of early ability. Their doing so is what produces the effects they report.

Both the measurement problems and the problems of spuriousness are accentuated by the time at which the variables are measured. It is always problematic to compare the effects of measures taken at different points in time, and this problem will be enormously accentuated if they are both part of an interrelated complex. While both SES and IQ are conceived theoretically as background characteristics, that is not how they are measured. The SES measure is dominated by events that occurred before or during the respondents' childhoods, but IQ is measured in 1980, when the respondents were between 14 and 21. The coefficients showing the relation of each to a state such as poverty are compared. This procedure introduces at least two main sources of bias into the estimates of the relative effects of SES and AFQT. The fact that SES is dominated by events from a much earlier in time means that its effect will appear weaker due to the noise of intervening events. Moreover, the effect of the late measure (AFQT) will be biased upward to the extent that poor test scores are correlated with the complex of cumulative deprivation.

The simple rule with regard to control is that to find the causal effect operating between two variables, you must control any variables that are causally prior to them, and you must not control any variable that intervenes between them. Taking the measures at different times will compound that problem with systematic biases. What legitimizes this peculiar comparison is Herrnstein and Murray's assumption that intelligence tests measure a biologically fixed individual capacity, so that it will not matter when it is measured. Otherwise, the symmetrical comparison of coefficients of two interrelated variables, with one measured from the distant past and the other measured contemporaneously, would be self-evidently mistaken.[321] Herrnstein and Murray wave aside issues of the age of testing IQ with the statement that IQ scores are "stable, although not perfectly so, over much of a person's life" (*The Bell Curve*, p. 23).[322] They stress the high correlation between intelligence measured at different points, and they conceive of intelligence as a biological constant, so that neither attenuation nor the influence of the environment seem to threaten their analyses. Although they note the effect of education on intelligence,[323] and sporadically control for education,[324] they do not pursue the matter systematically. However, the question of parameter bias cannot be answered by the correlation between an index and an underlying variable,[325] which is, in any case, assumed rather than demonstrated from the data.[326]

The National Longitudinal Survey of Youth has evidence relevant to whether there is a significant effect of either kind, although Herrnstein and Murray fail to consult it. For each subject, if there was any kind of test earlier in school, it is included in the data set. Some 1104 white respondents in the survey took some form of intelligence test at least once when they were in school, and the data set includes the centile score of the subjects on those tests. Some 290 of the subjects took intelligence tests during elementary school and the centile scores on those tests are in the data set. By looking at the earlier measures, we can eliminate at least part of the bias that results from comparing a late measure of cognitive performance to an early measure of socioeconomic status.[327] The school measures are, as the literature suggests, strongly correlated with AFQT scores,[328] but that does not mean that AFQT scores are unbiased; it does not mean that the AFQT scores can be substituted for the early scores in analyzing conditions such as poverty.

Figure A-6 shows the logistic equation and corresponding graphs that result from the substitution of school IQ into Murray and Herrnstein's analysis of poverty. The IQ scores are composites of various school IQ-type tests, measured in centiles and treated analogously to Herrnstein and Murray's treatment of SES. In the NLSY scores are listed for a dozen tests, but no more than a small fraction of the respondents have a score for any one of them. As in *The Bell Curve*, when more than one test was given, their centile scores were averaged.

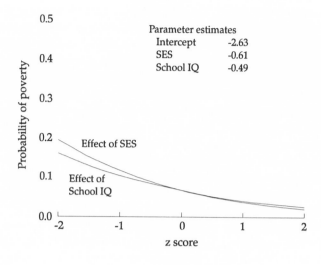

Figure A-6.
Replication of Herrnstein and Murray's analysis using school IQ.

It is evident that when one employs IQ estimates measured by the school composite, the difference between SES and IQ in their effect on poverty vanishes. Different measures of IQ at different times do not appear to be so closely correlated with each other than it does not matter when one measures IQ. It clearly does matter.[329] The bulk of the students for which school IQ data exist in the NLSY took tests in high school. AFQT (and the dependent variables) are measured in 1980, when the subjects ranged from 14 to 21. Thus, while Figure A-6 reduces some of the bias which results from comparing the effects of a very early measure of SES to those of a late measure of IQ, they do not eliminate very much of it. The main measures composing SES refer to events at least ten years earlier than high school. However, it is also possible to substitute relatively early measures. Figure A-7 shows the results of substituting intelligence scores from elementary school into the equation for poverty for the cases for which those test scores exist. In that case, not only does the difference between AFQT and SES vanish, so too does the effect of IQ, and the effect of SES increases proportionately.

Although the different measures of intelligence are intercorrelated, they behave strikingly differently when paired with SES in the equation for poverty. The adolescent measure (AFQT) makes it appear that cognitive ability is strikingly more powerful than SES; the middle measure makes it appear that SES and IQ have similar effects; and the early measure makes it appear that cognitive ability has no significant effect at all. The results suggest that Herrnstein and Murray's reported findings are artifacts. These data are certainly inconsistent with the thesis that IQ scores at different times are so stable that later scores may be substituted for earlier ones. These results are clearly more consistent with the model of cumulative causation than they are with any interpretation in terms of invariant biogenetic ability.

The early measures of IQ correlate quite highly with the AFQT; yet the secondary school measure has a much weaker relation to the dependent variables, such as poverty; and the elementary school measures have no relation at all. How can this be? We can think of no explanation which leaves any substantial portion of Herrnstein and Murray's argument intact.

Their argument leaves considerable ambiguity as to when social background and intelligence are supposed to have their effect. They assume that it will not matter when intelligence is measured, because it is genetically fixed, and their argument requires that assumption. While there is some ambiguity as to whether they are assuming that intelligence test scores are fixed by age 6, when children are in school, or by age 14, it is essential to their analysis that these various measures not only be correlated but that they have similar relations to the dependent variables. However, in contrast to that assumption, it would appear that those elements of AFQT scores that are highly correlated to the dependent variables (indeed, those elements that are correlated at all) are those that are

Figure A-7.
Replication of Herrnstein and Murray's analysis using early school IQ.

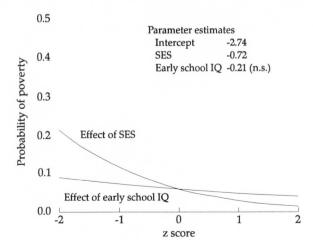

unrelated to measured IQ earlier. This grossly contradicts an interpretation of the effects of AFQT in terms of "native ability." Herrnstein and
Murray have a number of possible counters. They might argue that
AFQT is a "better measure" while the smaller number of cases and the
different tests of school IQ is an "inferior measure" which should be ignored. But for this argument to hold, the early tests have to be worthless,
and it is impossible to maintain that their SES measure has less measurement error than those tests. Some psychometricians have argued that IQ
crystallizes much later than age 6 and that later measures test native ability, while early measures just test home environment, but that argument
is inconsistent with the much smaller size of the effect of high school
tests.

   To see how the late measures can be closely related to poverty, while
the early ones, which are correlated with the later ones, are not, we must
consider what contributes to a good performance on a test such as the
Armed Forces Qualifications Test. Totally aside from any possible influence of innate ability, early scores will partly be correlated with later ones
because they influence schooling and they are correlated with the whole
mass of cumulative advantage or disadvantage that we have considered.
However, not everyone who scores well early will also score well later,
and we must consider why the small number of respondents who change
do so. To see why, imagine that a bright, college educated woman has
the misfortune to marry an abusive alcoholic, and that she and her bright,
sensitive children end up homeless, on the streets. For reasons that are
well understood, those children will attend inferior schools irregularly,
and they are likely to remain functionally illiterate, to do poorly on the
AFQT, and to display all the poor prospects of family dysfunction, unemployment and crime, associated with growing up on the streets. How
would such a situation appear within the Procrustean bed of Herrnstein
and Murray's conceptualization? Within that conceptualization, everything will appear upside down. Although the children's poor prospects
are caused by social disadvantage, they will have a high SES index, dominated by their parents' education a generation earlier, and so it will appear that environment has no effect. Although their poor performance
on the AFQT in 1980 resulted from functional illiteracy produced by the
cumulative disadvantage of growing up homeless, Herrnstein and Murray's conceptualization will take that performance in 1980, when the children are in their late teens or twenties, to be a measure of biologically
fixed capacity. A conceptualization which forces the hypothetical situation we have described to appear to be the effect of biological capacity is
clearly problematical. Similarly the case of a drug dealer whose riches allow his children to grow up in the suburbs will appear to be the children's

intelligence (high AFQT) triumphing over their poverty (low parental education).

Our example is hypothetical, but a conceptualization and operationalization of "native ability" and "social environment" that ignmres the early, defines the children as moderate to high in SES on the basis of parent's education, and takes the late test scores as measures of early ability is logically and conceptually flawed. Moreover, from examining how people get into and out of poverty, this hypothetical example is not extreme or atypical. Most people do not fall into poverty. But closed plants, failed marriages, injuries and addictions do not respect the genes of children. When we ascribe their effects to those genes, we legitimate them and victimize the children.

Indeed, we are now in the somewhat embarrassing position of having explained more than 100 percent of Herrnstein and Murray's finding. The structure of cumulative causation, many of which operate on the whole community, between generations, should produce a spurious effect even of intelligence measured very early. And the inclusion of better measures of social background, should reduce the effect of intelligence. But we find that a measure of intelligence even taken later than parents' education, has no significant effect at all, once one has controlled SES, even with Herrnstein and Murray's poor measure of SES. Possibly even a poorly constructed measure of SES will pick up many effects of environment, since we do not suppose that scoring well in early grades is an active disadvantage.

Sources of bias

Herrnstein and Murray base a series of assumptions on the conceptualization of ability as biogenetically fixed. They assume that poverty, unemployment, injury, welfare, school failure, divorce, illegitimacy, ineffective parenting, crime, and similar problems should be explained by the traits of individuals. They assume that cognitive capacity and socioeconomic status are the relevant traits to explain those behaviors, and that they are invariant and independent of other systematic forces of cumulative disadvantage. They assume that each of these traits are well measured by their SES index and by the AFQT test in 1980, and that the coefficients of these two indices should be compared, even though the two measures are dominated by measures of events that occurred at very different times. We have seen that these assumptions are highly problematical, and they raise issues that are not specific to *The Bell Curve*. These issues will come up with regard to other analyses over the course of the next decade. The issue of the causes of success and failure in jobs and education is one of the most highly studied questions in the social sciences. Social problems associated with disadvantage are also the subject of enormous literatures. The issue of race and ethnic differences in social success and in the incidence of social problems are both politically and theoretically important. And thus it is essential to be able to evaluate the kinds of arguments that are made in *The Bell Curve*. It proposes that there are differences in cognitive ability that account for success and failure and for social problems such as unemployment, illegitimacy, and crime; that racial and ethnic differences in cognitive ability account for racial and ethnic differences in success.

Since the message is one that many people wish to hear, we can confidently predict that there will be a number of replications over the next decade that will allege that Herrnstein and Murray are right about the nature, genetic basis, and importance of intelligence, and its application to racial differences and social problems. Since the analysis is reminiscent of the theories of the eugenicists and the Nazi theoreticians early in the century, and since it attacks the foundational insights of the social sciences during the twentieth century, there will also be a number of replications that will allege that Herrnstein and Murray are wrong. The present appendix has tried to show some of the technical issues involved. Technical decisions about the statistical analysis actually embody fundamental substantive assumptions about the causal processes going on. Such decisions may make the apparent effects of "IQ" or of the "environment" appear larger or smaller. Specifically, there are issues of how and when IQ and environment are measured, how the relationship between them is measured, what prior or contemporary conditions are included in the analysis, and how the effects are compared.

We can now give the reader a guide to some of the forthcoming debates in the form of a manual of "how to lie with statistics"—i.e. how to exaggerate or minimize the effect either of IQ or of environment. The aim is not to promote distortion, but to allow the reader to recognize it.

In terms of measurement, whenever there is a relationship between two variables, its apparent strength will depend partly on how well the variables themselves are measured. The relationship will usually appear stronger when the variables are well-measured and weaker when the variable is poorly measured. Similarly the passage of time acts somewhat like statistical error. All kinds of things happen with the passage of time; there are many slips twixt the cup and the lip. The intervention of time will ordinarily attenuate the effect of a variable, and so when a variable is measured recently, it will appear to have a stronger relation to the variable, and when it is measured remotely, it will appear to have a weaker one.[330]

Table A-1.
Measurement Error Sources of Bias

TO MAKE THE EFFECT OF IQ APPEAR STRONGER	TO MAKE THE EFFECT OF IQ APPEAR WEAKER
Measure IQ well.	Measure IQ poorly.
Measure environmental effects poorly.	Measure environmental effects well.
Measure IQ as late as possible.	Measure IQ as early as possible.
Measure SES as early as possible.	Measure SES as late as possible.
Correct SES for reliability.	Do not correct SES for reliability.

Not only does the passage of time create a kind of error, attenuating the apparent effect of anything measured remotely, but also when a complex of interrelated variables reinforce each other, it creates systematic biases. That is, besides measurement problems, another set of biases hinge on model specification. The central issue is how the specific measures of ability and environment interact with the complex of aspirations, identity, networks of friends, school, and social supports. Thus, the most effective means of manipulating the data are:

Table A-2.
Model specification sources of bias

TO MAKE THE EFFECT OF IQ APPEAR STRONGER	TO MAKE THE EFFECT OF IQ APPEAR WEAKER
Use few controls.	Use many controls.
Ignore all the concrete forms of environmental constraints.	Control a rich and varied set of environmental constraints.
Pick a measure of IQ affected by some rewards and constraints.	Pick a measure of IQ less affected by rewards and constraints.
Ignore contemporaneous conditions such as alcoholism.	Control contemporaneous conditions such as alcoholism.
Measure SES so that it is weakly correlated to social rewards and causation.	Measure SES so that it is strongly correlated to social rewards and causation.

Herrnstein and Murray purport to lean over backwards to provide a conservative test of their thesis, particularly in their construction of SES, their normalizing of AFQT and their use of "g-loaded" weighting of the subscales of AFQT. But in fact, they are conservative only with respect to technical choices that make no difference. On the choices that do make a difference, they make assumptions that exaggerate the effect of IQ.

Conclusion

The fact that quantitative data analysis operates within a framework of assumptions does not mean that it is less reliable than face-to-face experience. Face-to-face experience also operates within a framework of assumptions. In face-to-face experience, a person could assume that someone was stupid because that person could not read and write or because they could not do calculus problems. In our face-to-face interactions we may make assumptions similar to those in regression models about what kinds of things may affect poverty. Indeed, the assumptions in quantitative research are often more explicit and more subject to correction than those in our personal experience. Nevertheless, the assumptions of quantitative analysis are sometimes more dangerous. They may invest policy implications with the mantle of science, and we are more familiar with the problematic character of assumptions from daily living than with those that underlie quantitative research. That means that unless we take the time to become familiar with the latter, we can be imposed upon by an analysis such as that in *The Bell Curve*. However, the issues are too important for us to allow that to happen. In the same way that war is too important to be left up to generals, social research is too important to be monopolized by researchers.

The Bell Curve purports to show that low intelligence is a powerful cause of conditions such as poverty, unemployment, school failure, family failure, and moral failure. It invites its readers to join in the investigation of how much such conditions depend on intelligence, how much intelligence is biogenetic, and how much of the variation between groups and societies depends upon genetic endowment. But the view that *The Bell Curve* has shown any effects of intelligence at all confuses the assumptions it brings to the data with the conclusions that may be drawn. The idea that the data show any effect of intelligence whatsoever requires a peculiar, asymmetric, and implausible treatment of SES and IQ. IQ is measured very late, simultaneously to the dependent variables being explained, and it is compared to an index of SES dominated by parents' education. It is this implausible and unjustified procedure that produces the "findings" in Part II of *The Bell Curve*.

Appendix 2

The Scholarship of The Bell Curve

There is remarkable variation in the evaluation of *The Bell Curve*'s scholarship and coverage of prior and disagreeing theory. Of the nearly one-hundred reviews collected in Fraser (1995) and Jacoby and Glauberman (1995), the great majority criticize its coverage as biased, selective, and slanted.[331] However, some reviewers go out of their way to commend the book for broad, even-handed coverage.[332] And certainly, with an immense bibliography of some one-thousand items, it is clear that Herrnstein and Murray have gone to great trouble to create the impression of wide, almost encyclopedic coverage. Further, at many points they either rest their argument on what they claim is the scientific wisdom, beyond scholarly dispute,[333] or their argument gives the appearance of laying out opposed positions and leaving it to the reader to decide.

The variation in evaluation is partly due to whether the reviewer agrees with the conservative political program of *The Bell Curve* or with its central theses, and it is partly due to disciplinary affiliation. Theorists from psychology, economics, and political theory are somewhat more likely to accept its claims to give fair and adequate coverage; theorists from fields such as sociology, education, or social work are more likely to view its coverage as biased. In fields of study central to the argument of *The Bell Curve*, such as race relations, mobility, education, the family, or affirmative action, there is no unanimity as to what are the most essential scholarly works and positions to confront. Furthermore, even when there is general agreement as to the most central works in the field, it is possible to disagree about the responsibility of a work such as *The Bell Curve* to acknowledge or to deal with those works. A polemical work has a different responsibility from a work of general scholarship. Even among scholarly works, some theorists are more likely to emphasize the general scholarly responsibilities in research than others. For example, in constructing a regression equation, most social theorists would regard the model (the choice of what variables to include in the analysis and the interpretation of their relationships) as a product of prior theory and research, requiring a general review of the literature[334] while some would regard it as an essentially arbitrary choice of the researcher.

Thus, the question of bias in scholarship is not a simple one. Nevertheless, we do not think it is only or mainly a question of subjective judgment. On most of the topics *The Bell Curve* addresses, there are well-known, established bodies of scholarship. A balanced treatment has to address that scholarship. Nor is it only a question of citing the relevant works. A fair and honest treatment will not merely cite them but will come to terms with their analyses and findings. Herrnstein and Murray try to give an impression of balanced coverage, but that the impression is an illusion. They prominently cite and discuss a handful of works critical of their approach.[335] But in all cases they have ignored the bulk of the relevant theory and research, and even the works that they cite that disagree with their approach are often glibly dismissed, or ignored in their subsequent analyses. The appearance of balanced debate is a product of selecting a few scholarly works, giving a distorting spin to their argument, and then juxtaposing them to a series of marginal, racist works, widely recognized to be without scientific foundation. Herrnstein and Murray misrepresent the balance of scholarship in the fields of:

Race and Ethnic Relations

On no topic is Herrnstein and Murray's highly selective coverage of theory more evident than in the field of race and ethnic relations. Uncited and unacknowledged are the works of the Chicago School such as Park (1950) and Frazier (1966), as well as the related community studies and theory such as DuBois (1899). Nor do they include the works of Boas or his students, which established the modern anthropology of race (Boas, 1938; Harris, 1968; Montagu, 1974).

Although Herrnstein and Murray cite a very large number of works dealing with race, they do not cite, acknowledge, or address the work generally acknowledged as central to the analysis of race relations in the United States: Myrdal (1964). Nor do they acknowledge the bulk of the stream of research that followed it, such as Williams (1964), Pettigrew

(1964), Parsons and Clark (1966), Lieberson (1980), or Farley (1984). They cite Jaynes and Williams (1989), but they appear not to have read it.

Instead, the bulk of their references to literature on race is to writers such as Phillipe Rushton (11 citations), Richard Lynn (17 citations), Arthur Jensen (24 citations), and other members of the editorial board of *Mankind Quarterly* (20 citations). In an attempt to give the impression of coverage that is not entirely slanted, they refer to a few people critical of their position such as James Flynn (7 citations), John Ogbu (1 citation), and William J. Wilson (1 citation). In each of these cases, however, Herrnstein and Murray fail to cite the key findings or theoretical arguments. For example, Flynn is presented prominently but described as giving a finding about the drift of IQ scores that is not relevant to the analysis of group difference. His cross-sectional finding that the drift is greatest with "highly g-loaded," "culture-neutral" tests, such as Raven's Matrices, is neither acknowledged nor addressed even though it is a decisive obstacle for Herrnstein and Murray's central assumption that "g-loaded" tests measure genetic capacities.

Genetics

The Herrnstein and Murray coverage of the anthropology and sociology of race is matched by their complete failure to deal with the mainstream works on the genetics of race, such as Cavalli-Sforza (1994). Their coverage of genetic arguments and issues is even more selective.

We have discussed in the text their use, despite their own disclaimer, of within-group heritability as an estimate of the degree that group differences are genetic and individual characteristics are immutable. Their coverage of prior theorists is designed to support this treatment. The great bulk of the 1970s "IQ debate" is uncited and unacknowledged. A few figures such as Richard Lewontin, Leon Kamin, and Stephen J. Gould are prominently, but very selectively, cited. However, their work is often misrepresented, and is not acknowledged or discussed at points in the argument where it is most relevant.

In addition to misrepresenting and misinterpreting heritability, Herrnstein and Murray have completely ignored work of more than 20 years standing that provides evidence about the nature of genetic differences between races. This work (Lewontin, 1972; Nei and Roychoudhury, 1974) quite clearly demonstrates that the overwhelming bulk of genetic variation is within races, not between. That is, for a randomly selected gene, we expect very nearly as much variability from individual to individual within races as we would ever see between two individuals of different races. Were it not for the few genes that affect skin color, hair color and form, and facial traits, we would be unable to classify

individuals into anything resembling the races about which Herrnstein
and Murray appear to care so deeply. This work is nicely summarized by
Cavalli-Sforza *et al.* (1994, p. 19).

Social Mobility

The core argument of Part I of *The Bell Curve*, which plays a powerful
role as an organizing assumption elsewhere, is that there has been a basic
transformation (a "leveling") of social mobility processes in the United
States. There is an immense literature on social mobility, including such
classics as Lipset and Bendix (1959), Blau and Duncan (1967), Hauser
(1975), and Featherman (1976). In general this literature is inconsistent
with the analysis of *The Bell Curve* and it is entirely ignored in that work.
Particularly relevant is the widely accepted "Featherman-Hauser hypothesis," which claims that the main determinants of mobility are structural (i.e., mobility occurs when structural processes are making room at
the top) rather that variation in the amount of circulation mobility. (For a
review, see Kerckhoff, 1995.) This is also ignored in *The Bell Curve*. Instead, after citing eight studies to establish the uncontested fact that education plays a not insignificant role in some kinds of advancement,[336] *The
Bell Curve* depends mainly upon a short article in *Fortune* magazine
(Burck, 1976) to establish their key point.

Social Stratification and Poverty

The Bell Curve almost completely lacks references to the literature on
social structural determinants of poverty, including that of the Chicago
School of Urban Sociology. A useful summary of this work is James Short
(1971). An example of contemporary work in the same tradition is William J. Wilson (1987). While cited in *The Bell Curve*, its message is ignored.
Also omitted is literature tracing a link between causes of, and social policies on, poverty—for example, Danziger, Sandefur, and Weinberg (1986),
and Danziger, et al. (1994). There is a dearth of demographic studies of
poverty. While some of the more relevant U.S. Census publications are
cited, specifically Current Population Reports Series P60, they are used
quite minimally. The analyses of the Economic Policy Institute are completely ignored, although publications such as Mishel and Bernstein
(1993) are an excellent source of facts on poverty.

Education

There is an immense body of literature about success and failure in
education and about the determinants of the present gap between black

and white performance. Some of this analysis merges with more general analyses of mobility (Featherman, 1976; Hauser, 1976). Herrnstein and Murray bemoan the failure to include the analysis of intelligence in the explanations of educational success, but either fail to cite them at all (e.g., Manski and Wise, 1983) or they cite them without analysis only to dismiss them as the conventional environmental wisdom (e.g., Jencks, et al., 1979 cited and ignored in *The Bell Curve*, p. 52). While educational success and failure is complex and is somewhat different at different levels of education, it is strange for a book claiming to be scholarly to ignore panel analyses of reciprocal effects on cognitive flexibility (Miller, Kohn, and Schooler, 1986).

There is an extensive literature on the reasons for the relative lack of educational success by disadvantaged or black students in particular. Herrnstein and Murray give a relatively exhaustive review of those works that blame the failure on the students and then cite, but fail to describe or address, those works that blame the failure on the schools or on the students' situation (Kozol, 1992; Ogbu, 1991). They completely ignore the analyses of educational success in terms of pedagogical strategies and arrangements (e.g., Knapp and Shields, 1991; Stevenson and Stigler, 1992; Wallace, 1994).

Divorce, Women, and Illegitimacy

Herrnstein and Murray ignore analysis of social change in America as it has affected women and the family. Of particular relevance is Bianchi and Spain (1986) and Danziger and Gottschalk (1993). William Julius Wilson's classic study (1987) develops the social processes that trap people in welfare dependency. Among the more specific studies critical to understanding the rise of the single parent household, the high divorce rate and teenaged pregnancy are Furstenberg's two studies of teenaged mothers (1976, 1987). The latter book contains data that demonstrate that out of wedlock childbearing among low-income teenagers does not lead to permanent welfare dependency. Gelles and Pedrick's book (1985) develops the prevalence of domestic violence and the higher level of violence among low-income families, while Weitzman's (1985) discusses the legal changes that have contributed to the present difficulties of divorced women. Hartmann, Kraut, and Tilly (1987) look at the negative effects of the changing job market for women's earnings. The report of the National Criminal Justice Information and Statistical Service (1978) will help to set the record straight on crime. For a good account of family changes see Skolnick and Skolnick (1992).

Racism and Discrimination

Exceeding even the selectivity of *The Bell Curve*'s treatment of race is its treatment of prior research on racism.[337] With some oversimplification, we can describe the literature on racism and discrimination as composed of three streams. The first stream, running from such works as Allport (1954) and Adorno (1950) to Pettigrew (1982), Kleugel and Smith (1986) and Schuman, et al. (1985), analyzes *attitudinal prejudice*. *The Bell Curve* cites or acknowledges none of these works and seems to have overlooked their analyses. A second stream centers on processes that will produce discriminatory behavior even when the perpetrators are not prejudiced and have complete and accurate information. Thurow's analysis of *"statistical discrimination"* is illustrative of others (Spence, 1974; Hacker, 1992). For example, if women or minorities or any other group are 10 percent more likely to show up late for work, to quit, or to mug taxi drivers, then the rational employer or taxi driver may play the odds and decide not to hire them/pick them up. Even if this 10 percent of bad risks is a correct and unbiased perception of the reality, it will unfairly discriminate against the 90 percent of women, minorities, or other group who are not bad risks. *The Bell Curve* does not acknowledge or discuss the literature dealing with statistical discrimination.

A third stream of literature deals with *institutional racism*, sexism, or discrimination (e.g., Ezorsky, 1991; Ringer and Lawless, 1989; Ogbu, 1991). Such works argue that many structures, from business management to education, are now dominated by majority groups. These present a fundamentally hostile environment to anyone who is a token minority (e.g., Kanter, 1977). In general, by systematically refusing to examine any work that analyzes racism as a significant force, Herrnstein and Murray can assume that it no longer exists as a significant force.

These biases and omissions reflect the theses they desperately wish to get across. The form of their argument is often not to argue for a thesis but to present a series of positions from existing theory, leaving the question open. We have tried to give the reader a more balanced picture of the existing social research. Familiarity with that research demonstrates that Herrnstein and Murray have written an intensely polemical book disguised as an uncommitted and encyclopedic work of scholarship.

Notes

Notes to Chapter 1

1. Gingrich (1994), to be further discussed in Chapter Nine.

2. Social theorists define ascriptive roles or positions as those into which the occupant is born, in a way not modifiable by his or her choices. Thus, inequalities associated with race, sex, and accidents of birth are ascriptive.

3. After the Civil Rights movement, "colored person," or "Negro" tended to be replaced by "black." More recently, some people have advocated "Afro-American," "African American," or "person of color." In the 1982 General Social Survey, non-white respondents were asked, "What do you like to be called, 'black,' 'Colored,' 'African American' or does it make no difference?" Of those stating a preference, 77% chose "black," with the remainder about equally divided between "Negro," "Colored" and "African American." Therefore, though we cannot know what will be the dominant preference, we shall use "black."

4. In fact, Chapter Eight of *The End of Racism* (D'Sousa, 1995), "Institutional Racism and Double Standards: Racial Preferences and Their Consequences," is a roughly fifty page summary of the argument of *The Bell Curve*.

5. Gingrich (1995), p. 80. Gingrich's analysis will be the focus of Chapter Nine.

6. We shall see in Chapter Nine that the new political right in the United States is a complex of highly contradictory tendencies. Usually the political "left," advocating greater equality and redistribution, is distinguished from the "right," resisting such changes or advocating a return to earlier social forms. In the United States today, the center of the new right are the congressmen centered

around Newt Gingrich's *Contract with America* and its proposals to devolve most federal programs to the states.

7. Merton (1973).

8. As Herrnstein and Murray admit (*The Bell Curve*, p. 410) a well known case in which failure to use a capacity appears to lead to its extinction is language acquisition (e.g., Davis, 1947; Pines, 1981). Unless one learns to use language by a certain time, one will never be able to do so. Perfect pitch seems to be another case, and a major question is the degree to which cognitive functions are similar.

9. Hofstadter (1955). The nature of Social Darwinism and even whether there is a coherent strand of theory so designated, is contested by Banister (1979). Ultimately it is a matter of the definition and the purposes of the analysis. The family resemblance between the Social Darwinist theorists is unmistakable, but if one examines any two theorists closely enough, one finds that they differ.

10. Chase (1977).

11. Aristotle (1947), p. 553-563.

12. Spencer (1994).

13. Kevles (1985).

14. Chase (1977).

15. The psychometric movement of the early twentieth century was not politically uniform. The issue is not the psychology of intelligence but the sociology of intelligence, the ways that intelligence results from and contributes to social structures. Herrnstein and Murray insist on the distinction between a figure such as Lewis Terman, presented as neutral and liberal, and a figure such as Brigham (the founder of the Educational Testing Service), who adopted the racist distinction between Nordic, Alpine, and Mediterranean peoples to argue for restriction of immigration. As Mensh & Mensh (1991), among others, have pointed out, the different strands formed a single cable. The rapid success of intelligence testing, had little to do with science. Rather, the elite and middle class in the United States, threatened by immigration, welcomed measures that seemed to support their superiority and segregation.

16. Despite the claims of Herrnstein and Murray to the contrary, the broad streams of psychometric and eugenic analysis were connected to mass nativism (that is, opposition to immigration) and racism, through theorists such as Brigham and Harry Hamilton Laughlin. Nativism and racism provided the mass audience and political muscle that allowed the more academic movements to have powerful disastrous effects, both here and in Germany.

17. Lane and Miller in Jacoby and Glauberman (1995).

18. As Jencks (1980) points out, discussions stressing heritability often imply falsely that "due to genes" and "due to environment" are exhaustive and mutually exclusive categories. If skin color is heritable, then anything associated with it will be heritable; to infer that such things are not environmental and cannot be eliminated by social changes in a known fallacy. Herrnstein and Murray simply ignore Jencks' argument, but as Appendix 2 shows in other cases, even when they cite the relevant works, they ignore their consequences and implications.

19. *The Bell Curve*, p. 520.

20. Montagu (1974), especially the appendix on ethnic groups.

21. *The Bell Curve*, for example, pp. 312, 413.

22. Kaus (in Fraser, 1995, p. 136), notes that in the 1994 symposium, when this issue was raised, Murray said that he had not thought about that point. But Murray says that he has been working on this book for more than five years. It is hard to understand how he could have failed to think about a point so central to social policy debates about race and affirmative action.

23. Moreover he argues that all remedial programs, Civil Rights laws, or affirmative action programs make excuses for and therefore encourage those alleged cultural pathologies.

24. Kaus in Fraser (1995), pp. 130-9.

25. An earlier draft of this book contained a large number of extended quotations from *The Bell Curve*. Given the carefully constructed arguments and rhetoric of *The Bell Curve*, we believed that it was only fair to allow the authors to speak in their own words. However, when we wrote to Basic Books (MacMillan) for permission to quote from *The Bell Curve*, the permissions editor informed us the Murray would require to see the sections of our draft which are the context of the quotations. She emphasized that Murray was very concerned about the adverse publicity *The Bell Curve* received, and so he has set up a group to ensure that the text around any quotations does not misrepresent what he regards as the argument of *The Bell Curve*. We sent the relevant pages of our working draft and, after some delay, we received a restrictive permission for the exact phrasing of that draft, conditional on a fee of $300. The language of the permission required that any changes we make in the draft be submitted to Murray's group for approval, in order for us to use the quotations.

We reluctantly decided to eliminate most quotations, bringing them down to the normal guidelines of "fair use," substituting paraphrases and citations for direct quotations. We do not contest Murray's legal right to restrict or control use of quotations from *The Bell Curve* in any way he pleases, or to charge what he sees fit. Nevertheless, norms of science prohibit many practices that are legal, good business, and canny politics. Specifically, the norms of science are collectivistic and universalistic (Merton, 1973). We believe that Murray is attempting to use copyright law to allow only those works which view his arguments as valid to quote from *The Bell Curve*.

26. A majority of the sixty reviews collected in Jacoby and Glauberman (1995) would defend that characterization.

27. Indeed, D'Sousa constructs analogous policy implications from an argument that suggests blacks are culturally deficient. D'Sousa's argument is directed against "cultural relativism." His failure to understand anthropological cultural relativism is both cause and effect of his view that social scientists are judges, set up to evaluate the value of cultures and individual behaviors. But cultural relativism is not mainly about being a judge. One must understand cultures and behaviors if one is to explain or judge them. Many of the blunders of nineteenth century anthropology and sociology stemmed from being in too great a hurry to make a value judgement. Neither an environmental explanation nor a cultural understanding of ghetto behavior implies normative approval—i.e., "excusing it."

28. Obviously, the answer partly depends upon the definition of "racism." As we shall see in Chapter Six, Herrnstein and Murray, although they have no explicit discussion, implicitly define racism as a set of individual attitudes. Thus,

like D'Sousa, they deny the existence of institutional racism or, for that matter, institutional sexism, classism, or privilege of other kinds. In our concluding chapters, we will suggest that institutional racism, based upon vicious cycles of deprivation, often requires only government inaction to thrive. But even if racism is seen solely as attitudinal prejudice, it is hard to see how exposure to Herrnstein and Murray's arguments could do anything but increase racism, no matter how they are combined with the admonition to treat each person as an individual.

29. Snipp (1989).

30. In the social sciences, basic assumptions about what forces are involved in some process are often called a "model" (Blalock, 1979: 154-155; See Appendix 1, below). Some models are particularly potent, regardless of their empirical adequacy, due to their connection to policy proposals. *The Bell Curve* must be evaluated at several different levels because it proposes a reductionist analytical model linked to the individualistic world view of the New Right, and so any attempt to deal with only one aspect of its argument will fail to engage its main point.

31. In our Chapter Nine, we shall see that there is considerable tension between the orienting assumptions of different components of the New Right. The racist reductionism of white supremacist groups is in sharp contradiction to the individualism of libertarian intellectuals; both are in conflict with the moralism of the Christian Coalition. A key political role of right-wing intellectuals such as Murray is to construct positions within which these contradictions can coexist.

32. William Julius Wilson, "Public Policy Research and The Truly Disadvantaged" in Jencks and Peterson (1991b), pp. 461-481.

33. William Julius Wilson, "Studying Inner-City Social Dislocations," *American Sociological Review* 56 (1991a):1-14.

34. The main development of all the social sciences is based on the insight that we are social beings and that acquisitive, power-seeking, or gender-related behaviors, which seem innate and natural, are actually products of socialization and of cultural, familial, peer, and structural influences. We know this partly because different societies differ. This fundamental insight, which appeared in different forms in anthropology, history, political science and sociology, both in Europe and in the United States (Knapp, 1991), is continuously ignored by *The Bell Curve* which without argument assumes that the relevant determinants are innate in individuals.

35. Chase (1977).

36. Among the many critiques of individualistic culture of poverty accounts of social problems was Ryan (1976).

37. Weschler Adult Intelligence Scale.

38. Morgenthau (1994), p. 150. Along with the special issue of *The New Republic* devoted to *The Bell Curve*, this issue of *Newsweek* was one of the principal works that made *The Bell Curve* into a media event in 1994.

39. Neisser, et al., 1995; Blum, 1978; Mensh and Mensh, 1991. Herrnstein and Murray acknowledge that psychological theorists have long been split on the issue of the one-dimensionality of intelligence, but it is characteristic of their mode of argument that after citing one general work by Gardner (1983) and another by Sternberg (1988), they proceed to define themselves as "the classic tradition" and to ignore all the concrete works which directly bear on their arguments.

40. Sternberg (1985).

41. Many of the works collected in Fraser (1995) and Jacoby and Glauberman (1995) focus on the cognitive reductionism of Herrnstein and Murray's argument. A balanced selection of the range of opinion among psychologists is given in Sternberg (1995), and Sternberg's own position is briefly stated in Sternberg (1996). Works such as Gordon (1995) show the broader range of intelligent competencies and abilities that interest most employers or potential colleagues.

42. As we shall see, their argument is not entirely consistent on the relation of test performance and education. While some parts of their argument treat the SAT as a measure of fixed, biogenetic ability, other parts treat aggregate SAT scores as a measure of the effectiveness of education. While later portions of their analysis demonstrate an effect of education on such test scores, they underestimate those effects by a factor of two or three (Korenman and Winship, 1995; Neal and Johnson, 1994), and their earlier analyses either fail to control education as a cause of different test scores at all, or they run analyses for some subsets of respondents, according to educational degree, without any analysis of how education fits into the causal structure of deprivation.

43. We will review the analysis of Fischer *et al.* (1996) in chapter four. A careful analysis of the substantive content of the Armed Forces Qualifications Test shows that it manifestly concerns tasks from school. Test scores are much more highly correlated with schooling than with age, and in fact, once one controls schooling, they are *negatively* correlated with age. This is consistent with the fact that one forgets this material if one is away from it; it is inconsistent with Herrnstein's and Murray's interpretation that there is a developmental emergence of an innate ability, like hand-eye coordination. And Appendix 1, below, will show that early school test scores are entirely unrelated to the conditions and behaviors, such as poverty, which Herrnstein and Murray purport to explain in terms of a biogenetic cognitive ability. Rather, we shall see that the components of later test scores which are associated with the variables they ascribe to cognitive ability are those which are entirely uncorrelated with early measures which purport to measure such ability.

44. See the section, "Can IQ at Age 15 Be a Cause of Poverty at Age 30?" pp. 129-130 of *The Bell Curve*, and compare this to the demonstration, pp. 590-591, that even the most primitive measure of environmental support, number of years of education, has a significant effect on AFQT score. It is characteristic that what they assume in one place does not take account of what they say elsewhere.

45. Cavalli-Sforza (1994).

46. Chapter Nine will argue that these contradictions represent differences between different groups in the New Right. Specifically, the contradictions are the condition of possibility of an alliance between white supremacist groups and libertarian conservatives.

47. Thus, a condition of the alliance just mentioned is an enormous restriction of range of the meaning of the word "racism." The common element of *The Bell Curve*, *To Renew America*, and *The End of Racism* is to restrict the meaning of the term "racism" to a complex of ideas, excluding the possibility of institutional racism or of calling any actions "racist," except possibly insofar as the actions are motivated by racist ideas.

48. Loewen (1995).

49. The view that the essential problem faced by blacks in the United States is white racism has many defenders today, such as Blauner (1978), Ringer & Lawless (1989), and Steinberg (1995).

50. Despite many disclaimers, the view that blacks have been given equal opportunity but have not measured up to it is the central thrust of both *The Bell Curve* and *The End of Racism*.

51. Authors such as Steinberg (1995) are extremely critical of Myrdal for suggesting that low black standards of living, morals and manners reinforce white racism. While *An American Dilemma* absorbed the work of many American black and radical scholars such as Frazier, Drake, and Johnson, it also led to dismissing, as reductionist, works that centered on jobs, and it overlooked the central dynamic of the Civil Rights movement. No matter what arguments are ultimately produced about the source of those low standards, Steinberg believes, such arguments lead to blaming blacks for white racism. However, Myrdal is quite clear that the essential sources of inequality stem from white institutions: "It is thus the white majority group that naturally determines the Negro's 'place.' All our attempts to reach scientific explanations of why the Negroes are what they are and why they live as they do have regularly led to determinants on the white side of the color line." (1964 [1944] lxxv).

52. This system is what is often called a vicious cycle, but Myrdal noted that it is a highly unstable equilibrium which can work both ways (Myrdal, 1964 [1944]: 75-78, 1065-1070). In such a system of positive feedback, an increase in racism or a decrease in black standard of living will send the system into a pathological or vicious spiral, but an increase in black living standards or a decrease in racism can send the system into a spiral of improvement.

53. Myrdal (1964 [1944]), pp. 1065-1070.

54. There is a considerable literature discussing cumulative causation both in sociological theory and in economics. Moreover, it often overlaps with a newer explosion of theory on catastrophe, chaos, and complexity (e.g. Arthur, 1994). Skott and Auerbach (1995) have pointed out that the earlier forms of theory were often superior to the newer approaches that have sometimes reinvented the wheel without an adequate connection to historical and sociological dynamics.

Notes to Chapter 2

55. Herrnstein (1971), abridged in Jacoby and Glauberman (1995).

56. Herrnstein (1973).

57. Thus, Herrnstein's syllogism requires a remarkable transmutation of the concepts of "merit" or "meritocracy," which are central to their argument. For most people, the concept of "merit" and occupational advancement according to "merit" is attractive because it is associated with an open system in which hard work, motivation and one's ability to do the job determine one's position. But in a paradoxical set of transformations, Herrnstein and Murray associate merit to job productivity; job productivity to IQ test performance; IQ test performance to genes; and thus advocate as a "meritocracy" a hereditary caste system.

58. Herrnstein's formulation of the corollary appears in the reprinted, edited version of his article, on page 612 of Jacoby and Glauberman (1995).

59. Blumberg (1980).

60. Hochschild (1995).

61. *The Bell Curve*, pp. 110-113.

62. Blau (1994).

63. Their only evidence is a hypothetical calculation about Harvard/Radcliffe marriages and a hypothetical anecdote about elite law firms (*The Bell Curve*, pp. 110-113). They cite Mare (1980) as quantitative evidence for increased assortative mating, but in fact Mare argues that educational homogeny, while it increased from 1940 to 1970, may have stabilized or decreased in the 1980s (Mare, 1991, p. 24; Goldberger and Manski, 1995).

64. Whyte (1990). Herrnstein and Murray use Harvard students for their reference, but religious, racial, and ethnic barriers to intermarriage have weakened. Legal bans no longer exist. Increasing geographical mobility, diversity of organizational memberships, or heterogeneous work environments would suggest that heterogeneity of marital partners may be increasing.

65. Chase (1977). In Chapter One we saw that eugenicists such as Davenport analyzed tuberculosis, pellagra (a vitamin B deficiency), or mental retardation in terms of genetic predisposition. These analyses focused on the individual characteristics (i.e., genes) allegedly causing the diseases to run in families. Often the analyses were grossly mistaken and absurdly over-generalized. For example, retardation ("feeble-mindedness") was conceived as a unitary phenomenon, simplistically measured by performance on a paper-and-pencil test, without a clinical evaluation of overall function, and explained monocausally through genetic predisposition. In fact, retardation is often exceedingly complex. Both prenatal traumas (such as those caused by German measles or alcohol) and infant traumas (such as infectious diseases, nutrition, or lead paint) can play a powerful or dominant role.

66. The classic example is the debate about equality of educational opportunity. Coleman (1966) argued that equal educational resources made relatively little difference, on the basis of comparing standardized statistics of the relation of educational resources to educational performance with statistics concerning the relation of family characteristics to educational performance. Among others, Cain and Watts (1968) pointed out that the relevant policy question is the effect of devoting resources to equalizing access to educational resources as opposed to devoting resources to other things.

67. See Goldberger and Manski (1995).

68. Chase (1977).

69. Smith (1985); Chase (1977).

70. Kamin (1974); Mensh and Mensh (1991).

71. Blum (1978, p. 119) notes that "g" had been conceived both as the common factor of intelligence tests and as a general cognitive ability. The fundamental problem of the psychometric movement was the relation between these. Instead of research addressing this relation, figures such as Arthur Jensen and Herrnstein merely equivocated from one meaning to the other, often in subsequent sentences.

72. It is not clear how important this assumption of one-dimensionality is for their argument. In theory, they might be able to construct an argument leading to their policy implications without it. However, the unidimensional concept of IQ produces most of the caste-like implications of their analysis, and is required by their implausible analyses of mating, productivity, and race.

73. Block and Dworkin (1977); Flynn (1980); Gardner (1983); Gould (1981).

74. Gardner (1983).

75. Taylor (1980); Mensh and Mensh (1991).

76. A discussion of the Burt affair may be found in Gould (1981). For an interesting aside on the lasting effects of Burt's fraud, see Paul (1987).

77. Bouchard et al. (1990).

78. McKusick (1994).

79. The statistical measure called the *variance* is used to quantify variation (see Appendix 1).

80. Algebraically, heritability $= V_G/(V_G + V_E)$, in which V_G and V_E are the genetic and environmental contributions to variation, referred to as the genetic and environmental variances.

81. In this discussion we are following Herrnstein and Murray in the implausible assumption that the goodness or poorness of the environment can be measured on some simple linear scale. When they speak of the environments of different groups as having become more similar, they need some such assumption; but as we shall see, the assumption is simplistic and improbable.

82. Jencks, 1980; and see Chapter Six, below.

83. Block and Dworkin (1977); Blum (1978); Gould (1981); Kamin (1974); Lewontin et al. (1984); Mensh and Mensh (1991); Schiff and Lewontin (1994); Taylor (1980); Tucker (1994).

84. There are a number of different forms of the argument that it makes no difference. For example, they suggest a "thought experiment" to show why they believe that it makes next to no difference whether genes are part of the reason for the observed differences. They ask the reader to imagine that tomorrow it is discovered that the black/white difference in measured intelligence is entirely genetic in origin. They ask what difference would that make in the way the reader would approach the question (*The Bell Curve*, p. 312). Here, the question of public policy and of long-term effects is collapsed to individual behaviors and their short-run consequences. Most Germans did not treat most Jews differently as a consequence of Nazi theory, but that does not mean that it had no effect.

85. In the later stages of Herrnstein and Murray's argument, the supposed fact that some people are not very smart, regardless of how they came to be that way, is used to urge the simplifications of moral standards by the reassertion of traditional morality. For example, they say that "the difference between people of low cognitive ability and the rest of the society may be put in terms of a metaphor: everyone has a magnetic compass, but some of those compasses are more susceptible to magnetic storms than others" (*The Bell Curve*, p. 543). Here, the kind of "intelligence" at issue is considerably different from that in the first five-hundred pages of the book.

Notes to Chapter 3

86. Thurow (1996), p. 2.

87. Wilson (1991a); Danziger and Gottshalk (1993); Bartlett and Steele (1992).

88. Tucker (1994); Chase (1977); Kevles (1985); Kamin (1974).

89. For example, they suggest that the most efficient way to raise the IQ of the society is for smarter women to have a higher birthrate than duller women. But they claim to be apprehensive about what might happen if the government decides to social-engineer who has babies. (*The Bell Curve*, pp. 548-549).

90. Ruggles (1988). Also see Chapter Four below.

91. The section, "Dealing with Demography" argues that the United States has in place policies that encourage the "wrong women" to have babies (*The Bell Curve*, pp. 548-549). While Aid to Families with Dependent Children is particularly objectionable to Herrnstein and Murray, all services for low income children are suspect.

92. Their analysis is without foundation. See Chapter Two.

93. One function will not appear for many hundreds of pages. Then Part IV of The Bell Curve, will develop a pseudo-populist castigation of the cognitive elite: liberals, academic social scientists, or readers of The New York Times are members of the cognitive elite. Their support for liberal policies such as affirmative action programs is a reflection of a more general separation from the experiences and real issues of common men and women, who are exposed to the threats of the "cognitively disabled."

94. Mishel and Bernstein (1993), pp. 281-285.

95. Blau and Duncan (1967). See Appendix 2 below.

96. It is not quite correct to say that Herrnstein and Murray or that D'Sousa believe that structures of institutional racism have disappeared. It would be more correct to say that they believe that they never existed in the first place. For instance, D'Sousa says, "Since racism is an ideology of biological superiority, 'institutional racism' is a nonsense phrase that avoids the real problems" (1995, pp. 335-336). Since D'Sousa has narrowed the definition of "racism" to individual beliefs in biological superiority, he can consistently argue that there was nothing racist about slavery. But of course as an institutional system, regardless of a few black slave holders, slavery was a racist system.

97. Such time series and interpretation of trends are notoriously sensitive to choices of beginning and end points. These are never explicitly acknowledged or justified in *The Bell Curve*. Herrnstein and Murray use 1920, the mid 1930s and mid 1960s, and the early 1980s as their primary points of comparison.

98. For example, Cooley reprinted in Jacoby and Glauberman (1995).

99. The argument that is generated is both causal and normative, returning to the main arguments of Spencer. It is argued that laissez faire competition gives everyone a fair chance, so that those with ability get ahead and those who do not get ahead lack ability. At the same time, an elitist moral argument is implied. The language, the images and the main arguments undermine any form of equal moral concern, social egalitarianism or support for equalization of opportunities.

100. That is, 3.5 million out of 11 million (*The Bell Curve*, p. 60).

101. Burck (1976).

102. The question is whether Herrnstein and Murray's scholarship and literature reviews are broad, fair-minded coverage of the main relevant works or slanted and biased selections. The issue is so important that we have devoted Appendix 2 to the question. Here, Herrnstein and Murray willfully ignore the great mass of mobility studies in favor of a biased selection of a few studies to give a misleading impression. Appendix 2 suggests that this is true of their scholarship throughout the book.

103. Hunter (1979; 1980; 1985).

104. Hartigan and Wigdor (1989).

Notes to Chapter 4

105. Center for the Study of Policy Attitudes (1994). The CSPA study commissioned by the producers of the PBS special "America's War on Poverty," was based on focus groups, phone interviews, and data from other surveys accessed through the Public Opinion data base of the Roper Center, University of Connecticut.

106. Jennifer Hochschild refers to programs that seriously attempt to equalize opportunities as "facing up to the American Dream" (1995). In contrast, the line of thought in *The Bell Curve* could be described as using lip service to the American dream to justify elitism. At stake are widely accepted commitments to social equality, legal equality (e.g., the view that one's treatment by the courts should not depend on one's wealth), equality of political power and equal moral concern. Despite differences in the ways that egalitarianism is conceived and defended, Amartya Sen has formulated a position that would receive widespread acceptance: insofar as capabilities are socially generated, they should be equal (Sen, 1992).

107. The Contract with America was widely touted as having used social surveys and focus groups to select only positions with wide public acceptance. Many politicians and citizens were influenced by the false assurance that these were all broadly accepted positions. It was not until nearly a year later that this broad popular support was exposed as a fraud. Gingrich employed the survey results of Frank Luntz, who merely tested highly biased, argumentative and leading questions and slogans, not the provisions of the "contract" (*Philadelphia Inquirer*, November 10, 1995, p. A29).

108. Aldrich and Nelson (1984).

109. Huff (1993).

110. As Appendix 1 describes, a standardized slope is just a measure of the relation between two variables when they are measured in standard deviations from the mean. This is supposed to make it possible to compare their causal effect. However, this notion of comparing causal effects conceals a number of implausible assumptions about the causal forces producing conditions such as poverty or illegitimacy.

111. Cain and Watts, 1970.

112. *The Bell Curve*, pp. 417-46.

113. Herrnstein and Murray have a detailed discussion of the distribution and the slight skew of their measure of intelligence (i.e., using the AFQT89, one tenth

of 1 percent of the highest scorers are given a standardized score of 1.7 rather than 2.8). They do not discuss the distribution and extreme cases of SES.

114. Fischer et al. (1996), Hechman (1994) and Korenman and Winship (1995), among others.

115. Mishel and Bernstein (1993), pp. 281-285.

116. Within the framework of psychometric assumptions, the question is how "reliable" the measures of IQ or SES are. Korenman and Winship (1995) have shown that after correcting for reliability the difference between the effects of SES and IQ disappear. We suggest that it is not even appropriate to conceive of SES as a stable individual trait.

117. In the social sciences, these assumptions are referred to as a "model," and the failure of these assumptions is referred to as "model specification error."

118. Model specification error occurs if there is a discrepancy between the causal processes actually operating and the coefficients one calculates. Pedhazur (1982); Berry (1993).

119. For example, they estimate that a three-point rise in IQ would decrease high school dropouts by 30 percent and illegitimacy rates by 15 percent.

120. As Appendix 1 shows, when the relationships are as weak as those Herrnstein and Murray display, the danger of inappropriately controlling a mediating variable is slight. And in any case, it is only by carrying out the multivariate analyses that one can see whether it is a problem, and it is simple to estimate the degree to which it is one.

121. Even this statement is not true without qualification. Herrnstein and Murray are ambiguous and confusing about whether it is direct effects or total effects that they are estimating. As Appendix 1 shows, even if the effect of education were entirely "due to intelligence" in the sense that the correlation between education and intelligence was due only to the effect of intelligence on education, that would not mean that changing education could not affect outcomes. One way to show this would be to extend the hypothetical example we used in Chapter One, in which blue eyes leads to attention, which leads to verbal ability, which leads to rewards. In that case, if one were to control for verbal ability, blue eyes would have no effect. From a policy standpoint, this would mean that if one equalized attention (i.e. gave equal amounts to brown-eyed children) then blue eyes would not affect rewards.

122. E.g., Zorbaugh (1929); Shaw et al. (1929). Summary of Chicago School literature in Short (1971).

123. Wilson (1991a).

124. For example, Knapp, One World (New York, Harper Collins, 1994).

125. Summary statement in Robertson (1987), pp. 443-444.

126. Easterlin (1987).

127. Mishel and Bernstein (1993), p. 290.

128. U.S. Bureau of the Census, Current Population Reports (1991), pp. 1, 4, and 24.

129. Eitzen and Zinn (1993), pp. 373-374; Mishel and Bernstein (1993).

130. Other useful treatments of the mythology of poverty include Bane and Jencks, 1973, and Fischer et al., 1996.

131. There is nothing intrinsically racist about these myths, and, with the exception of Kleugal and Smith (1986), we are not aware of research that explores how closely correlated they are with racial prejudices and stereotypes. Nevertheless, in the United States today, myths of lazy, sexually promiscuous, dependent, immoral welfare recipients are entwined with racism in many ways, principally by the myth that most welfare recipients are black. This represents the fundamental implicit cooperation between *The Bell Curve* and *The End of Racism*.

132. Moffitt (1992).

133. Mishel and Bernstein (1993), p. 208.

134. U. S. Department of Health and Human Services, Social Security Administration. *Annual Statistical Supplement to the Social Security Bulletin, 1994* (Washington, D.C., Government Printing Office, 1994), pp. 443-446; U. S. Bureau of the Census, *Statistical Abstract of the United States, 1995* (Washington, D.C., Government Printing Office, 1995), pps. 388, 481.

135. Ruggles (1988), p. 18.

136. The Luxembourg Income Study shows how far government programs can reduce childhood poverty rates. Most industrialized nations would have double-digit poverty rates like America's, were it not for their more extensive government poverty programs. Rainwater and Smeeding (1995), Appendix Table A-2.

137. For a good example of unemployment studies using structural factors in the analysis, see Layard (1994) and Schervish (1983).

138. Mishel and Bernstein (1993), p. 146.

139. Costrell (1988).

140. Byrne, Foust, and Therrien (1992).

141. *The Bell Curve*, p. 548. They know that there is no evidence that welfare encourages births and considerable evidence that it does not, but they appeal to the myth that it does so by asserting that the United States has in place policies that socially engineer births.

Notes to Chapter 5

142. For an introduction to logistic regression, see Aldrich and Nelson (1984).

143. At times the subgroups used by Herrnstein and Murray in argument contain quite small numbers. For example, the category of mothers who were separated, divorced, or never married is only 215 of the original sample of 3367. From this small subsample, the authors proceed to argue differences between the bottom 2 or 3 percent and the upper 2 or 3 percent. Two percent of 215 is only four cases—a very small number from which to draw conclusions for the entire United States. A comparison of the top and bottom 5 percent would involve approximately sixteen cases.

144. Malinowski (1927). One need only remember the traditional Chinese family structure, with its multiple wives and concubines, to know that the model of legal marriage of the United States is just one example of family, not the only way society can order its relationships between parents and children. Herrnstein and Murray cite Malinowski in support of their limited view of marriage but ignore the documentation Malinowski provides of the separation of pregnancy from parenting in primitive societies.

145. There is a difference in the ratio of males to females between the white population and the black. In 1992, at the ages of ten to 14, whites had a ratio of 105.2 while the black ratio was 102.5. This difference continues to grow over the age range, with females outnumbering males after the age of 20 for the black population. By the age of 29, the white ratio is 100.9, while the black ratio is 91.4. Under conditions of extreme poverty the sex ratio is even more unequal (*Statistical Abstract*, 1993, p. 20).

The differential expectation of death among babies born alive between males and females and between whites and blacks (rate per 1000 live births in 1990) are at birth for whites 8.55 for males and 6.59 for females, while the rate for blacks is 19.68, for males and 16.30 for females. These differences continue across the lifespan, with males and blacks having higher death rates. By 30 the rate for white males is 1.76 and for females 0.61. For blacks the rate for males is 4.39 and for females, 1.65 (*Statistical Abstract*, 1993, p. 88).

146. Danziger and Gottschalk (1993), pp. 19-97.

147. For a discussion of the relative merits of marriage by a group of low-income women, see Kronick, Family Life and Economic Dependency, Report to the Welfare Administration (1964). See also Furstenburg (1976).

148. Data taken from the study of Kronick (1962).

149. Gelles and Pedrick (1985), pp. 73-74.

150. Weeks (1989), pp. 9-10.

151. Weitzman (1985).

152. In 1989, 3,056,000 marriages were terminated by divorce. In the same year, there were 2,531,000 remarriages (*Statistical Abstract*, 1993, p. 387). On that same page of the Statistical Abstract is evidence that there are more men in arrears on child-support payments among the non-poor than among the poor.

153. In 1950, the U.S. population was 150, 694, 361. By 1990, it was 248, 709, 873 (*Statistical Abstract*, 1993, p. 8). Given a changing population base, the numbers of people who engage in any form of behavior can be expected to rise with the increase of population, without any change in the rate of incidence of such behavior.

154. See the discussion of illegitimacy in Ellwood (1988), pp. 70-72.

155. Luker in Skolnick and Skolnick (1992), pp. 160-172. Their own development is interrupted by childbearing, and they are unlikely to parent the child as adequately as older women. Finally, parenting interrupts education for teenagers, making it difficult for them to complete high school and thus have the credentials essential either to working at a job with adequate pay.

156. Goode (1960).

157. Herrnstein and Murray present illegitimacy as a rapidly rising curve. They plot the percentage of births that are illegitimate over time. This distorts what has occurred. The rising curve is almost entirely due to a falling overall birthrate and a dramatic drop in legitimate births while illegitimate births have remained relatively stable, with black illegitimate births actually declining. The rise in illegitimate births is small and the result of a slightly higher illegitimate birthrate among whites. In 1950 the birthrate per 1,000 was 24.1. By 1990, the birth rate was 16.7 (*Statistical Abstract*, 1993, p. 76). The birthrate for teenagers between the ages of fifteen and nineteen has fallen from 68.3 in 1970 to 59.9 in 1990. Further,

the poorer the woman, the less they want children. Among professional women only 26 percent said they do not intend to have more children. In contrast, 63.8 percent of those who are not high school graduates say they do not intend to have more. Overall, 63.4 percent of black women say they do not want more children (*Statistical Abstract*, 1993, p. 83). More informative graphs showing the numbers of black and white illegitimate births in relation to total births are found in Ellwood (1988, p. 69).

158. *The Bell Curve*, pp. 548-549.

159. See Kronick (1962).

160. See the Committee on Ways and Means, U.S. House of Representatives, *Overview of Entitlement Programs*, 1993 Green Book for statistics on the characteristics of welfare recipients.

161. A nutrition program in Philadelphia intending to improve the diets of unmarried, poor, teenaged pregnant women discovered they could not present meals requiring access to a stove or a kitchen because most of these women had no parents and no home. They were living on the street or moving from place to place, sleeping wherever a casual acquaintance would give them a bed. Instead they had to teach them to choose wisely among the foods available from street vendors.

162. Oppenheimer (1970).

163. See the Manpower studies published annually by the Department of Labor in the 1960s.

164. duRivage (1992).

165. Women with children under six have been entering the labor force in increasing numbers: in 1960, 18.6 percent were working; in 1970, 33.3 percent; in 1980, 45.1 percent; in 1993, 59.6 percent. The fastest-growing employment market for these women is as home health aides, human service workers, and personal and home care aids, all fields where wages are very low, close to if not the minimum wage (*Statistical Abstract*, 1993, pp. 391, 394). In 1990, over one million women lost their jobs (p. 417). While median weekly earnings of white females in 1990 was $355, of black women, $308, private household workers earned an average of $171 a week in 1990 (p. 429). The average AFDC (welfare) payment per month in 1990 was $396 in the United States, with some states having a payment as low as $115 (Alabama). Work pays better than welfare in all states (*Statistical Abstract*, 1993, p. 384).

166. For a concise history, see DiNitto (1995), especially Chapter Six.

167. In 1990, 14.5 percent of Americans were living below the poverty line of an annual income of $13,359 (*Statistical Abstract*, 1993, p. 441). Fifteen percent of white children were living below the poverty line; 44.2 percent of black children. For black children living with both parents, 34.7 percent were in poverty, while 65.3 percent were who lived with single parent—and 61.3 percent of those living with the mother alone were in poverty (p. 475). The highest percentage of children in poverty are in the poorest states of Alabama, Mississippi, Arkansas, New Mexico, and Louisiana—and our nation's capital, Washington, D.C. (p. 477).

168. Case example from the files of Kronick (1962).

169. U. S. Department of Agriculture, Agricultural Research Service (1965).

170. Hirschi and Selvin (1967).

Notes to Chapter 6

171. Schwartz in Dunbar (1984), p. 61.

172. Murray's colleague, D'Sousa, in *The End of Racism*, makes the argument that, "Racism undoubtedly exists, but it no longer has the power to thwart blacks or any other group in achieving their economic, political and social aspirations" (1995, p. 525). D'Sousa makes the implausible argument that the cases such as Colin Powell and Clarence Thomas show that race is no longer a master status. Neither did the case of Frederick Douglas show that race was not a master status in the 1860's. D'Sousa's book fleshes out, elaborates and supplements *The Bell Curve*'s assertion of a great social leveling. It is equally implausible.

173. For D'Sousa, the only area where one is entitled to equal treatment and concern is in the law. But it is evident that in a system of cumulative causation, color blind forms of law, combined with ignoring the larger structures of inequality, will not even provide equal treatment by judges and police, let alone equal social capabilities.

174. Quadagno (1994).

175. As we shall see, racism should not be identified with individual attitudinal prejudice and sentiments. Changes in political organization and mobilization, including the mobilization and action of white supremacist groups, are relatively independent of changes in prejudiced attitudes in the population at large. Moreover, institutional structures and policies that are not motivated by prejudice may have a racist impact.

176. Jaynes and Williams (1989) document the limited changes. White opposition to black-white contact in the 1980s ranges from 3 percent in the case of jobs, through 10-15 percent in the case of schools and housing, and it reaches 60 percent in the case of marriage. Loewen (1995) gives a good historical analysis.

177. Edsall and Edsall (1992); Greenberg (1994).

178. Jackman (1994); Kleugal and Smith (1986).

179. This is, of course, a misleading view of the role of environmental variation, since heritabilities will depend on the variation in traits caused by environmental variation, and not with the environmental variation itself.

180. The concept of institutional racism was introduced by Charmichael and Hamilton (1967), who contrasted individual racist actions with a subjective racist intent (the bombing of a black church) with more pervasive institutional structures (ghetto segregation and slum housing). The concept was rapidly extended to cover such institutional arrangements as jobs, education, courts, government, political parties, medicine and housing (Knowles and Prewitt, 1969; Blauner, 1972), and analogous concepts such as institutional sexism were developed.

181. Although not as a function of color-blind policy, for the policies would have to countervail those forces.

182. We have simplified some aspects of Myrdal's analysis of the practical problem of discrimination. He argues that discrimination breeds more discrimination in at least two other ways. First, whenever there is a wall of inequality and segregation, unprejudiced persons may be motivated to contribute to it. Unprejudiced counselors or even parents may steer blacks away from careers where they will be excluded later on. And if there is a wall in housing, jobs or social life, many blacks may gravitate to any break in the wall, leading whites who have no

objection to an integrated situation to maintain an unbroken wall in order to avoid being inundated and placed within an all-black neighborhood, job or institution. Considerable subsequent analysis of non-prejudiced discrimination and institutional racism is ignored by Herrnstein and Murray. D'Sousa mounts a determined defense of such discrimination.

183. Myrdal (1964 [1944]), pp. 207-209, 308-309, 320, 435-483, 623.

184. That both positive and negative spirals are possible was the core of Myrdal's analysis, and it is related to the work for which he later won his Nobel Prize. Many examples of positive and negative spirals have occurred. The idea that "The only good Indian is a dead Indian" did not spring full fledged from Western culture. Rather, as Indians were segregated, marginalized, impoverished and deprived of political power, the stereotype of violent, lying, thieving beggars could grow, and resistance to the theft of land and livelihood could lead to coercion and genocide. The case of the Hawaiian Portuguese becoming "native" is probably another example of a negative spiral (Geschwender, 1988). Among a number of cases of positive spirals, there is the case of the Mississippi Chinese (Loewen, 1995).

185. As we have noted, D'Sousa, Herrnstein, and Murray take the increase in the black middle class and the formation of an elite consisting of figures such as Colin Powell or Clarence Thomas as evidence for the end of racism.

186. See Jaynes and Williams (1989). D'Sousa takes the growth of the black middle class as evidence for the end of racism. He can do so only by defining anyone not poor as "middle class." For example, "As of 1994, only about one third of blacks were poor; the rest were middle class or better off" (1995, p. 329). Apparently D'Sousa is using the federal poverty line (around $14,000 for a family of four) as the boundary of middle class, even though the great majority of those living at the poverty line are chronically malnourished. Thus, he ignores precisely the group that has been most damaged by the loss of jobs and social services, namely the black working class (Massey and Denton, 1993; Wilson, 1991a).

187. For example, the 1977 Commission on Civil Rights report, *Last Hired, First Fired*, showed that when three recessions and severe government cutbacks in the 1970s combined with seniority systems, an enormous number of the blacks hired in the late 1960s and the early 1970s were then fired.

188. Jaynes and Williams (1989).

189. Cavalli-Sforza *et al.* (1994).

190. Montagu (1974).

191. They imply that the lower test scores cannot be due to racism, because Asians (and Jews) were exposed to racism, but now have high scores. Herrnstein and Murray thus assume that "racism" like any difference in environments, is a simple and uniform quantity. Chapter Two has shown the implausibility of that assumption. Specifically, they ignore differences in stereotypes and identities and their different effects on test performance.

192. *The Bell Curve*, p. 277.

193. Their series of questionable or mistaken treatments of these data are documented in Hauser (1995).

194. They say that earlier chapters have shown that low cognitive ability "raises the risk" of "living in conditions" or "acting in ways" that society hopes to change

(*The Bell Curve*, p. 369). Here, as elsewhere, their ambiguity about one issue covers up their sleight of hand about another. They say that they don't know whether it is the conditions or the behaviors that are at fault, but in either case, they say, they have shown that low cognitive ability raises the risk, in the same way that a high level of cholesterol raises the risk of heart disease. They have shown no such thing. They have merely shown that poor test scores are correlated with those conditions or those ways of acting, which is a different matter. See Appendix 1 below.

195. This is a different form of the "It matters little" ploy that we analyzed in Chapter One. On the one hand, they produce a biological determinist argument, replete with the classical eugenic implications that nothing can be done by changing ghetto conditions, that births should be discouraged and immigration halted. On the other, they slide to radically different arguments about culture and law, saying it matters little. We have argued that the scientific and intellectual dishonesty of the argument is the precondition of the political alliance between those who believe in black biological inferiority, those who believe in black cultural inferiority, and those who do not believe in black inferiority but wish to reduce government social programs.

196. Despite this disclaimer, the authors have already made a wrong-headed use of heritability as an estimate of how much different environments would have to explain the difference between the races (*The Bell Curve*, p. 299).

197. That is, here we will assume that the norms of reaction all have the same slope. For example, we assume that there are not some plants that benefit from a lot of sun while others are damaged. While the assumption of no interactions is probably not true, it provides the case most friendly to the argument in *The Bell Curve*.

198. See, for instance, Lewontin (1994).

199. Lewontin (1972), Nei and Roychoudhury (1974), Cavalli-Sforza *et al.* (1994).

200. Even some scholars such as Flynn (1980) have suggested that the analogy requires that one show that there are two greenhouses; i.e., that there is a significant environmental difference for blacks and whites. But a host of studies have shown that perceived race is an extremely salient characteristic, a "master status" that, independently of socio-economic status, influences how one is treated.

201. Again, Jencks (1980) shows why it is misleading to suppose that effects that are heritable and genetic are, thereby not environmental.

202. With regard to the presumption that intelligence should be regarded as a one-dimensional fixed characteristic of individuals, Sternberg (1995) gives a popular summary of his reasons for considering intelligence a multidimensional ability poorly measured by AFQT-type tests. His massive *Encyclopedia of Intelligence* examines some of the research and theory relevant to that claim. Fischer *et al.* (1996) have shown some of the ways that a multidimensional and process-oriented view leads to a coherent explanation of many features of the NLSY data which are quite mysterious within Herrnstein's and Murray's framework.

203. For example, Flynn (1980).

204. This section is indebted to the many good psychological analyses of *The Bell Curve* such as Gardner, Gould, and Nisbett, in Fraser (1995).

205. The point has been made in many ways. Baron Von Zetnikoff's "Proposal to Resolve the Nature-Nurture Controversy" (Journal of Abnormal Sociology, reprinted in Blum, 1978) suggested taking 200 children from upper IQ parents and 200 children from lower IQ parents and randomly giving them controlled environments. For example, the poor environments would have to systematically lower self-esteem, self-confidence, and academic motivation by random penalties. The experiment is clearly unethical.

206. Our discussion follows Richard Nisbett, "Race, IQ, and Scientism" in Fraser (1995). The seven major studies are Scarr and Weinberg, "The Minnesota Transracial Adoption Studies," *Child Development* 54 (1983):260-267; Tizard, et al., "Environmental Effects on Language Development" *Child Development* 43 (1972):342-343; Scarr, et al., "Absence of a Relationship between Degree of White Ancestry," *Human Genetics* 39 (1977):73-77, 82-83; Loehlin, et al., "Blood Group Genes and Negro-White Ability Differences," *Behavior Genetics* 3 (1973):263-270; Witty and Jenkins, "Educational Achievements of a Group of Gifted Negro Children, *Journal of Educational Psychology* 25 (1934):548; and Willerman, et al., "Intellectual Development of Children from Interracial Mating," *Behavior Genetics* 4 (1974):84-88.

207. For example, the Tizard study is known to lack some of the flaws that Scarr, among others, has pointed to in Scarr and Weinberg. All children were raised in the same enriched environment. Tizard found the white children with somewhat lower IQs than the mixed race children, who were somewhat lower than the black children.

208. For most studies, they depend on the ambiguous summary in Loehlin, Lindsey, and Spuhler (1975).

209. Flynn (1991); Stevenson and Stigler (1992).

210. Mercer (1984); Ogbu (1991).

211. Recall that a correlation of 0.22 explains only about 5 percent of the variation in the dependent variable, even if it represents a simple causal influence.

212. Fischer *et al.* (1996, pp. 183-203). Specifically, they compare some 17 ethnic groups, who differ in social status but often not in biological ethnicity in terms of their test scores. For example, they compare Burakumin to non-Burakumin Japanese, as well as Koreans to native Japanese in Japan; they compare Jews to Arabs and Eastern Jews to Western Jews in Israel; and they compare Blacks, Latinos and American Indians in the United States. In all cases, the groups of lower status, regardless of their ethnicity, do more poorly in schools and on academic tests.

Notes to Chapter 7

213. Chapter Nine will detail the fact that on the far right wing of American politics today, there is a complex and turbulent interaction of many groups. None of them is entirely new, and the resulting configuration has not stabilized. We use the catch-all term New Right to refer to this configuration.

214. *The Bell Curve* has a two-page preface that argues that opposition to theories of genetic intellectual inequality stems from a commitment to the view of human equality and from support of policies that are based upon that commitment, and that the main motivation of *The Bell Curve* is to defeat those policies:

"solutions founded on better education, on more and better jobs..." ignore the role of intelligence "to grope with symptoms instead of causes, to stumble with supposed remedies that have no chance of working." (*The Bell Curve*, pp. xxii-xxiii).

215. Kleugel and Smith (1986).

216. *The Bell Curve*, p. 414.

217. As is well known, the forced sterilization laws of the United States at the time served as the model for the sterilization and euthanasia laws in Nazi Germany [Kevles (1985) and Kamin (1974)], and those then served as the opening wedge to legitimize policies of extermination.

218. The alleged inefficiency is supposed to stem from the greater productivity of those with high scores on IQ tests, but as Goldberger and Manski (1995) point out, their arguments about productivity contain elementary fallacies. *The Bell Curve* says that "An employer that is free to pick among applicants can realize large economic gains from hiring those with the highest IQs. An economy that lets employers pick applicants with the highest IQs is a significantly more efficient economy" (p. 64). However, one cannot validly get from the first claim to the second. What is true of each employer is not true of the whole economy.

219. Despite Murray's advocacy of juvenile incarceration as the cost effective and efficient response to juvenile delinquency, neither he nor the political Right as a whole calculates the cost to the society of the immense prison population in the United States. That cost involves not only direct expenses of prisons, but also forgone incomes and indirect expenses of a police state.

220. Kozol (1992).

221. Many poor children, in the richest country in the world, had never seen a doctor or dentist, never enjoyed an adequate diet or played with art material or seen children's books. Many needed glasses, hearing aids, or medical treatment.

222. Schorr (1988). Their analysis reflects the limitations of some early "culture of poverty" rationales for compensatory programs, which had suggested that early exposure to positive models would transform children's identities, including their IQ scores, without having to change their situation (Zigler and Muenchow, 1992). It is a cheap shot to evaluate a program against such unrealistic claims.

223. This argument merely recapitulates Jensen (1987).

224. They imply but do not say that the increase in openness of people taking the SAT mainly involved minority students, and so they restrict their explanation to whites. They say that during much of the period of declining SAT scores, the pool of white respondents taking the SAT was declining. (In fact, it increased slightly during the 1970s, but they suggest that since parental income and education remained constant that increase cannot be responsible for declining SATs.)

225. Recall that they implicitly promise readers that they and their children are cognitively gifted given that they are reading *The Bell Curve*.

226. They use the funding priorities of the Elementary and Secondary Education Act to suggest that education for the gifted is not receiving the resources and attention it deserves. This is like arguing that since need-based scholarships at Harvard go to relatively needy students, the whole of Harvard policy is oriented to the needs of needy students.

227. Wallace and Graves (1995).

228. Fischer *et al.* (1996 p.45) give the simple but not unrealistic example of choosing to admit ten students from among the 20 hypothetical students with the SAT scores listed below. If the two black students are the ones starred, and if the admissions criteria were exclusively SAT scores, admitting all students above 1000 and rejecting all those below, then the difference between mean white and mean black scores will be about as they appear in Herrnstein and Murray's data. Thus, even a strict, mechanical reliance on SAT scores will produce the kinds of distributions that Herrnstein and Murray find.

| 1300 | 1225 | 1200 | 1175 | 1150 | 1125 | 1100 | 1075 | *1050 | 1025 |
| 1000 | 975 | 950 | 925 | 900 | 875 | 850 | 825 | *800 | 750 |

229. That is, they suggest that there are underprivileged blacks (South Bronx) and privileged blacks (Scarsdale), underprivileged whites (Appalachia) and privileged whites (also Scarsdale). They suggest that policies ought to help both the South Bronx and the Appalachian applicants but now help the Scarsdale blacks instead.

230. Harris notes that this move, which might be termed abolishing affirmative action in the name of affirmative action, was central to the California initiative. The framers of the California initiative could trade on ambiguity and ignorance. Voters in California supported the initiative two to one because it claims to make preferences illegal, but oppose it two-to-one if its abolition of affirmative action is evident (*New York Times*).

231. Ezorsky (1991); Wilson (1991a). It is individual racism when a school turns down a qualified candidate because of a sentiment of racism on the part of a school official. It is institutional racism when a school fails to recruit at black schools or adopts recruitment criteria that will reject most black candidates, even if this occurs from nonracist individual motives.

232. Mills (1994); Ezorsky (1991); Pettigrew, et al. (1982).

233. D'Sousa is concerned to protect the rights of cab drivers or employers to protect their rational self interest. His argument, if accepted, guarantees the rights of teachers, doctors, store owners, employers, or other purveyors of essential services to deny them to any minority on the basis of fears of threat, damage, or disadvantage. However, even if the perception is correct that the group member might be a poor risk or might not fit in, the action is still discriminatory and extends to the entire group what may be true of some members of it. Moreover, contrary to D'Sousa's view, there is considerable evidence that the perceptions are often stereotyped and incorrect. The view that the perceptions are almost always correct is a consequence of D'Sousa's implausible view of opportunity and of his narrow conception of "racism."

234. For instance, Kanter (1977) showed that token women in predominantly male administrative positions faced a systematically disadvantageous situation, regardless of the particular motives of the men with whom they worked.

235. *The Bell Curve*, p. 547. Thus, the discrimination is "fair" from the standpoint of the employer or other discriminator, to the extent that it really does reflect the odds for the group. But it is unfair from the standpoint of the members of the group who are discriminated against because of actions of other members of the group. D'Sousa enormously exaggerated the incidence of "rational

discrimination," providing no evidence that many or most employers who think they are discriminating rationally are not actually motivated by prejudice.

236. Sen (1992).

237. In later cases, the notion of powerful adverse impact came to be specified in different ways, such as the four-fifths rule of the 1989 Code of Federal Regulations, which established that a requirement whose selection rate for any race, sex, or ethnic group was less than four-fifths that of the dominant group, was one with powerful adverse impact. See Edwards (1995, pp. 103-125).

238. A more elaborate argument, showing the same distortion of the 80 percent criterion, is D'Sousa's: "The Equal Opportunity Commission uses an eighty percent rule to enforce proportional representation: companies whose minority recruits are less than four-fifths of the ratio in the population are automatically presumed to be discriminating based on race" (The End of Racism, p. 298, Cf. p. 290). But, in the first place, the eighty percent criterion serves only to shift the burden of proof; it is not sufficient proof. In the second place, the comparison is to the pool of qualified applicants, not to the general population.

239. The force of D'Sousa's and Herrnstein and Murray's rejection of the concept of institutional racism comes from two intuitions, both of which are false. The first is that the discrimination is fair because "they" have to control "their" people. This implies that the black fare who is not picked up or the black or female applicant who is not hired is somehow responsible for the black mugger or the problematic black or female worker. Of course, those most able to influence the problematic behaviors are not those who would be penalized. The second intuition is that to explain pathological behaviors by environment or by institutional racism involves excusing and therefore encouraging them. Environmental explanations do not imply normative approval. Punitive responses do not always reduce the problems.

240. "We'd Love To Hire Them But," based on open-ended interviews, usually with the highest ranking official of the establishment, in Cook County (Kirschenman and Neckerman, 1991).

241. Wilson (1991a).

242. For example, beliefs about training or responsibility or ability to cooperate can be a self-fulfilling prophecy. "[P]roductivity is not an individual characteristic; rather, it is shaped by the social relations of the workplace. What begins as irrational practice based on prejudice or mistaken belief may end up being rational profit-maximizing behavior." (Kirschenman and Neckerman, 1991).

243. It devotes part of an appendix to arguing that Phillipe Rushton is not a "crackpot or a bigot" (The Bell Curve, pp. 642-643). Rushton argues that some species have few children and they care for them, while other species have many children for whom they do not care. He has tried to show that this is relevant to white/black differences by arguing that blacks have larger genitals and smaller brains, and tried to prove this argument (echoing one in Spencer) by handing out questionnaires about genital size in supermarkets.

Notes to Chapter 8

244. The Bell Curve, pp. 532-523.

245. Patterson (1995), pp. 198-206.

246. Some of the main passages are repeated in Jacoby and Glauberman (1995).

247. *The Bell Curve*, pp. 509-511.

248. K. Davis and W. Moore (1945).

249. For example, M. Tumin (1985).

250. Fischer et al. 1996 pp. 126-8.

251. Myrdal, 1944. Myrdal does not emphasize and did not foresee the escalating conflicts and mass mobilization which can result (Steinberg, 1995), but those considerations merely accentuate the degree to which large disparities of political power are inhospitable to the peaceful operation of the democratic process.

252. Richard Titmuss. Commitment to Welfare (New York: Pantheon, 1968).

253. The emphasis on fundamental, biological inequality between individuals always resonates with the beliefs of those who believe that different groups are biologically unequal. Works such as Kamin (1974) and Mensh and Mensh (1991) show the interconnection of the individualist and racial commitment to inequality with regard to the psychometric movement early in the century. Kleugal and Smith (1986) and Jackman (1994) show that individualism is the principal ideological basis for opposition to programs designed to equalize opportunities.

254. Spencer (1954 [1851]).

255. "To separate pain from ill-doing is to fight against the constitution of things, and will be followed by far more pain. Saving men from the natural penalties of dissolute living, eventually necessitates the infliction of artificial penalties." (Spencer, 1994 [1884], p. 80).

256. Spencer was not interested in really reducing dependency, any more than is Gingrich or the New Right. In fact, Spencer heartily approved the hat-in-hand gratitude and dependency of the recipient at the mercy of private philanthropy. One of his strongest objections to public provision of social services was that the recipient is not dependent, but comes to believe that he or she has a right to them, and so the edifying moral interchange between a grateful recipient and a superior philanthropist does not occur.

257. Spencer (1954 [1851]).

258. Thus figures such as Lester Ward, the first president of the American Sociological Society, argued for "telesis," planned development and change. And this position was consistent with his championing of universal public education, in opposition to the eugenicists.

259. Chase (1977).

260. Chapman (1988); Compare Allen (1986).

261. Patterson (1995), p. 197.

262. Kevles (1985).

263. Bellant (1988).

264. Schwartz (1976).

265. Reich (1981).

266. Edsall (1992).

Notes to Chapter 9

267. Barkun (1994).

268. Harrison and Bluestone (1988).

269. Thurow (1992).

270. Berry (1991).

271. Sen (1992).

272. Lowi (1995).

273. While the movement to focus on genetic mechanisms is powerful within the academy, this is not identical to the earlier eugenics movement. Intelligence and ability testing are fairly rooted in schools and large-scale organizations, but this differs from the psychometric movement.

274. Wills (1990).

275. Himmelstein (1990).

276. Gingrich (1995).

277. The defect, however, is conceived as a defect in values and motivation, as in Murray (1984), rather than a biological incapacity.

278. *To Renew America*, p. 8. We have given the most plausible interpretation, that an opportunity society will eliminate the need for welfare. Gingrich sometimes seems to defend the less plausible position that abolishing welfare will equalize opportunity.

279. *To Renew America*, pp. 44-49. Gingrich claims that Deming invented the structure of management that the Japanese then copied. It is an implausible thesis about Japan.

280. Toffler (1971); (1990).

281. Olasky (1992).

282. Danziger and Gottschalk (1996).

283. Thurow (1992) has stressed the fact that the United States simply cannot successfully compete by driving wages below those of the Third World and so if we are to compete, it must be on the basis of a skilled and committed work force, not an impoverished and polarized one.

284. Many social theorists believe that inclusive citizenship or inclusive societal community is the key to development. In the nineteenth century, the United States leaped forward by provisions such as universal free public education. More recently countries such as Japan and Germany have been more effective at institutionalizing the real inclusion of all members of the society. For example, Pettigrew (1964); Parsons and Clark (1966); Sen (1992); Thurow (1992); Danziger and Gottschalk (1996).

285. Dahl (1985). Herrnstein and Murray follow the mainstream of conservative thought, representing the welfare state as the basic threat to democracy in our time. "In its less benign forms, the solutions will become more and more totalitarian" (1995, p. 526, Cf. P. 532). Dahl has shown that all the main transitions from democracy to lack of democracy in the twentieth century have been associated with excess inequalities and attendant social problems.

286. Thurow (1992); Reich (1981).

287. For example, Fischer et al. 1996 distinguish the visible policies relevant to inequality (mainly redistributive policies) from invisible policies such as subsidies for home ownership, health care arrangements, or support or opposition to unionization. In the absence of countervailing forces, public policy often reinforces existing inequalities, while publicizing the small number of transfers that go to

the poor. It is this larger structure of policy to which cumulative causation is most relevant.

Notes to Appendix 1

288. *The Bell Curve*, p. 298. In Chapter Six, we have pointed out that this is a peculiarly bad argument. Most readers find it difficult to get a clear handle on the argument simply because of the way that it is posed. To pose a fallacious argument in scientific or scientific-appearing terms is one defining characteristic of pseudo-science.

289. That is ($1,000 - $3,000)/SD = -2,000/1,054 = -1.90.

290. Blalock (1979); Berry (1993); Pedhazer (1982).

291. The peculiarity of the scattergram, that all of the higher income respondents are given the same income, is an artifact of the ways that the National Longitudinal Survey of Youth coded respondents. All the respondents above a certain value were assigned the same value. This means that the data are intrinsically unreliable at high incomes, and creates difficulties for any analysis that emphasizes extreme values.

292. Specifically, to treat the relationship between AFQT as an effect of cognitive ability on income, Herrnstein and Murray must not only assume that AFQT is a fixed measure of native ability, but they must also assume "uncorrelated error terms." This means that they must assume that there is nothing that affects both income and AFQT scores. Their conceptualization of intelligence is designed to promote the idea that nothing affects AFQT scores, but even granting their assumptions about intelligence, these further assumptions are so implausible that Herrnstein and Murray must obscure the fact that they are making them.

293. What this means technically in Figure A-3 is that the variation of each case from the regression line is 95.2 percent of the total variation from the mean. This can be expressed in causal terms by saying that 4.8 percent of the variation in income can be statistically "explained" by AFQT. A great deal of the plausibility of Herrnstein's and Murray's argument rests on illegitimate implicit inferences. From the fact that some (i.e., about 5 percent) of the variation in income can be statistically explained by AFQT, they suggest that intelligence is a main cause of variation of variables such as income.

294. This finding is well-known (e.g. Bowles and Gintis, 1971) and has been clearly demonstrated for the kinds of data used in *The Bell Curve* by Dickens, Kane, Schultze (1995), and Fischer *et al.* (1996).

295. They show that such variables as poverty, illegitimacy, failure in school, and injury are somehow related to intelligence, and then fail to include them in the analysis of any other variable.

296. While no rescaling can eliminate the problem of measurement error, which is particularly acute at the very low range of SES, a more plausible set of assumptions about the measurement of SES and AFQT would only assume ordinal measurement for the purposes of comparing them. In that case, the poverty proportions of the bottom deciles of SES and AFQT would be compared, then the next decile, and so on. Equal areas on the polygon would then correspond to

equal numbers of cases, and the difference between the two curves would be much reduced.

297. However, the difference is smaller than that in Herrnstein and Murray or in Figure A-2 because the curves portray bivariate relations between poverty and AFQT or SES. In Herrnstein and Murray's analyses the bivariate relations will be less different than the multivariate ones they present.

298. We have noted that their SES index is heavily weighted with parental education which shows little relation to respondent's later poverty.

299. Many of the respondents at very low levels of AFQT score are almost certainly functionally illiterate. They scored worse than randomly on the test, especially on the later parts of it. Fischer *et al.* (1996) have suggested that this shows they had stopped trying. This is not necessarily unintelligent behavior for those paid to take a tedious test.

300. While multiple regression is a versatile and useful method of analyzing data, there are complexities to it that the reader can pursue in any good textbook, such as Blalock (1979), Aldrich and Nelson (1990), and Goldberger (1991).

301. At each level of one of the independent variables, the plane would cut it in straight lines (simple regressions) with the same slope, but possibly different means, due to the different levels of the variable on which one is making the sections. While it is difficult to visualize more than two independent variables, the mathematical techniques work with any number of variables.

302. There are an infinite number of possible regression coefficients expressing the effect of one variable on another, depending what other variables are analyzed. Social scientists analyze this choice in terms of model specification and spurious relationships.

303. As we have noted, the assumptions require that all the other forces operating on the dependent variable or variables not have systematic effects, that the error terms be uncorrelated (see Blalock, 1979). As we shall see, if there are systematic forces affecting many of the variables in the analysis, as is presumed by a model of cumulative disadvantage, then the procedures Herrnstein and Murray use will give systematically biased estimates, and that these problems will be accentuated by other issues concerning the measures they use.

304. Specifically, their analyses consist of multiple regressions, in which a dependent variable, such as poverty or unemployment is predicted as a function of three other variables: age, AFQT89 (the subjects' score on the 1980 Armed Forces Qualification Test, rescaled according to the weighting of the 1989 test), and SES (socioeconomic status in 1980). Since age is ignored after it is used to construct the regression equations, we shall focus on the effects of AFQT89 and SES.

305. For a lucid discussion of some of the problems of their causal model, see Goldberger and Manski (1995).

306. We noted that the relation between AFQT and income could occur because of an effect of AFQT, and effect of income, or an effect of any other, unmeasured variable. Although the national Longitudinal Survey of Youth has considerable resources for the analysis of the interplay over time of various measures of cognitive function and income, Herrnstein and Murray chose to ignore these resources. They also ignore the existing literatures that have carefully looked at the reciprocal interplay of cognitive flexibility and jobs or other social situations such as that

of Kohn and his collaborators. Instead, on the basis of a priori assumptions they choose to take the correlation of income and AFQT scores as an effect on income of cognitive capacity. From the standpoint of their thesis, this begs the question. But it motivates the policy arguments that there is reverse discrimination.

307. Garfinkle (1990).

308. These conceptual shifts are analogous to the well-known magic tricks involving a little ball which the magician can find magically transported to different locations. It looks as though the same little ball, cognitive capacity, has been examined and found in different contexts. In fact, what has happened is that by clever rhetoric one ball has been palmed and another substituted.

309. For example, they reject the view that explanations that focus on the individual characteristics of the poor "blame the victim" (*The Bell Curve*, p. 131). This dominant approach in the social sciences, which Herrnstein and Murray wish to counter, corresponds to what we termed "Aristotle's fallacy" in Chapter One. No matter how brutalized you find slaves to be, it is slavery that brutalizes slaves, not the characteristics of slaves that produce slavery.

310. For example, in Chapter Three we showed that Herrnstein and Murray make the unlikely and unsubstantiated assumption that schools, jobs and all other social institutions have been radically transformed to eliminate vestiges of privilege and to give everyone an equal chance. It is only on the basis of assumptions such as this that school failure can be ascribed to individual inadequacy.

311. For example, Herrnstein and Murray, 1995, pp. 366-368. Here, as elsewhere, the language is Pickwickian and misleading. They assert that while they cannot say what "would" happen, they can show what "does" happen in the NLSY sample. This language seems to falsely imply that the large causal effects described in the text and table are matters of fact. However, since they have systematically failed to consider the social changes and the differences between different societies in the behaviors they wish to explain, they can only say what "does happen" and what swings in social problems "can result" on the basis of unlikely and unsubstantiated individualist assumptions.

312. Even a measure that emphasized income would be limited. As Oliver and Shapiro (1995) have shown, the inequalities most relevant to housing, education, and other cumulating processes are usually those of wealth rather than income. Racial differences in wealth have narrowed little, if at all.

313. Data were most often missing for parental income and occupation. In practice, therefore, the scale was most heavily based on parents' education.

314. These errors were exacerbated by the treatment of missing cases of family income.

315. The effect will often be greater when a non-linear method, such as logistic regression, is employed, because this bias is accentuated by any form of analysis that concentrates on a very small number of extreme cases.

316. For example, see the text example of a hypothetical analysis of the effects of fire engines on fire damage, beginning on p. 70.

317. Although such problems are relatively straightforward when there are few variables, the central problem of the social sciences is that usually important processes involve a large number of variables. It is widely recognized that even the simple measurement of something like job discrimination, involves estimating a

model of some thirty or forty variables. This is at the limit of our ability to conceptualize and measure.

318. Hackman, 1995; Hauser, 1995.

319. The figure also shows why multiple regression, controlling further variables, is similar to the procedure which Herrnstein and Murray employ for education, running separate regressions for those with different degrees. Failing to analyze a variable which is bound up with one that you do analyze can be misleading.

320. That is, assume that shooting people in the heart causes them to bleed to death which causes them to die. Then, if one were to examine the effect of shooting, controlling bleeding, one would find that it had no effect. One would interpret this result to indicate that shooting does cause death; it causes death by causing people to bleed to death. But as a matter of policy, if one could immediately staunch the bleeding and hook people up to heart lung machines, shooting them in the heart would not cause death. The fact that shooting them in the heart, controlling bleeding, has no effect really means as a practical matter that if we could control bleeding we would eliminate the deaths. Herrnstein make the fallacious and counter-factual inference that since test scores affect education, controlling education would not influence the conditions of deprivation.

321. Non-biological fixed abilities, such as those resulting from early socialization into a cognitive identity or moral standpoint can produce exactly the same model as the biogenetic one, a point that Murray stresses when he wishes to downplay the biogenetic character of the argument, but ignores when it is time to examine the stability itself.

322. They suggest that intelligence scores correlate powerfully ($r = .8$ to $.9$) and that test-retest correlations should fall somewhere between the reliability of the test ($=.9$) and its square root ($=.81$) (*The Bell Curve*, pp. 129-130).

323. It is, perhaps, an overstatement to say that they ignore the effects of education. One of the peculiarities of the book is that it often fails to take account in one place of the findings and qualifications it has acknowledged in others. While there are two discussions of the effect of education on IQ, these are separated by several hundred pages from the actual analyses in Part II and are never acknowledged in those discussions, which stress the relative constancy of IQ scores.

324. Hauser (1995b) notes that less than half of the analyses have any controls, even for number of years of education. The possibility that different kinds or qualities of education might have different effects is nowhere acknowledged or pursued, and related known effects are systematically ignored.

325. A measure with substantial error may be unbiased, if the error terms are uncorrelated with those of the other variables being considered. Conversely a measure that is very highly correlated may be significantly biased. To the extent that test scores and SES are part of a system of cumulative causation, the question of bias rather than test-retest reliability is relevant.

326. Herrnstein and Murray believe that IQ is a biological trait and stable within the limits of measurement error. However, they say that IQ up to age five is "not much use in predicting adult IQ" (*The Bell Curve*, p. 130), and that it is only after age fifteen that IQ scores are "as deeply rooted a fact about subjects as their height" (ibid.).

327. One must first rearrange the NLSY data by grade rather than type of test, and then pool them. See Knapp (1996).

328. The correlation of AFQT with all school IQ tests combined was R = .76, and its correlation with school tests given in grades K - 6 was R = .63, both comparable with well accepted results.

329. These findings with regard to poverty are typical. The much weaker relation of childhood measures of IQ than of adult measures is well known, and the reversal of the apparent causal importance between SES and IQ if one uses the earlier measure is true of most of Herrnstein and Murray's effects (Knapp, 1996).

330. These effects may be accentuated by a non-linear method such as logistic regression. Since logistic regression plots a logarithmic function, it can exaggerate problems of measurement or interactions with unmeasured variables. The bivariate relation of SES and AFQT to poverty are almost identical, but their coefficients in a multiple logistic regression differ by nearly a factor of three. While it is not certain that all logistic or non-linear effects will be in the direction of exaggerating the effects of IQ, it is certainly the case that measures that are sensitive to extreme values (such as partial statistics of non-linear kinds) will accentuate these biases.

Notes to Appendix 2

331. For example, Gould and Gardner, and Rosen and Lane in Fraser (1995).

332. For example, Sowell and Glaser in Fraser (1995).

333. This is most obviously the case in their assumptions about intelligence. There, *The Bell Curve* opposes the "received wisdom" of Stephen J. Gould and his allies to "a scholarly consensus." It characterizes the received wisdom as "all that tests really accomplish is to label youngsters, stigmatizing the ones who do not do well and creating a self-fulfilling prophecy" (*The Bell Curve*, p. 13). It characterizes the scholarly consensus as intelligence is a one-dimensional ability, is genetic to a considerable degree, and is measured in an unbiased way by IQ tests (*The Bell Curve*, p. 14, citing Snyderman and Rothman, 1988).

334. For example, Blalock (1979).

335. Such as Lewontin (1994); Gould (1981); Mercer (1984); and Ogbu (1991).

336. *The Bell Curve*, footnote 19, p. 673.

337. Murray and Herrnstein almost entirely fail to acknowledge or take account of any social scientific analyses of racism. Often they seem to assume that if racism ever existed, it does no longer.

Bibliography

Adorno, T., E. Frankel-Brunswick, D. Levinson, and R. Sanford. *The Authoritarian Personality* (New York: Harper and Row, 1950).

Aldrich, J., and F. Nelson. *Linear Probability, Logit and Probit Models*. Sage Series in Quantitative Applications in the Social Sciences, No. 45 (Beverly Hills, Calif.: Sage, 1984).

Allen, G. "The Eugenics Record Office at Cold Spring Harbor, 1910-1940," *Osiris* 2 (1986). [Reprinted in Jacoby and Glauberman (1995).]

Allport, G.W. *The Nature of Prejudice* (Cambridge, Mass.: Addison-Wesley, 1954).

Aristotle. *Introduction to Aristotle*, edited by R. McKeon (New York: The Modern Library, 1947).

Arthur, N. B. *Increasing Returns and Path Dependence in the Economy* (Ann Arbor: University of Michigan Press, 1994).

Banister, R. *Social Darwinism* (Philadelphia: Temple University Press, 1979).

Barkun, M. *Religion and the Racist Right: The Origins of the Christian Identity Movement* (Chapel Hill: University of North Carolina Press, 1994).

Bartlett, D.L., and J.B. Steele. *America: What Went Wrong?* (Videocassettes; Alexandria, Virg.: Public Broadcasting Service, 1992).

Bellant, R. *Old Nazis, the New Right and the Republican Party* (Boston: South End Press, 1988).

Berry, B.J. *Long-Wave Rhythms in Economic Development and Political Behavior* (Baltimore, Md: Johns Hopkins University Press, 1991).

Berry, W.D. *Understanding Regression Assumptions* (Newbury Park, Calif.: Sage, 1993).

Bianchi, S.M., and D. Spain. *American Women in Transition* (New York: Russell Sage, 1986).

Blalock, H.M., Jr. *Race and Ethnic Relations* (Englewood Cliffs, N.J.: Prentice-Hall, 1982).

Blalock, H.M., Jr. *Understanding Social Inequality* (Newbury Park, Calif.: Sage, 1991).

Blalock, H.M., Jr. *Social Statistics* (New York: McGraw Hill, 1979).

Blau, P. *Structural Contexts of Opportunity* (New York: Wiley, 1994).

Blau, P., and O.D. Duncan. *The American Occupational Structure* (New York: Wiley, 1967).

Blauner, B. *Racial Oppression in America* (New York: Harper, 1972).

Block, N.J., and G. Dworkin (eds.). *The I.Q. Controversy: Critical Readings* (London: Quartet Books, 1977).

Blum, J.M. *Psuedoscience and Mental Ability* (New York: Monthly Review Press, 1978).

Blumberg, P. *Inequality in an Age of Decline* (Oxford: Oxford University Press, 1980).

Boas, F. *General Anthropology* (New York: D. C. Heath Co., 1938).

Bouchard, T.J., Jr., D.T. Lykken, M. McGue, M. Segal, and A. Tellegen. "Sources of Human Pschological Differences: The Minnesota Study of Twins Reared Apart," *Science* 250 (1990):223-228.

Bowles, S. and H. Gintis. "IQ in the US Class Structure," *Social Policy* 3 (1973):65-96.

Burck, C. "A Group Profile of the Fortune 500 Chief Executives," *Fortune* (May 1976):173- 177.

Byrne, J.A., D. Foust, and L. Therrien. "Executive Pay," *Business Week* (March 30, 1992), p. 52.

Cain, G., and H. Watts. "Problems in Making Policy Inferences from the Coleman Report," *American Sociological Review* 35 (2, 1970):228-242.

Cavalli-Sforza, L.L., P. Menozzi, and A. Piazza. *The History and Geography of Human Genes* (Princeton, N.J.: Princeton University Press, 1994).

Center for the Study of Policy Attitudes (CSPA), *Fighting Poverty in America: A Study of American Public Attitudes* (Washington, D.C.: CSPA, December 8, 1994).

Chapman, P.D. *Schools as Sorters: Lewis M. Terman Applied Psychology and the Intelligence Testing Movement, 1890-1930* (New York: New York University Press, 1988).

Charmichael, S. and C. Hamilton. *Black Power* (New York: Vintage, 1967).

Chase, A. *The Legacy of Malthus: The Social Costs of the New Scientific Racism* (New York: Random House, 1977).

Cherlin, A.J. *Marriage, Divorce and Remarriage* (Cambridge, Mass.: Harvard University Press, 1981).

Coleman, J.S., E.Q. Campbell, C.J. Hobson, et al. *Equality of Educational Opportunity* (Washington, D.C.: USGPO, 1966).

Committee on Ways and Means, U.S. House of Representatives, *Overview of Entitlement Programs*, 1993 Green Book (Washington, D.C.: USGPO, 1994).

Costrell, Robert. *The Effects of Industry Shifts on Wage Growth* (Washington, D.C.: Joint Economic Committee, 1988).

D'Sousa, D. *The End of Racism* (New York: The Free Press, 1995).

Dahl, R.A. *A Preface to Economic Democracy* (Berkeley: University of California Press, 1985).

Danziger, S., G.D. Sandefur, and D.H. Weinberg (eds.). *Confronting Poverty: Prescriptions for Change* (New York: Russell Sage Foundation, 1994).

Danziger, S., and P. Gottschalk. *America Unequal* (Cambridge, Mass.: Harvard University Press, 1995).

Danziger, S., and P. Gottschalk (eds.). *Uneven Tides: Rising Inequality in America* (New York: Russell Sage Foundation, 1993).

Danziger, S., and D.H. Weinberg. *Fighting Poverty: What Works and What Doesn't* (Cambridge, Mass.: Harvard University Press, 1986).

Davenport, C. "Euthenics and Eugenics," *Popular Science Monthly* (Jan. 1911):19.

Davis, K. "Final Note on a Case of Extreme Isolation," *American Journal of Sociology* 52 (1947):432-437.

Davis, K., and W. Moore. "Some Principles of Social Stratification," *American Sociological Review* 10 (1945):242-249.

Dickens, W.T., T.J. Kane, and C.L. Schultze. "Does *The Bell Curve* Ring True?" *Brookings Review* (Summer, 1995).

DiNitto, D.M. *Social Welfare Politics and Public Policy* (Boston: Allyn and Bacon, 1995).

DuBois, W.E.B. *The Philadelphia Negro* (New York: Schocken, 1899).

Dunbar, L. (ed.). *Minority Report* (New York: Pantheon, 1984).

duRivage, V.L. *New Policies for the Part-time and Contingent Workforce* (Armonk, N.Y.: M. E. Sharpe, 1992).

Easterlin, R. "The New Age Structure of Poverty in America: Permanent or Transient?" *Population and Development Review* 13 (1987):195-208.

Edsall, T.B., with M.D. Edsall. *Chain Reaction: The Impact of Race, Rights, and Taxes on American Politics* (New York: W. W. Norton, 1992).

Edwards, J. *When Race Counts: The Morality of Racial Preference in Britain and America* (London: Routledge, 1995).

Eitzen, S.D., and M.B. Zinn. *In Conflict and Order: Understanding Society* (Boston: Allyn and Bacon, 1993).

Ellwood, D. *Poor Support: Poverty in the American Family* (New York: Basic Books, 1988).

Eyefarth, K. "Leistungen ver schiedener Gruppen von Besatzungskindermn in Hamburg-Wechsler Intelligenztest für Kinder. Archiv für dir gesamte. *Psychologie* 113 (1961):222-241.

Ezorsky, G. *Racism and Justice: The Case for Affirmative Action* (Ithaca, NY: Cornell University Press, 1991).

Farley, R. *Blacks and Whites: Narrowing the Gap?* (Cambridge, Mass.: Harvard University Press, 1984).

Featherman, D.L., and R.M. Hauser. *Opportunity and Change* (New York: Academic Press, 1978).

Fischer, C., M. Hout, M. Jankowski, S. Lucas, A. Swidler, and K. Voss. *Inequality by Design* (Princeton: Princeton University Press, 1996).

Flynn, J.R. *Asian Americans* (Hillside, N.J.: Erlbaum, 1991).

Flynn, J.R. "Massive IQ Gains in 14 Nations," *Psychological Bulletin* 101 (1987):171-191.

Flynn, J.R. *Race, IQ, and Jensen* (London: Routledge, 1980).

Fraser, S. (ed.). *The Bell Curve Wars: Race, Intelligence, and the Future of America* (New York: Basic Books, 1995).

Frazier, E.F. *The Negro Family in the United States* (Chicago: University of Chicago Press, 1966).

Furstenberg, F. *Adolescent Mothers in Later Life* (New York: Cambridge University Press, 1987).

Furstenberg, F. *Unplanned Parenthood: The Social Consequences of Teenaged Childbearing* (New York: Free Press, 1976).

Gardner, H. *Frames of Mind: The Theory of Multiple Intelligences* (New York: Basic Books, 1983).

Gelles, R., and C. Pedrick. *Violence in Families* (Beverly Hills: Sage, 1985).

Geschwender, J.A., R. Carroll-Sequin, and H. Brill. "The Portugese and Haoles of Hawaii," *American Sociological Review* 53 (1988):515-527.

Gibson, M., and J. Ogbu (eds.). *Minority Status and Schooling: A Comparative Study of Immigrant and Involuntary Minorities* (New York: Garland, 1991).

Gingrich, N. *Contract with America* (New York: Times Books, 1994).

Gingrich, N. *To Renew America* (New York: Harper Collins, 1995).

Gingrich, N. and R. Armey. *Contract with America* E. Gillespie and B. Schellhas, eds. (New York: Times Books, 1994).

Goldberger, A. *A Course in Econometrics* (Cambridge, Mass.: Harvard University Press, 1991).

Goldberger, A., and C. Manski. "Review Article: *The Bell Curve*," *Journal of Economic Literature* 33 (1995):762-776.

Goleman, D. *Emotional Intelligence* (New York: Bantam, 1995).

Goode, W.J. "Illegitmacy in the Caribbean Social Structure," *American Sociological Review* 25 (1960): 21-30.

Gould, S.J. *Mismeasure of Man* (New York: Norton, 1981).

Greenberg, S. *Middle Class Dreams* (New Haven, Conn.:Yale University Press, 1994).

Hacker, A. *Two Nations: Black and White, Separate, Hostile, and Unequal* (New York: Scribner's, 1992).

Harris, M. *The Rise of Anthropological Theory: A History of Theories of Culture* (New York: Crowell, 1968).

Harrison, B. and B. Bluestone. *The Great U-Turn: Corporate Restructuring and the Polarizing of America* (New York: Basic Books, 1988).

Hartigan, J.A., and A.K. Wigdor (eds.). *Fairness in Employment Testing* (Washington, D.C.: National Academy Press, 1989).

Hartmann, H., R. Kraut, and L. Tilly. *Computer Chips and Paper Clips* (Washington, D.C.: National Academy Press, 1987).

Hauser, R., H. F. Taylor, and T. Duster, "Symposium on *The Bell Curve*," *Contemporary Sociology* 24 (2, 1995):149-161.

Hauser, R. "*The Bell Curve*: A Perspective from Sociology, *Focus* 17 (1995b).:25-28.

Herrnstein, R.J. "I.Q.," *Atlantic Monthly* (September, 1971):43-64. [Reprinted in Jacoby and Glauberman (1995).]

Herrnstein, R.J. *I.Q. in the Meritocracy* (Boston: Little, Brown, 1973).

Herrnstein, R.J., and C. Murray. *The Bell Curve: Intelligence and Class Structure in American Life* (New York: Free Press, 1994).

Herrnstein, R.J., and C. Murray. "Race, Genes and I.Q.: An Apologia," *The New Republic* 211 (#18, October 31, 1994):27.

Hilton, S. *Senator for Sale* (New York: St. Martin's Press, 1995).

Himmelstein, J.L. *To the Right: The Transformation of American Conservatism* (Berkeley: University of California Press, 1990).

Hirschi, T., and H. Selvin. *Delinquency Research: An Appraisal of Analytic Methods* (New York: Free Press, 1967).

Hochschild, J. *Facing Up To the American Dream* (Princeton: Princeton University Press, 1995).

Hofstadter, R. *Social Darwinism in American Thought* (Boston: Beacon Press, 1955).

Huff, D. *How to Lie with Statistics* (New York: Norton, 1993).

Hunter, J.E. "An Analysis of Validity," Report to the Federal District Court, Alvarez vs. City of Philadelphia, 1979.

Hunter, J.E. "Test Validation for 12,000 Jobs," U.S. Employment Service, U.S. Department of Labor (Washington, D.C.: GPO, 1980).

Hunter, J.E. *Differential Validity Across Jobs in the Military* (Rockville, Md.: Research Applications, 1985).

Hunter, J.E. *Methods of Meta-Analysis* (Newbury Park, N.J.: Sage, 1990).

Jackman, M. *The Velvet Glove* (Berkeley: University of California Press, 1994).

Jacoby, R., and N. Glauberman (eds.). *The Bell Curve Debate: History, Documents, Opinions* (New York: Times Books, 1995).

Jaynes, G.D., and R.M. Williams, Jr. (eds.). *A Common Destiny: Blacks and American Society* (Washington D.C.: National Academy Press, 1989).

Jencks, C. *Rethinking Social Policy* (Cambridge, Mass.: Harvard University Press, 1992).

Jencks, C., and P.E. Peterson (eds.). *The Urban Underclass* (Washington D.C.: The Brookings Institution, 1991).

Kamin, L.S. *The Science and Politics of I.Q.* (Potomoc, Md.: Lawrence Erlbaum Associates; distributed by Halsted Press, New York, 1974).

Kamin, L.S., and Eyesenck, H.J. *The Intelligence Controversy* (New York: Wiley and Sons, 1981).

Kanter, R.M. *Men and Women of the Corporation* (New York: Basic Books, 1977).

Kerckhoff, A. "Institutional Arrangements and Stratification Processes in Industrial Societies," *Annual Review of Sociology* 21 (1995):323-347.

Kevles, D.J. *In the Name of Eugenics: Genetics and the Uses of Human Heredity* (New York: Knopf, 1985).

Kirschenman, J., and K. Neckerman. "We'd Love To Hire Them But," in C. Jencks, and P.E. Peterson (eds.), *The Urban Underclass* (Washington D.C.: The Brookings Institution, 1991).

Kleugel, J., and E. Smith. *Beliefs About Equality* (New York: Hawthorne, Aldine, 1986).

Knapp, M., and P. Shields. *Better Schooling for the Children of Poverty* (Berkeley, CA: McCutcheon Publishing Co., 1991).

Knapp, P. "Age, IQ, and Ability." Paper presented at the American Sociological Association's Annual Meetings, 1996.

Knapp, P. *One World-Many Worlds: Contemporary Sociological Theory* (New York: Harper Collins Publishers, 1994).

Knowles, L.L., and K. Prewitt (eds.). *Institutional Racism in America* (Englewood Cliffs, N.J.: Prentice-Hall, 1969).

Kohn, M., K. Slomczynski, and C. Schoenback. "Social Stratification and the Transmission of Values in the Family: A Cross-National Assessment," *Sociological Forum* 1 (1, 1986):73- 102.

Korenman, S., and C. Winship. "A reanalysis of *The Bell Curve*." Working paper 523, (Cambridge: NBER, 1995).

Kozol, J. *Savage Inequalities: Children in America's Schools* (New York: Harper Collins Publishers, 1992).

Kronick, J.C. *Attitudes Toward Dependency: A Study of 105 ADC Mothers*, Final Report to the Social Security Administration (Bryn Mawr: Bryn Mawr College, 1962).

Kronick, J.C. *Family Life and Economic Dependency, Report to the Welfare Administration* (Bryn Mawr: Bryn Mawr College, 1964).

Laughlin, H.H. *Eugenical Sterilization in the United States* (Chicago: Psychopathic Laboratory of the Municipal Court of Chicago, 1922).

Layard, R. *The Unemployment Crisis* (New York: Oxford University Press, 1994).

Levins, R., and R. C. Lewontin. *The Dialectical Biologist* (Cambridge, Mass.: Harvard University Press, 1985).

Lewontin, R. C. "The apportionment of human diversity," in *Evolutionary Biology*. Vol. 6. Th. Dobzhansky, M. Hecht, and W. Steere, eds., pp. 381-398, (New York: Appleton-Century-Crofts, 1972).

Lewontin, R. C. *Inside and Outside: Gene, Environment, and Organism* (Worcester, Mass.: Clark University Press, 1994).

Lewontin, R. C., S. P. Rose, and L. J. Kamin. *Not In Our Genes: Biology, Ideology, and Human Nature* (New York: Pantheon Books, 1984).

Lieberson, S. *A Piece of the Pie: Blacks and White Immigrants Since 1880* (Berkeley: University of California Press, 1980).

Lipset, S. M. *Social Mobility in Industrial Society* (Berkeley: University of California Press, 1959).

Loehlin, J. C., G. Lindzey, and J. N. Spuhler. *Race Differences in Intelligence* (San Francisco: Freeman, 1975).

Loehlin, J. D., S. G. Vandenberg, and R. T. Osbourne. "Blood Group Genes and Negro-white Ability Differences," *Behavior Genetics* 3 (1973):263-70.

Loewen, J.W. *Lies My Teacher Told Me: Everything Your American History Textbook Got Wrong* (New York: The New Press, 1995).

Lowi, T.J. *The End of Liberalism: The Second Republic of the United States* (New York: W. W. Norton, 1979).

Luntz, F. *Philadelphia Inquirer*, November 10, 1995:A29.

Malinowski, B. *Sex and Repression in Savage Society* (New York: Meridian Books, 1955; first published in 1927).

Manski, C. and D. Wise. *College Choice in America* (Cambridge, Mass.: Harvard University Press, 1983).

Mare, R.D. "Five Decades of Assortative Mating," *American Sociological Review* 56 (1991):15-32.

Massey, D., and N. Denton. *American Apartheid: Segregation and the Making of the Underclass* (Cambridge, Mass.: Harvard University Press, 1993).

McKusick, V.A. *Mendelian Inheritance in Man* (Baltimore, Mar.: Johns Hopkins University Press, 1994).

Mensh, E., and H. Mensh. *The IQ Mythology: Class, Race, Gender, and Inequality* (Carbondale: Southern Illinois University Press, 1991).

Mercer, J. "What is a Racially and Culturally Nondiscriminatory Test?" in C. Reynolds and R. Brown (eds.), *Perspectives on "Bias in Mental Testing"* (New York: Plenum Press, 1984).

Merton, R.K. *The Sociology of Science: Theoretical and Empirical Investigations* (Chicago: University of Chicago Press, 1973).

Miller, S. "Review of *Losing Ground*," *Contemporary Sociology* 14 (1985): 684-668.

Mills, N. (ed.). *Debating Affirmative Action: Race, Gender, Ethnicity, and the Politics of Inclusion* (New York: Dell Publishing, 1994).

Mishel, L., and J. Bernstein. *The State of Working America: 1992-93* (Economic Policy Institute Series, Armonk, N.Y.: M..E. Sharpe, 1993).

Modgil, S., and C. Modgil. *Arthur Jensen: Consensus and Controversy* (New York: Falmer Press, 1987).

Moffitt, R. "Incentive Effects of the U.S. Welfare System: A Review," *Journal of Economic Literature* 30 (1, 1992):1-61.

Montagu, A. *Man's Most Dangerous Myth: The Fallacy of Race* (New York: Oxford University Press, 1974; first edition published in 1945).

Morgenthau, T. "I.Q.: Is It Destiny?" *Newsweek* (October 24, 1994).

Murray, C. *Losing Ground: American Social Policy, 1950-80* (New York: Basic Books, 1984).

Myrdal, G. *An American Dilemma.* (New York: McGraw-Hill, 1944).

National Criminal Justice Information and Statistical Service. *Myths and Realities about Crime* (Washington, D.C.: Department of Justice Law Enforcement Assistance Administration, 1978).

Nei, M., and A. K. Roychoudhury, "Genetic variation within and between the three major races of Man, Caucasoids, Negroids, and Mongoloids." *Am. J. Hum. Genet.* 26:421-443.

Neisser, U., et al. *Intelligence: Knowns and Unknowns.* Report of the Task Force of the Board of Scientific Affairs of the American Psychological Association (Washington, D.C.: APA, 1995).

Nisbett, R. "Race, IQ, and Scientism," in S. Fraser (ed.), *The Bell Curve Wars* (New York: Basic Books, 1995).

Often, J. (ed.). *Political Writings* (Writings of Herbert Spencer) (New York: Cambridge University Press, 1994).

Ogbu, J. *Minority Status and Schooling* (New York: Garland, 1991).

Olasky, M.N. *The Tragedy of American Compassion* (Washington, D. C.: Regnery Gateway, 1992).

Oliver, M., and T. Shapiro. *Black Wealth/White Wealth* (New York: Routledge, 1995).

Oppenheimer, V.K. *The Female Labor Force in the United States: Demographic and Economic Factors Governing its Growth and Changing Composition* (Berkeley: University of California Press, 1970).

Park, R.E. *Race and Culture* (Glencoe, Ill.: Free Press, 1950).

Parsons, T. and K.B. Clark (eds.). *The Negro American* (Boston: Houghton Mifflin, 1966).

Paul, D. B. "The Nine Lives of Discredited Data." *The Sciences* (May, 1987):26-30.

Pedhazur, E.J. *Multiple Regression in Behavioral Research: Explanation and Prediction* (New York: Holt, Rinehart and Winston, 1982).

Pettigrew, T., G.M. Fredrickson, D.T. Knobel, N. Glazer, and R. Ueda. *Prejudice* (Cambridge, Mass.: Belknap Press, 1982).

Pettigrew, T. *A Profile of the American Negro* (Princeton, N.J.: Van Nostrand, 1964).

Pines, M., "The Civilization of Genie." *Psychology Today* (September, 1981):28-34.

Public Papers of the Presidents of the United States: Lyndon B. Johnson, USGPO, 1966, p. 636.

Quadagno, J. *The Color of Welfare* (New York: Oxford University Press, 1994).

Rainwater, L., and T.M. Smeeding. *Doing Poorly: The Real Income of American Children in Comparative Perspective*, Working Paper No. 127, Luxembourg Income Study (Syracuse, N.Y.: Maxwell School of Citizenship and Public Affairs, Syracuse University, 1995).

Reich, M. *Racial Inequality: A Political-Economic Analysis* (Princeton, N.J.: Princeton University Press, 1981).

Ringer, B., and E. Lawless. *Race, Ethnicity, and Society* (New York: Routledge, 1989).

Robertson, I. *Sociology* (New York: Worth Publishers, 1987).

Rose, A.M. *The Negro in America* (New York: Harper and Row, 1964).

Ruggles, P. *Measuring the Duration of Poverty Spells* (Washington, D.C.: The Urban Institute, 1988).

Ryan, W. *Blaming the Victim* (New York: Vintage Books, 1976).

Scarr, S., S. Pakstis, H. Katz, and W.B. Barker. "Absence of a Relationship between Degree of White Ancestry," *Human Genetics* 39 (1977):73-77, 82-83.

Scarr, S., and R. Weinberg. "The Minnesota Transracial Adoption Studies: Genetic Differences and Malleability," *Child Development* 54 (1983):260-267.

Schervish, P.G. *The Structural Determinants of Unemployment: Vulnerability and Power in Market Relations* (New York: Academic Press, 1983).

Schiff, M., and R.C. Lewontin. *Education and Class: The Irrelevance of IQ Genetic Studies* (New York: Oxford University Press, 1986).

Schorr, L.B., with D. Schorr. *Within Our Reach: Breaking the Cycle of Disadvantage* (New York: Anchor Books, 1988).

Schwartz, M. *Radical Protest and Social Structure* (New York: Academic Press, 1976).

Sen, A. *Inequality Reexamined* (New York: Russell Sage Foundation, 1992).

Sewell, W. H. *Education, Occupation, and Earnings: Achievement in the Early Career* (New York: Academic Press, 1975).

Sewell, W.H., R. Hauser, and D. Featherman (eds.). *Schooling and Achievement in American Society* (New York: Academic Press, 1976).

Shaw, C.R., H.M. Zorbaugh, H.D. McKay, and L.S. Cottrell. *Delinquency Areas: A Study of the Geographic Distribution of School Truants, Juvenile Delinquents, and Adult Offenders in Chicago* (Chicago: University of Chicago Press, 1929).

Short, J.F., Jr. (ed.). *The Social Fabric of the Metropolis: Contributions of the Chicago School of Urban Sociology* (Chicago: University of Chicago Press, 1971).

Skolnick, A., and J. Skolnick. *Family in Transition* (New York: Harper Collins, 1992).

Skott, P., and P. Auerbach. "Cumulative Causation and the 'New' Theories of Economic Growth," *Journal of Post-Keynesian Economics* 17:381-402 (1995).

Smith, J. David. *Minds Made Feeble: The Myth and Legacy of the Kallikuks* (Rockville, Md.: George Mason University Press, 1985).

Snipp, C. M. *American Indians: The First of This Land* (New York: Russell Sage Foundation, 1989).

Snyderman, M., and S. Rothman. *The IQ Controversy: The Media and Public Policy* (New Brunswick, N.J.: Transaction Books, 1988).

Spence, A. M. *Market Signaling: Informational Transfer in Hiring and Related Screening Processes* (Cambridge, MA: Harvard University Press, 1974).

Spencer, H. *Man vs. The State*, reprinted in J. Often (ed.), *Political Writings* (New York: Cambridge University Press, 1994 [1884]).

Spencer, H. *Social Statics; or the Conditions Essential to Human Happiness Specified, and the First of Them Developed* (New York: Schalkenback Foundation, 1954 [1851]).

Steinberg, S. *Turning Back: The Retreat from Racial Justice in American Thought and Policy* (Boston, Mass.: Beacon Press, 1995).

Sternberg, R.J. "What We Should Ask About Intelligence," *The American Scholar* (1996).

Sternberg, R.J. (ed). *Encyclopedia of Intelligence.* (New York: Macmillan, 1994).

Sternberg, R.J. *The Triarchic Mind: A New Theory of Human Intelligence* (New York: Penguin, 1988).

Sternberg, R.J. *Beyond I.Q.: A Triarchic Theory of Human Intelligence* (Cambridge: Cambridge University Press, 1985).

Stevenson, H.W., and J.W. Stigler. *The Learning Gap: Why Our Schools Are Failing and What We Can Learn From Japanese and Chinese Education* (New York: Summit Books, 1992).

Taylor, H. *The IQ Game* (New Brunswick, N.J.: Rutgers University Press, 1980).

Thurow, L.C. *The Future of Capitalism* (New York: William Morrow, 1996).

Thurow, L.C. *Head to Head: The Coming Economic Battle Among Japan, Europe, and America* (New York: Morrow, 1992).

Titmuss, R.M. *Commitment to Welfare* (New York: Pantheon, 1968).

Tizard, B., A. Cooperman, and J. Tizard. "Environmental Effects on Language Development: A Study of Young Children in Long-stay Residential Nurseries," *Child Development* 43 (1972):342-343.

Toffler, A. *Future Shock* (New York: Bantam Books, 1971).

Toffler, A. *Powershift: Knowledge, Wealth, and Violence at the Edge of the 21st Century* (New York: Bantam Books, 1990).

Tucker, W.H. *The Science and Politics of Racial Research* (Chicago: University of Illinois Press, 1994).

Tufte, E.R. *Visual Display of Quantitative Information* (Cheshire, Conn.: Graphics Press, 1983).

Tumin, M. *Social Stratification* (Englewood Cliffs, N.J.: Prentice Hall, 1985).

U.S. Bureau of the Census. *Current Population Reports*, Series P60, No. 175. Poverty in the United States, 1990 (Washington, D.C.: USGPO, 1991).

U.S. Department of Agriculture, Agricultural Research Service. *Food Consumption of Households in the United States of America, 1965.* (Washington, D.C.: U.S. Department of Agriculture, ARS, 1965).

U.S. Bureau of the Census, *Statistical Abstract of the United States, 1992* (Washington, D.C.: USGPO, 1993).

U.S. Department of Health and Human Services, Social Security Administration. *Annual Statistical Supplement to the Social Security Bulletin, 1994* (Washington, D.C.: USGPO, 1994).

U.S. Commission on Civil Rights. *Last Hired, First Fired* (Washington, D.C.: USGPO, 1977).

Wallace, B., and W. Graves. *Poisoned Apple: The Bell Curve and How Our Schools Create Mediocrity and Failure* (New York: St. Martin's Press, 1995).

Wallerstein, J., and S. Blakeslee. *Second Chances: Men, Women and Children a Decade After Divorce* (New York: Ticknor and Fields, 1989).

Weeks, J.R. *Population: Introduction to Concepts and Issues* (Belmont, Calif.: Wadsworth Publishing Co., 1989).

Weitzman, L. *The Divorce Revolution* (New York: Free Press, 1985).

Whyte, M.K. *Dating, Mating and Marriage* (New York: Aldine de Gryler, 1990).

Willerman, L., A.F. Naylor, and N.C. Myrianthopolous. "Intellectual Development of Children from Interracial Mating," *Behavior Genetics* 4 (1974):84-88.

Williams, R.M. *Strangers Next Door: Ethnic Relations in American Communities* (Englewood Cliffs, N.J.: Prentice-Hall, 1964).

Wills, G. *Under God: Religion and American Politics* (New York: Simon and Schuster, 1990).

Wilson, W.J. "Studying Inner-City Dislocation," *American Sociological Review* 56 (1991a):1- 14.

Wilson, W.J. "Public Policy Research and The Truly Disadvantaged" in C. Jencks and P.E. Peterson (eds.), *The Urban Underclass* (Washington, D.C.: The Brookings Institution, 1991b), pp. 461-481.

Wilson, W.J. "Poverty and Family Structure: The Widening Gap between Evidence and Public Policy Issues," IRP Conference Paper (Madison, Wisc.: University of Wisconsin Press, 1984).

Wilson, W.J. *The Truly Disadvantaged: The Inner City, the Underclass, and Public Policy* (Chicago: University of Chicago Press, 1987).

Wilson, W.J. (ed.). *The Ghetto Underclass: Social Science Perspectives* (Newbury Park, CA: Sage, 1989).

Witty, P.A., and M.D. Jenkins. "The Educational Achievements of a Group of Gifted Negro Children" *Journal of Educational Psychology* 25 (1934):586.

Wolfgang, M., N. Weiner, and P. Cook (eds.). *Criminal Violence* (Beverly Hills: Sage, 1982).

Zigler, E., and S. Muenchow. *Head Start* (New York: Basic Books, 1992).

Zorbaugh, H.M. *The Gold Coast and the Slum* (Chicago: University of Chicago Press, 1929).

Index

About the Authors

PETER KNAPP, Professor of Sociology at Villanova University, is the author of works on social theory such as *One World, Many Worlds* (1994).

JANE C. KRONICK, Professor of Social Work and Social Research at Bryn Mawr College, is a well-known researcher in the area of social policy.

R. WILLIAM MARKS, Associate Professor of Biology at Villanova University, specializes in genetics.

MIRIAM G. VOSBURGH, Emeritus Professor of Sociology at Villanova University, is a demographer focusing on family studies.

ISBN 0-275-95545-1

90000>

HARDCOVER BAR CODE

T06261/ND MAG 0.80 BWR .0020in
AI-2012 KNAPP, PETER